SOCIAL ENTERPRISE

This book introduces students and others to the discipline of social entrepreneurship, which encourages the creation of enterprises that are socially inclusive yet economically and ecologically sustainable.

In each chapter there is a mix of case studies about internationally well-known enterprises and other more local enterprises which are totally new. The book leads its readers to understand and appreciate entrepreneurial issues and to engage themselves in community-based activities. *Social Enterprise* helps readers to:

- analyse and articulate the blend of social, environmental and economic values which are present in all kinds of enterprise
- understand the issues involved in translating good intentions with multiple goals into focused, sustainable and practical actions
- propose alternative social enterprise management strategies based on their own analysis of case studies of entrepreneurial endeavours that are perceived to be 'social'

The authors take a pragmatic yet critical approach, and this book should be core or recommended reading for Social Entrepreneurship and Social Enterprise modules at advanced undergraduate, postgraduate and MBA levels.

Malcolm Harper is Emeritus Professor of Enterprise Development at the Cranfield School of Management, UK.

Nadiya Parekh is Assistant Professor of Management and Social Entrepreneurship at Sonoma State University, California, USA.

SOCIAL ENTERPRISE
Cases and Analysis for Understanding Social Business

Malcolm Harper and Nadiya Parekh

Routledge
Taylor & Francis Group

LONDON AND NEW YORK

First published 2022
by Routledge
2 Park Square, Milton Park, Abingdon, Oxon OX14 4RN

and by Routledge
605 Third Avenue, New York, NY 10158

Routledge is an imprint of the Taylor & Francis Group, an informa business

British Library Cataloguing-in-Publication Data
A catalogue record for this book is available from the British Library

Library of Congress Cataloging-in-Publication Data
Names: Harper, Malcolm, 1935– author. | Parekh, Nadiya, 1984– author.
Title: Social enterprise : cases and analysis for understanding social
    business / Malcolm Harper and Nadiya Parekh.
Description: New York, NY : Routledge, 2022. | Includes bibliographical
    references and index.
Identifiers: LCCN 2021014455 (print) | LCCN 2021014456 (ebook)
Subjects: LCSH: Social entrepreneurship. | Sustainable development. |
    Strategic planning.
Classification: LCC HD60 .H386 2022 (print) | LCC HD60 (ebook) |
    DDC 658.4/08—dc23
LC record available at https://lccn.loc.gov/2021014455
LC ebook record available at https://lccn.loc.gov/2021014456

ISBN: 978-0-367-46959-7 (hbk)
ISBN: 978-0-367-46960-3 (pbk)
ISBN: 978-1-003-03222-9 (ebk)

DOI: 10.4324/9781003032229

Typeset in Classical Garamond
by Apex CoVantage, LLC

CONTENTS

List of figures   viii
List of tables   ix
About the authors   x
Preface   xii

1   What enterprises are *really* social?   1

     1.1 Deconstructing the concept of 'social enterprise' 1
     1.2 Case studies 5
         Case 1.2.1 Social enterprises in the United Kingdom 5
         Case 1.2.2 XYZ: a great social enterprise 10
     1.3 Follow-up activity 14
     1.4 References 14

2   Mixing making profits and doing good   16

     2.1 Social equity through entrepreneurship 16
     2.2 Case studies 20
         Case 2.2.1 Ben and Jerry's – social, commercial or
                 both? 20
         Case 2.2.2 Kings Active Foundation – a British social
                 enterprise 22
     2.3 Follow-up activity 25
     2.4 References 26

3   Profits can be social   27

     3.1 Understanding the social dimensions to profit 27
     3.2 Case studies 31
         Case 3.2.1 Micro-finance Credit Rating International
                 (M-CRIL) – inclusive micro-economics 31
         Case 3.2.2 Eton College 34
     3.3 Follow-up activity 36
     3.4 References 37

4 Social aims and social deeds   38

   4.1 Social enterprises: do definitions matter? 38
   4.2 Case study 43
        Case 4.2.1 SKDRDP – a faith-based social enterprise
                   in southern India 43
   4.3 Follow-up activity 59
   4.4 References 59

5 Impact investment   60

   5.1 The capital to do good 60
   5.2 Case study 70
        Case 5.2.1 Aavishkaar 70
   5.3 Follow-up activity 74
   5.4 References 75

6 Emerging models and confusing solutions   76

   6.1 Why is social entrepreneurship popular? 76
   6.2 Case studies 80
        Case 6.2.1 Milk Mantra – a socially conscious dairy
                   business 80
        Case 6.2.2 The Better Meat Company – another
                   approach to cattle 84
   6.3 Follow-up activity 87
   6.4 References 87

7 The need for innovation   88

   7.1 Innovations in social finance 88
   7.2 Case study 94
        Case 7.2.1 The Peterborough social impact bond – the
                   world's first 94
   7.3 Follow-up activity 101
   7.4 References 102

8 Impact assessment   103

   8.1 Impact: understanding and investing in positive change 103
   8.2 Case study 107
        Case 8.2.1 The Not for Profit Finance Fund (NFF) 107
   8.3 Follow-up activity 113
   8.4 References 113

9 Legal structure choices   115

   9.1 Incorporation of social enterprises 115
   9.2 Forms of incorporation: the United States, United Kingdom and
        India 122

9.3 *Case studies 126*
    *Case 9.3.1 BASIX – for profit and for
              good – together? 126*
    Case 9.3.2 Rang De – from non-profit to for-profit 131
9.4 *Follow-up activity 140*
9.5 *References 141*

10 The social enterprise life cycle   142

10.1 *The nature of change and its inevitability 142*
10.2 *Case study 158*
    Case 10.2.1 The Body Shop 158
10.3 *Follow-up activity 164*
10.4 *References 165*

11 The way ahead   167

11.1 *Who invests in social businesses and why do they do it? 167*
11.2 *Case studies 176*
    *Case 11.2.1 Worktree – a social enterprise at many
              crossroads 176*
    *Case 11.2.2 Elon Musk – visionary, multi-billionaire: is
              he also a social entrepreneur? 179*
11.3 *Follow-up activity 182*
11.4 *Conclusion 182*
11.5 *References 183*

Index   184

FIGURES

2.1   Failure of Subsidised Poor-Lending Initiatives   18
7.1   Greatest Challenges Facing the Impact Investment Market   89
8.1   Schematic of a Typical Impact Value Chain Model   103
10.1   Inter-disciplinary Nature of Value   143
10.2   Three Value Dimensions for an Enterprise   143

TABLES

2.1   The Kings Active Foundation Income Statement 2019   25

4.1   Scale of SKDRDP Operations   50

7.1   Estimate of Annual Cost Per Prisoner in Different Countries   95

8.1   Income Statement NFF 2019   111

8.2   Balance Sheet NFF as on December 31, 2019   111

9.1   Suggestions for Legal Structure Choices for Social Enterprises   122

ABOUT THE AUTHORS

Malcolm Harper was educated at Oxford University, the Harvard Business School and the University of Nairobi. He worked for nine years in a medium-sized household hardware manufacturing business in England, mainly in marketing. He then taught in Nairobi, from 1970 to 1974, before coming to Cranfield School of Management, where he was Professor of Enterprise Development. Since 1995 he has worked independently, mainly in India. He has published some twenty-five books and numerous articles on various aspects of self-employment, enterprise development, microfinance, value chains and homeless children. His research and consultancy work have been supported by a wide range of national, international and non-government development agencies.

He has advised and evaluated a number of enterprise development and microfinance programmes and institutions in India and in East and West Africa, Latin America and the Caribbean, the Middle East and Gulf area, South and South East Asia, as well as in the United Kingdom. From 1996 until 2006 he was Chairman of BASIX Finance of Hyderabad, a leading 'new generation' microfinance institution, and he is Chairman of M-CRIL of New Delhi, the pioneer of microfinance credit and social rating in Asia.

He was also the founding editor-in-chief of the journal *Small Enterprise Development* (now *Enterprise Development and Microfinance*) and has been chairman, director and trustee of a number of other institutions, including Homeless International; Musoni, a Netherlands based cashless microfinance group operating in East Africa; and APT Action against Poverty in the United Kingdom. His work has been mainly in India, but he has recently worked in a number of other countries, on Islamic microfinance, livelihoods and value chain development, including Pakistan, Somaliland, Yemen, Angola, Sudan, Tibet, China and Morocco.

Nadiya Parekh was educated at the management schools of Indian Institute of Technology, Madras, and National Institute of Technology, Calicut. After her doctoral studies she worked as Assistant Professor in Social Entrepreneurship academia in India. Later she has worked in the impact investment industry in the United States in the research and analytics domain. Currently she is working as Assistant Professor, Management and Social Entrepreneurship at the School of Business and Economics, Sonoma State University, California (http://sbe.sonoma.edu/about-us/nadiya-parekh-phd). Her research publications have been predominantly in the field of microfinance sustainability and social enterprise financing. She has authored *Sustainability of Indian Microfinance Institutions: A Mixed Methods Approach* Springer, New York, 2014) and co-edited *Technology and Innovation for Social Change* (Springer, New York, 2015).

PREFACE

We cannot be sure that more enterprises are social, or 'doing good', than there were ten or twenty years ago, but what is certain is that the terms 'social enterprise' and 'social entrepreneur' are being more widely used. There may have been a time when academic labels and the titles of books and of university courses followed the general acceptance of meanings, but it is nowadays clear that they precede it, that it is a growing field not only in the real world, but in a world that asks and wonders about reality.

We must leave it to our readers to decide whether we have thrown any light on what is a confusing field, but we do hope that we have thrown some light on the issue, and, if nothing else, that we have demonstrated how unclear it is. We do not want nor would pretend in this book to be offering a definition or even a choice of definitions; one of our teachers once told us that what matters is asking the right questions, and the answers are not so important.

Our theme of social enterprise is ill-defined and unclear. In attempting to write about it, we have perhaps fallen into the trap of suggesting some inappropriate generalisations, but we have included a number of examples and case studies in the hope that our readers can draw their own conclusions as to what is and is not a social enterprise.

We are not ourselves social entrepreneurs, unless we chose to define the term so broadly as to make it more or less useless, so we have inevitably depended very much on the experience, the generosity and the insights of a number of people who very definitely are social entrepreneurs. They have done us and our readers a great favour by sharing their time and experiences with us and with our readers, and they are all of course with their very different enterprises sharing their talents and time and indeed their careers with society at large.

- Manoj Kumar of the Society for Children
- Frances and Sanjay Sinha of M-CRIL
- Veerendra Heggade and Dr Manjunath of SKDRDP
- Vineet Rai of Aavishkaar
- Sri Kumar of Milk Mantra
- Ben Sadler of Alive and Kicking

- David Taylor and Richard Holmes of the Kings Active Foundation
- Smita and Ram Ramakrishna of Rang De
- Tom Bulman of Worktree

Thank you, to all of them, and to all the social entrepreneurs who are trying in one way or another to make the world a better place, regardless of whatever title they and society may use to describe them.

And thanks also to our friends and family – Marley, Digger, Uschi and 'our' 250 or so children in Odisha (see www.orissa.org.uk), and Meeraah, Dhaarmin and our parents – who helped us to stay 'social' while exploring what is 'social' in enterprises.

All the royalties on sales of this book are donated to 'Friends of the Children of Orissa' (www.orissa.org.uk), a small UK-based charity which was started by one of the authors in 1992. It supports a residential school for several hundred orphans and other destitute girls, and a group which rescues and rehabilitates around a thousand children every year from the streets and railways in Odisha state of India, which used to be called Orissa.

Malcolm Harper, Nadiya Parekh, Filgrave and Sonoma
February 2021

1 WHAT ENTERPRISES ARE *REALLY* SOCIAL?

1.1 Deconstructing the concept of 'social enterprise'

The term 'social enterprise' is widely used to describe entities that are run on business lines but whose aim is to 'do good'. Traditionally, there were 'charities' whose founders aimed to achieve some social goal, to 'do good' in some way, and which depended on donations and grants for their income, and there were 'businesses', which were set up to sell goods or services, in order to make a profit for their founders, staff and investors.

However, today we are moving into a new phase, where society expects entrepreneurial entities, whether they are charities or businesses, to pursue multiple goals. Many business entrepreneurs whose earlier motivation was only to make a profit feel obligated to move beyond the creation of economic value for their shareholders and customers, and to demonstrate their commitment to social value creation. And at the same time many so-called 'charities' or other entities which might earlier have been expected only to 'do good' are now under pressure to be 'financially sustainable' and to move beyond their role as creators of social value alone. This is a positive and promising transition, which significantly widens the possible scope of activities and options for the growth of enterprises of all kinds. People who follow this new hybrid path in their entrepreneurial ventures are coming to be known as 'social entrepreneurs'.

We still have businesses and we still have charities, but there is a growing middle ground between those who aim to be 'pure' for-profit entrepreneurs, to start and to build businesses which obey the law and the usual tenets of morality but whose goal is to maximise profits for their founders and investors, and these new social entrepreneurs, who build so-called 'social enterprises'. Their aim is 'social', however that is defined, to 'do good', but at the same time to cover their costs and to earn a living for their employees and a profit or return on their effort and on the capital, which has been contributed by their founders and investors.

One problem with 'new' terminologies and with trying to decide whether certain entities or people should or should not be described with them is that we tend to believe that the things our new words describe are as clear as other

DOI: 10.4324/9781003032229-1

things for which we have generally accepted labels; there may be some uncertainties at the margins, but we are generally agreed that cats are cats and that dogs are dogs. We argue endlessly about normative terms, whether something is good or is bad, or is a virtue or a vice, but we understand that the meaning of such terms depends on our opinions and that such terms are used differently from more objective words. When we say that a particular entity is a 'social enterprise', we are generally not praising or criticising it; we believe that we are saying something objective about it.

It would not be possible, or useful, to try to 'fix' a definition of 'social enterprise', in the hope that users of the term would agree what is and what is not 'social'; any undertaking which involves more than one person is after all 'social' in a strict dictionary sense of the word. But we must be aware of the dangers of using the term 'social enterprise' as if it was clear and definitive.

There are many different criteria we can use to decide whether a given enterprise is 'social' or is not: the sources of its funding and of its income, its founder's or its employees' motives, the remuneration levels of its staff, how its results are measured, the impact, actual or intended, of its activities on its 'clients' or on society in general, its legal form and many others.

Enterprises which might be deemed to be 'social' by one of these criteria can very clearly fail to qualify under another, and we must avoid stereotypes; an enterprise which pays its managers what seem to be enormous salaries or another which has made its founders into multi-millionaires may benefit large numbers of needy people. The term 'social enterprise' is also sometimes used as if it was a way of saying that an enterprise is run in a 'business-like' way, properly controlling costs and measuring results, holding staff to certain standards of performance, with the unspoken implication that traditional 'charities' are almost inevitably sloppily managed, without any quantitative measures, because 'doing good' cannot be measured in the same way as profits. This can be dangerous because it gives any for-profit business the scope to make a small or merely cosmetic change to its existing way of doing business, and to add an environmental, social or governance dimension to it so that it can qualify as a 'sustainable' investment.

It also gives any charity the scope to add an income-generating off-shoot to its existing donation-based model and to proclaim that it is a 'social enterprise' and thus to attract more commercial capital. Though this transition to sustainability may not be harmful in the short run, tensions can arise because of the lack of a clarity of the meaning of the term 'social enterprise'. This can lead to many entities masquerading as 'do-gooders' when in fact there is no legitimacy to their claims in the long run, other than may be contained in their self-serving 'impact' reports.

Academic researchers have not thus far been successful in resolving this very practical issue, although their failure is perhaps to be expected given the wide and expanding usage of the terminology. The broad definitions given by academia, such as demarcating social enterprises as organisations with a strong social mission which offer innovative entrepreneurial solutions to existing social problems in a sustainable way (Dees 1998; Light 2008; Nicholls 2008) are actually no more than attempts to suggest what a social enterprise <u>should</u> be. Such definitions do not clarify what a social enterprise is or is not in practice. Because of this lack of clarity, other writers have said that the concept (Defourny and Nyssens 2010) and the practice (Kerlin 2013) of social entrepreneurship may vary across regions and institutional contexts. It can also be defined by its market orientation or by the nature of its innovations (Bacq and Janssen 2011; Dees and Anderson 2006). This leaves us with an endless definitional debate as to what the terms 'social enterprise' and 'social entrepreneur' really mean.

It can also be argued that cooperatives are social enterprises, because they are owned and managed by their staff, or by their customers or their suppliers, rather than by their investors and shareholders whose main interest, it is assumed, is financial profit rather than 'doing good' in any particular way. Some cooperatives are indeed highly 'social', and many of them have been promoted, supported and in some ways managed by external authorities or promoters who wish to avoid the exploitation which is so often associated with investor-owners who have no links to an enterprise apart from their wish to make a profit.

We prefer, however, not to broaden the definition in that way; many cooperatives are set up with highly social motives, and some although by no means all have been very successful in improving the lot of employees, customers or suppliers. Cooperation is of course necessarily social, since it requires people to work together; hence in that sense cooperatives should be called social. There is however nothing inherently social or 'good' about the intentions of people who have come together to start a business, nor do members of a cooperative necessarily limit their own earnings from it in the interest of achieving any particular social good; a cooperative of prostitutes or burglars is nonetheless a cooperative because the products or services which its members offer are generally deemed not to be at all social in the accepted sense of the word. 'Social enterprise' is no doubt a useful term or conceptualisation to describe what in some ways is a new institutional model to which many socially minded entrepreneurs may aspire. But the term must be used with caution, and we must not assume that entities which are labelled in this way are necessarily 'good', or 'bad', or, perhaps more important, that businesses which we do not call 'social' are for that reason not doing a great deal of good.

One approach to deciding whether or not a given enterprise is 'social' is to find out how it is funded. If its customers pay the full cost of whatever product or service it provides, it could be argued that it is not a 'social enterprise', in the most commonly accepted sense. Sometimes, however, both the users of a service and society as a whole benefit from people's use of it. Classic examples include public toilets or rubbish collection. Mass suburban transport is similar, in that if there were no such service, the amount of road traffic would be intolerable for society as a whole. In such cases, a significant proportion or even all the costs of the service may have to be paid for from a 'social' source, such as charitable donations, or by government, because a large proportion of the people who are expected to need the service either cannot afford its full cost or will be unwilling to pay for it. It may seem reasonable to label this as a social enterprise.

There are two very large and well-known such enterprises, however, one in the United States and the other in the United Kingdom, both of which are probably familiar to many of our readers, and which would be called 'social enterprises' by that criterion. Both of them, as it happens, provide the same essential social service, one in London and the other in New York City. The London enterprise costs the pounds sterling equivalent of about $13 billion a year to operate, and the similar operation in New York costs around $17 billion a year. In both cases, the users of the services pay approximately 50 percent of the total cost, while the balance is covered by the respective city authorities.

Many of their customers might be both willing and able to pay the full cost of their services, but the social costs in terms of disadvantage to poorer people and inconvenience and environmental damage caused by people using alternatives are judged to be such that it is worthwhile for the cities to cover half their costs. The services in question are urban bus and subway transport, as many readers may realise. Transport for London, and the New York Metropolitan Transport Authority provide similar services, although the New York authority also manages and charges toll fees for the various tunnels which serve Manhattan[1]

These are not social enterprises, by any commonly accepted definition, perhaps because they are owned and operated by public authorities, not by independent private social entrepreneurs, and we would not propose that they should be. These examples do demonstrate, however, the 'fuzziness' which surrounds the terminology, and the danger of accepting over-rigorous or simplified definitions.

If we really want to recognise social enterprises as a new and desirable form of institution, then we must come up with more analytical evidence rather than anecdotal claims as to why social enterprises are structurally and functionally better equipped to do more good than 'ordinary' businesses and thus can qualify to be called more 'social' than their for-profit or 'pure' non-profit counterparts. The results should speak for themselves without any bias based on labels. Until then the term 'social enterprise' as a type of entity which does more good than other institutional forms must be treated with caution as such entities do not necessarily do more good or less harm.

In theory, such enterprises might be viewed as institutions that can solve social problems by marrying social and business methods. In practice, social entrepreneurship as a field is still emerging and is subject to many institutional instabilities and ambiguities. This leaves social entrepreneurs and their enterprises more vulnerable to misconceptions and exaggerated expectations than other institutional forms as the field is still dominated by many funders who prioritise economic value capture over social value creation, although in theory the whole concept is based on an optimal mix of the two aims.

Commercial enterprises on the other hand have a clear business logic and measurable value propositions that makes their results verifiable. As Milton Friedman says, clarity of purpose is critical for performance and for for-profit businesses "the business of business is to do business." He adds,

> There is one and only one social responsibility of business – to use its resources and engage in activities designed to increase its profits so long as it stays within the rules of the game, which is to say, engages in open and free competition. without deception or fraud.
>
> (Friedman 1970)

In that sense, unlike social enterprises, a commercial business has no competing purposes logic. Hence, its business model and goals are convincing to those who finance it. It may itself do good, or its founders and investors may acquire far more resources than social entrepreneurs whose motives are unclear, and may therefore do more 'good', that is, be more 'social', than those who are labelled as such, although that may not have been their primary intention.

It is useful to consider what 'social' really means in the context of actual enterprises; every chapter in this book ends with one or more case studies. This chapter concludes with two very different case studies. The first describes the social enterprise scene in the United Kingdom, where such enterprises are probably more recognised and organised as such than in most other countries, and the second describes a very large United States–based international enterprise, whose operations benefit millions of people throughout the world, but has never to our knowledge been identified as a 'social enterprise' by its founder or its beneficiaries.

1.2 Case studies

Case 1.2.1 Social enterprises in the United Kingdom

This first case study is not an account of an individual enterprise, social or otherwise; it is a critical review and summary of the social enterprise 'sector' in the United Kingdom, drawn mainly from a publication entitled "The Future of Business: State of Social Enterprise Survey, 2017." This report was produced and published by Social Enterprise UK, a voluntary association which is funded by its members; they include social entrepreneurs, interested individuals and institutions. The characteristics of the sample of 1,581 enterprises, their legal form, the nature of their activities and so on in itself provides a good picture of what a social enterprise really is, in the context of the United Kingdom but also internationally (Social Enterprise, UK 2017).

The United Kingdom is internationally regarded as a pioneer of social enterprise and the related activity of social investment. This view may or may not be justified, but social enterprises in the UK are certainly more organised and legally recognised as such than in many other countries. British government statistics identify around 70,000 social enterprises in the UK, contributing the sterling pound equivalent of over $30 billion to the economy and employing nearly a million people. Independent research which was carried out by the National Council for Voluntary Agencies for 'Big Society Capital' identified a not very different total of 67.000 so-called 'asset-locked social companies', which means enterprises whose capital is legally committed to the undertaking of social activities. During the twelve years between 2005 and 2017, about 13,000 so-called Community Interest Companies[2] were founded, which is another indicator of the growth of the movement.

Given the uncertainty and increased division, inequality and lack of certainty in both national and international affairs, social enterprise can play a significant part in the creation of a more positive future. Social enterprises are not a panacea, but they can answer some of society's challenges, by showing how it is possible to make the most efficient and at the same time the most equitable use of individual countries' and the world's resources, to create opportunities for everyone, and to demonstrate how business can be carried out more equitably. Social enterprises do business in different ways, and they have also shown strong commercial resilience in difficult conditions. The social enterprise 'sector', if it can be called a separate sector, does better than 'ordinary' mainstream businesses when measured by a range of business metrics, such as growth in turnover, innovation, business optimism, start-up rates, and by its racial, gender and other indicators of the diversity of its leadership.

The sample for the 2017 study of British Social Enterprises consisted of 1,591 social enterprises; almost 1,000 of them were contacted and interviewed by telephone, while the others completed on-line questionnaires. They were initially contacted from a list provided by their association. The enterprises used a fairly wide range of institutional forms; 39 percent of them were what is known as 'companies limited by guarantee', which offers similar protections and obligations to those applying to regular limited companies, except that the directors are not entitled to receive a share of any surplus, but they are responsible for the institution's liabilities, but only to a strictly limited nominal amount.

Twenty two percent were 'community interest companies', which have a defined and specific relationship to the communities they serve; this form is used mainly by entities which aim to serve a particular local group, which is often related to housing.

Sixteen percent were 'companies limited by shares'. This is a form of organisation which is used by many private for-profit businesses as well as social enterprises; it is similar to the more familiar public company, except that its shareholders' liabilities are limited to the amount its owners have invested. Nine percent were registered as 'industrial provident societies', a legal form which was in 2019 superseded by various form of cooperatives. The remaining enterprises were registered under a variety of other forms, or not at all. They included some sole proprietorships and some straight for-profit companies. This diversity illustrates the flexibility of the legal requirements, and the diversity of legal forms which social entrepreneurs can chose. There is no specific form of incorporation for a social enterprise; the respondents identified themselves as social entrepreneurs, and their membership of the various umbrella organisations to which they belonged was in some sense a confirmation of this.

The survey included questions about the activities and perceptions of the social entrepreneurs who ran the enterprises. The public sector was the main source of business for almost 60 percent of the enterprises with a turnover of more than £5 million, or about $6.5 million, to finance was their main problem, but they were in general faring better than the similar sample of 'non-social' counterparts to whom the questionnaire was also administered in order to compare them with the social enterprises. Almost half of the social enterprises were growing, as opposed to about a third of the comparative sample, and half of them had introduced new products or services in the previous twelve months, as opposed to a third of the others. This may in part at least be because the social enterprises were more recently established than the others and were thus more likely to be in their growth phase, but it does suggest that they were generally healthy.

Over 70 percent of the sample of social enterprises which were surveyed had made a profit or had covered all their costs in the preceding year, which was about as good a performance as that of small and medium enterprises in general in the country. Three-quarters of the sample earned more than 75 percent of their income from trading as opposed to relying on donations, and there was a higher proportion of start-ups than in the general enterprise population; three times as many of them had been started in the preceding three years as in the comparative sample. One-third of the social sample served a strictly local market, while the remainder sold to national and in some cases international customers. Two-thirds were engaged mainly in the provision of services while one-third sold physical goods, which were at least in part manufactured by themselves.

This data suggests that the social enterprises were generally more successful in a purely business sense than their counterparts, but they also shared many characteristics which are generally associated with being 'social' and which might conventionally have been expected to have reduced their success as businesses.

Forty-one percent of them were managed by a woman, 80 percent had women directors, and one-third of their directors were from what is sometimes known as BAME, or 'black, Asian and minority ethnic' communities. Over a third had directors who were in some way disabled, and just over a half were staffed mainly by women. In spite of these traditionally low income or marginal characteristics, the average salary of their chief executives was £36,000, or about $47,000. This was not a large sum in 2017, but it was not typical of small charities or marginal businesses.

The results of this survey should be treated with some caution, since Social Enterprise UK recently broadened its qualification for membership to include enterprises which aspired to fulfil the strict criterion relating to the share of their income which came from sales as opposed to grants and donations, so that enterprises which aspired to achieve the standard were admitted as well as those which had already achieved it. Membership is also free of charge to enterprises with a turnover of less than £100,000, or about $130,000, but it is reasonable to assume that all or at least most of the member enterprises understand and aspire to be 'real' social enterprises, so that their characteristics do represent a reasonable picture of the 'sector' as a whole.

This survey of social enterprises in an industrialised, 'modern' or 'developed' society demonstrates that such enterprises are not the struggling remnants of an earlier era, nor are they a last resort for people and places which have lost their place in the modern environment. They are flourishing, growing in themselves and in overall numbers, and they show quite clearly that 'modern' traditional businesses, owned by and generally run for the benefit of their shareholders, are not the only means whereby people can find satisfactory employment and the needs of modern society can be effectively served.

The survey, and the strong and generally well-recognised position of social enterprises in the United Kingdom does however pose some important questions, including:

1   Does formal recognition of social enterprises as a definite and definable class of business strengthen their position, or is there a risk that it may weaken other 'ordinary' businesses' commitment to or interest

in 'being social', because it encourages the notion that 'socialness' is a separate and identifiable type of activity, rather than being a more general quality and type of activity in which any entrepreneur might share?

2   In particular, the enterprises which are classed as 'social' in the UK and form the basis of this study are generally fairly small and tend to be run by people who would not generally be expected to own or manage successful independent businesses. Might these characteristics discourage more conventional entrepreneurs and larger or more 'mainstream' businesses from engaging in 'social' activities?

3   Generally, how does the UK's social enterprise 'scene' as it appears from this data differ from the situation in other countries with which readers may be familiar; is it as strong and well recognised, and well documented, or not, and what might the authorities and social entrepreneurs themselves do to improve the environment for such enterprises?

The British institution uses the term 'social enterprise' in its own title, but we should also recognise that this term can easily be misinterpreted; there is no clear or universally agreed definition as to what entities should and should not be known as 'social enterprises'. But the term itself can also be confusing, as is demonstrated by the British institution's own broadening of its key membership criterion from enterprises that actually earn half or more of their income from sales to those which aspired to do so.

The word 'social' actually means involving more than one person, and there is no necessary association of doing good for people with the word itself. Similarly, the word 'enterprise' is very broadly used to describe more or less any undertaking, such as a journey or an examination, although there is usually some implication that an enterprise necessarily involves something that is rather difficult to do. The English language is particularly and often confusingly replete with synonyms, whose meanings may differ not at all or only very slightly from other words, but it is important to try to be clear when we are attempting to describe the uses and interpretations of terms which describe novel entities which have not previously been clearly regarded as phenomena which merit their own name and definition.

There is a fairly clear continuum between a 'pure' for-profit or commercial business, whose owners' objective is only to make a profit, so long as its activities are legal in the place where it operates and morally acceptable to those who work for it, and a 'pure' charity, whose only objective is to 'do good' for others in some way. Our subject in this book, however, is the hybrid, whose objectives include making a profit, or earning enough money from its activities in order to survive and possibly to grow, including remuneration for its staff and payment of some kind for its finance, as well as doing the 'good' which usually was the cause which motivated its investors and employees to start it.

The terminology at both ends of the spectrum is clear; we know what we mean when we use the words 'charity' and 'business', and even lawyers are fairly clear, using terms such as 'foundation' and 'corporation', but there is no equivalent noun which is clearly understood to refer to such a hybrid. The British association uses the two words, 'social' and 'enterprise', and in this book we use a number of different adjectives, such as 'hybrid', but there is no equivalent single word.

We do not propose to nominate such a word, although and many of our readers will no doubt have their own preferences, but it is important to recognise that there is no universally or even generally accepted single word to describe the type of entity which is our subject.

Our second example is very different: it describes but also disguises one well-known multi-national and hugely social enterprise; it is probable that every reader of this book has in some way benefitted from its activities but may have never perceived it as a 'social enterprise'.

Case 1.2.2 XYZ: a great social enterprise

XYZ is probably the world's largest social enterprise. It serves hundreds of thousands and even millions of the world's less fortunate people in a whole variety of different ways, and it would be impossible to measure its total positive global impact.

XYZ provides a direct livelihood to around over 2 million people, many if not most of whom would find it difficult if not impossible to avoid total destitution if they were not assisted by XYZ. A major part of its work is for poorer communities in the United States, but over a third of the beneficiaries are outside North America, mainly in Latin America, but with a large and growing number in Africa and a growing presence in India and elsewhere.

XYZ has a highly positive and practical approach to gender and to the advancement of women, such that about three-quarters of their direct beneficiaries are women.

In addition to its direct beneficiaries, XYZ also works with and assists about 100,000 partner organisations, a high proportion of which are located in developing countries such as Bangladesh, Vietnam and poorer communities in China. Some of these partners and thus their beneficiaries are wholly dependent on XYZ, whereas others are also partners with others and usually rather smaller organisations; it is not possible to measure the exact numbers of XYZ's partner's beneficiaries, or to assess the extent to which the assistance they receive from these partners originates from XYZ, but it is possible that the number of these indirect beneficiaries comes close to the total of XYZ's direct beneficiaries.

These partners are administered by skilled and well-qualified people, as is XYZ itself, and their level of remuneration is similar to that received by people who carry out similar tasks in the same countries. The bulk of those who benefit from the activities of XYZ's partners in poorer countries, however, are poor people for whom there is usually no other source of livelihood, many of whom have migrated into slum communities in rapidly growing urban centres. These beneficiaries do not get the same level of assistance as do XYZ's direct beneficiaries in the United States and other wealthier countries, but their only alternative is often dire poverty or even starvation in their rural villages, or irregular, badly paid day labouring on slightly better-off people's farms.

The largest number of beneficiaries who receive assistance from XYZ, however, are those who chose to avail of the very low-cost services which are available from its over nine thousand locations, worldwide. Some of these people may only receive help from XYZ on an occasional basis, perhaps once in a year or even less when they are in need, while others rely on XYZ for assistance almost every day. It is not possible to state the exact number of these people, but they certainly outnumber the direct beneficiaries by a large margin, perhaps ten or twenty times, and it is similarly impossible to estimate the value of the help they receive, but this may be the most valuable form of assistance provided to the poor by XYZ, although it is not directly quantifiable.

Because XYZ is so large, it has inevitably attracted many imitators, and its leaders acknowledge that XYZ's own assistance programmes are sometimes based on the services which other organisations offer. As a result, its millions of direct and indirect beneficiaries usually have a choice; there are many other organisations which offer similar services. XYZ's leaders have become used to this however, and they regard it as evidence of their own success. If millions of poor people can access two or possibly even more sources of assistance, this is surely better for them than if they depend wholly on XYZ, and it also ensures that XYZ's staff worldwide are keen to offer generous and useful assistance, which millions of people will benefit from because they have a choice.

A number of XYZ's operations are subject to various local taxes in different jurisdictions. XYZ estimates that in addition to the monetary value of their own and their partners' assistance to direct and indirect beneficiaries, they pay nearly $5 billion in taxes every year to the governments of the United States and of the other countries where they work. It is of course impossible to state how this money is used, and to what extent it also contributes to the alleviation of poverty, but it can reasonably be included in any estimate of the total benefit which society globally receives from the organisation.

Questions to consider:

1   Is XYZ actually a social enterprise? Which of its characteristics suggest that it is, or is not, a genuine social enterprise?
2   What additional information is needed to determine more definitely whether XYZ is or is not a social enterprise? The case study is of course very brief, but from the information which is provided it is clear that XYZ does indeed satisfy what might be considered the 'common sense' requirements of a social enterprise: it works with and benefits poor people, including those in rich countries such as the United States as well as in some of the world's poorest countries and its beneficiaries are not compelled to benefit from its services, in spite of its large size.

We are not given any exact figures about the remuneration of its management, and there is no information about the sources of the finance that is presumably invested in it, nor about whatever reward those sources have received from their investments. It is clear, however, that XYZ clearly does a great deal of good, in many different ways, for very large numbers of needy people.

It may be useful at this point also to consider what difference it might make to the decision as to whether or not XYZ is a social enterprise if the case had included the missing information. If XYZ's top management were being paid over some particular sum per year, or if their earnings were over some multiple of the wages paid to its lower paid staff, would this in some sense 'disqualify' XYZ from being called 'social'? Or, if the individuals or institutions which had provided its finances were receiving interest payments or some other remuneration which was over some particular rate of return, would that be a disqualification?

Some readers may by this point appreciate that they have been 'tricked', and that XYZ is not a charity or social enterprise at all. It is, in fact, a thinly disguised description of the retail giant Walmart,[3] which is never considered to be a social enterprise. Walmart is in fact regarded by many people as a typical and so far, highly successful or perhaps exploitative pure for-profit business, whose success has enormously enriched its owners and senior employees. Nobody would consider its business model to be 'social', and many people, probably including some of its customers and employees, would consider the company to be actively anti-social.

In this disguised description, the word 'beneficiary' is used to describe all three of the very large groups of people, worldwide, who do in fact benefit from their association with the company and have 'voted with their feet' to do so. That is, the direct employees of Walmart, the employees of Walmart's suppliers, and, most numerous of all, Walmart's customers. While the Walton family, the company's founders, and some senior management, are in no sense poor or disadvantaged, the company is well known for attracting large numbers of poorer people as its rank-and-file staff, and for the low incomes of the employees of its suppliers, particularly in Bangladesh and other low-income countries. Above all, of course, Walmart could never be described as a supplier to high-income people.

Walmart's mission is stated to be "to save people money so that they can live better" (Ferguson 2015), and this is true not only of its customers, the people who buy from the company because of its low prices, but of its staff, many of whom might otherwise be unemployed, and also of its suppliers' employees.

Walmart and other mass-market retailers are often criticised for forcing down the prices of the goods they source from poorer countries, and thus the wages paid to their suppliers' employees. It can be argued, however, that there are few if any alternative employment opportunities available to these people; one of the co-authors of this book worked for some time in rural Bangladesh, trying to assist local small businesses. The majority of the people to whom we talked, however, and in particular the women, made their job choices very clear.

The least preferred but most likely form of employment was part-time casual labour in their own village. Second was a full-time job in one of the small workshops in local towns which we were trying to promote. Their third choice, which most people considered to be very desirable but unattainable for most, was work in a garment factory in the capital city of Dhaka, which might well have been supplying Walmart. Their ultimate choice, which was something of a dream, and least likely to be attained, was a job in Dubai or another Gulf state.

However, in most public perception, Walmart is still that wicked corporate giant that adversely impacts local businesses in many regions by their competitive low-priced business model, which may be thought to be due more to extractive low-wage practices than operational efficiencies.

Public perceptions and academic definitions may not classify it as a social enterprise, insofar as we are aware Walmart has never claimed to be such a thing. But its performance forces us to reflect and revisit the question – What entities are really 'social'?

Maybe that leads us from Milton Friedman's 'Share Holder Interest' to Michael Porter's 'Shared Value Initiative'. Maybe the reality is simpler than these theories – perhaps many if not most businesses merely realise where they can do better and behave more 'socially' when it seems to be possible, and they do so without worrying about labels. Does that make them less social?

We shall explore all this and more in the ensuing chapters.

1.3 Follow-up activity

Pick an organisation with which you are familiar and which in your understanding is a social enterprise, or an individual who is a social entrepreneur or perhaps was or intends in the future to be one. The organisation or individual need not be qualified as 'social' according to any theory or by other people's opinions except your own. Make a note of why you believe the organisation or individual is 'social'.

Then after you have read each chapter and its accompanying case or cases, ask yourself whether you still believe the enterprise or individual is social, and whether your perception of what is and what is not social has changed or not. If it has changed, in what ways, and if not why not?

Notes

1 For more details refer: (a) "How We Are Funded." n.d. Transport for London. Accessed February 7, 2021. www.tfl.gov.uk/corporate/about-tfl/how-we-work/how-we-are-funded (b) "MTA Operating Budget Basics." n.d. MTA. Accessed February 7, 2021. https://new.mta.info/budget/MTA-operating-budget-basics.

2 A community interest company (CIC) is a type of limited company introduced by the United Kingdom government in 2005 under the Companies (Audit, Investigations and Community Enterprise) Act 2004. It is designed for social enterprises which trade with a social purpose, or to carry on other activities for the benefit of the community. For more details refer: "Office of the Regulator of Community Interest Companies: Information and Guidance Notes." Accessed November 5, 2020. https://assets.publishing.service.gov.uk/government/uploads/system/uploads/attachment_data/file/626088/cic-12-1333-community-interest-companies-guidance-chapter-1-introduction.pdf.

3 For more details refer: "Walmart.Com | Save Money. Live Better." Accessed November 5, 2020. www.walmart.com/.

1.4 References

Bacq, Sophie, and F. Janssen. 2011. "The Multiple Faces of Social Entrepreneurship: A Review of Definitional Issues Based on Geographical and Thematic Criteria." *Entrepreneurship & Regional Development* 23(5–6): 373–403. https://doi.org/10.10 80/08985626.2011.577242.

Dees, J. Gregory. 1998. "The Meaning of Social Entrepreneurship." *Stanford University: Draft Report for the Kauffman Center for Entrepreneurial Leadership.* www.fuqua.duke.edu/centers/case/documents/dees_SE.pdf

Dees, J. Gregory, and B. Anderson Beth. 2006. "Framing a Theory of Social Entrepreneurship: Building on Two Schools of Practice and Thought." In *Research on Social Entrepreneurship: Understanding and Contributing to an Emerging Field*. Association for Research on Nonprofit Organizations and Voluntary Action (ARNOVA) 1(3): 39–66. BookChapter_Dees_FramingTheoryofSE_2006.

Defourny, Jacques, and Nyssens Marthe. 2010. "Conceptions of Social Enterprise and Social Entrepreneurship in Europe and the United States: Convergences and Divergences." *Journal of Social Entrepreneurship* 1(1): 32–53. https://doi.org/10.1080/19420670903442053.

Ferguson, Edward. 2015. "Walmart's Mission Statement & Vision Statement, Generic & Intensive Strategies." *Panmore Institute* (blog), August 12, 2015. Accessed February 2, 2019. http://panmore.com/walmart-vision-mission-statement-intensive-generic-strategies.

Friedman, Milton. 1970. "A Friedman Doctrine – The Social Responsibility of Business Is to Increase Its Profits." *The New York Times*, September 13, 1970, sec. Archives. www.nytimes.com/1970/09/13/archives/a-friedman-doctrine-the-social-responsibility-of-business-is-to.html.

Kerlin, Janelle A. 2013. "Defining Social Enterprise Across Different Contexts a Conceptual Framework Based on Institutional Factors." *Non-profit and Voluntary Sector Quarterly* 42(1): 84–108. https://doi.org/10.1177/0899764011433040.

Light, Paul C. 2008. *The Search for Social Entrepreneurship*. Washington, DC: The Brookings Institution.

Nicholls, Alex (ed). 2008. *Social Entrepreneurship: New Models of Sustainable Social Change*. Paperback Edition. Oxford: Oxford University Press.

Social Enterprise, UK. 2017. "The Future of Business – State of Social Enterprise Survey 2017." Accessed November 5, 2020. https://sewfonline.com/wp-content/uploads/2017/09/2017-State-of-Social-Enterprise.pdf.

2 MIXING MAKING PROFITS AND DOING GOOD

2.1 Social equity through entrepreneurship

We all have our own views about how the world *should* work. When we express these views, we often touch on the topic of 'social equity'. However difficult such an expression can be, or however diverse our comprehension of social equity is, if we are asked for our view of how the future should be, most of us probably envision a rather more equal society and economy than that which we have today. That need not be and certainly hardly ever is an economy in which everyone earns or possesses an equal amount of money, but nearly everyone believes that every person should have enough, however that is defined, and that a high degree of inequity leads to all manner of social problems.

Some of us believe that it is the state's responsibility to ensure some degree of equity, through taxes and subsidies and by other means, while others believe it to be part of the responsibility of not-for-profit entities, foundations. charities or whatever we choose to call them, but an increasing number of people are reflecting on the hitherto often unexplored role of businesses in the process of building an equitable society.

"Redefining the C-Suite: Business the Millennial Way", a recent study by American Express, surveyed 1,363 'Millennials' – people born between 1980 and 1996 – in the United States, the United Kingdom, France and Germany, and 1,062 so-called 'Gen Xers', that is, people who were born between 1965 and 1979. They found that the majority of the 'Millennials', that is, the younger group, believe that businesses should make one of their priority goals to have a 'double bottom line', to 'do well and to do good' (American Express 2017).

But are businesses meant to mix profits with a social purpose? Recently, the traditional view of business where the pursuit of profit has been viewed as the over-riding goal has been confronted by a newer concept known as 'social entrepreneurship'. This suggests that entrepreneurs should above all pursue a social purpose as their priority, and profitability should be the means whereby this is done, rather than the overall goal in itself. It is argued that enterprises which take a market approach and mix making profit with doing

DOI: 10.4324/9781003032229-2

good – 'social enterprises' – are expected to be in a better position to contribute to 'social equity' than are other types of enterprise, such as government or not-for profit entities, or commercial businesses.

One obvious example of a field where such social enterprises are active is the relatively new business of microfinance. Microfinance institutions provide financial intermediation to low-income people, usually but not always through some form of group approach that is both marketable and scalable, and, critically, is potentially profitable. These microfinance institutions can cover all their operation costs, including the relatively high costs of disbursing, managing, and recovering what are tiny sums when compared with traditional banking, as well as the cost of finance, even from commercial markets, and the cost of defaults. They can also charge what are generally seen as very reasonable interest rates, particularly when these are compared with the charges levied by local loan sharks or moneylenders who are the only alternative source of credit for poorer people.

This 'social enterprise' approach is generally more effective and scalable than earlier and traditionally 'charitable' microfinance institutions which distributed subsidised funds at below market interest rates. These institutions lost money on every transaction, their loans were often misused, exploited by political interests or hijacked by local elites, and their growth was limited by the amount of the losses which their donors were willing to bear (Ledgerwood 2001). The whole edifice demonstrated perhaps better than any other intervention that a 'social enterprise' approach, which covers its costs and probably makes a reasonable profit, can actually carry out what was previously seen as a totally social or charitable task, on a much larger scale, and more effectively, than a not-for-profit entity, as is shown in Figure 2.1.

This particular model for lending to poor people who previously had no access to secure and reasonably priced financial services has proved itself to be reasonably profitable and has been widely recognised and applied globally. One successful application, however, does not necessarily answer the larger question – how many businesses in reality can afford to mix oil (purpose) with water (profits)?

It may be that the model of the for-profit social enterprise fits the 'green' business sector, such as waste management, renewable energy, organic food and other activities related to climate change, and businesses such as microfinance which have the dual goals of growth and welfare, rather than more traditional or 'ordinary' types of business. But we should ask whether the social purpose really is the priority for these businesses, or are traditional profit-oriented entrepreneurs entering and exploiting unexplored commercial markets which merely happen to have a beneficial natural or social impact and are partly for that reason innovative and marketable? Is profit merely a means to achieve the social benefit in a financially sustainable way, or are such 'social entrepreneurs' merely exploiting a new market, with a very large economic potential as well as an environmentally attractive impact which

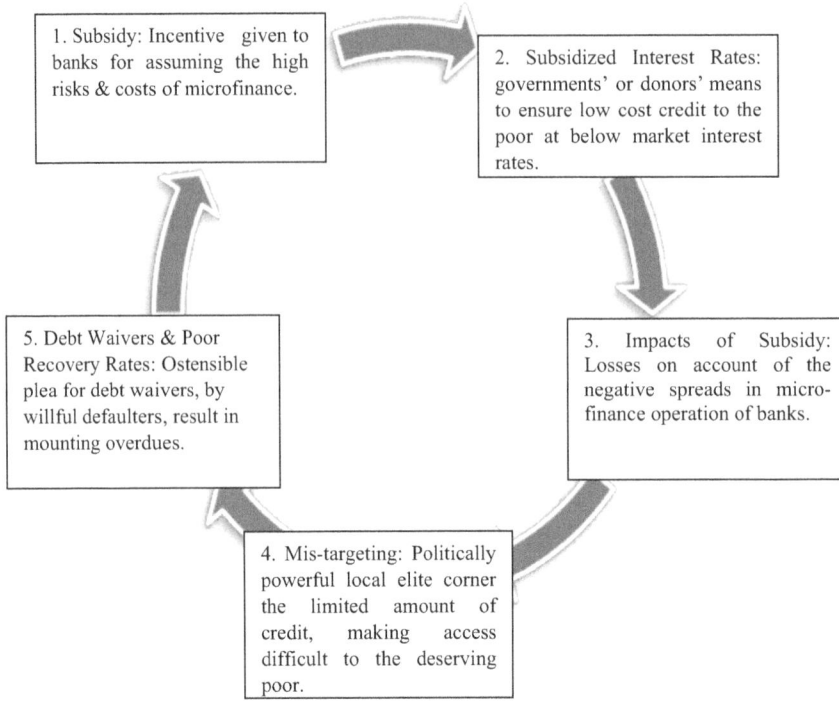

Figure 2.1 Failure of Subsidised Poor-Lending Initiatives

Source: Sketched by Authors.

Note: The sequence of content is based on the book: Ledgerwood, Joanna. 2001. Microfinance Handbook: An Institutional and Financial Perspective. Washington DC: World Bank.

constitutes a remarkable 'unique selling point' which can be 'sold' to financial investors, to client municipalities, to 'green' individuals or other 'socially conscious' customers?

We are not of course arguing that the pursuit of profits is in itself anti-social. The fundamental issue is whether the social enterprise model is being exploited as the best fit for for-profit causes which have an apparent social or environmental dimension which in itself can serve as a commercial advantage. This may be whether in attracting capital, or employees, or customers, all or any of whom may willing to provide such a business with a lower price or better service because of the social dimension of whatever good or service it provides. Are such so-called 'social enterprises' actually any different or 'better' than any other kind of commercial business except for the fact that the service they provide can in some way be shown to be 'social', just as other businesses provide services which are enjoyable, or 'necessary' or have some other feature which makes them attractive to potential investors, employees, suppliers or customers?

Can a traditional not-for-profit enterprise, such as a charity or foundation which addresses social equity issues such as poverty, health, education, homelessness, gender or child development operationalise the theoretical concept of social enterprise and thus become profitable and therefore 'sustainable' in practice? What does the evidence from social entrepreneurs tell us? Though there have been some attempts to add a revenue-generating arm to not-for-profit enterprises in order to make them more 'market-oriented', in the majority of cases the 'social enterprise' concept is only seen to be sustainable because society's value systems in some way fail to put a sufficiently high price on the achievement of social goals, so that an element of 'charity', goodwill, sacrifice or social subsidy has to be involved in order to make the activity viable. If 'social enterprises' are in practice no more than a necessary remedy for what we should hope are temporary failures in society's value systems, then why should we in any way consider 'conventional commercial enterprises' to be in some way less 'good' or in fact less 'social' when their primary goal is to maximise their profits? Is every business not a 'social business' in that sense?

By consistently satisfying the under-served needs in society, by innovating to cut costs and by contributing to social equity through employment generation, and by serving otherwise neglected social purposes sustainably for extended time periods, are 'ordinary' for-profit businesses not already creating a massive beneficial social impact? Is a business any less 'social' just because the social purpose in its operations was not spelled out or articulated when it started?

As we saw in the previous chapter in the case of Walmart, why do we tend to forget the 'socialness' of an enterprise the moment we hear that it has a 'commercial purpose' and can make huge profits for its owners and senior employees? On the same note, why do we attribute 'socialness' to not-for-profit enterprises without examining how well their actual operations are aligned with their self-proclaimed social mission? Again, when we do find a genuine not-for-profit institution that is performing a genuinely social task very effectively, on a very large scale, but we discover that its founders or senior executives are earning as much or even more than most managers of 'ordinary' for-profit businesses, why do we doubt their bona fides, or hesitate to donate to them?

What are we really looking for in our pursuit of social equity through business entrepreneurship? When we ask, 'What is social in an enterprise?' or attempt to decide whether a certain enterprise is 'social' or not, what are we trying to evaluate? We acknowledge the problems and contradictions that arise when the management of any institution state that one of their major objectives is both to make profits and to achieve social goals. The most useful way to address these questions is to look at individual cases. Ben and Jerry's[1] is our first case study through which we hope to prompt our readers to examine these issues.

Ben and Jerry's is a well-known and very successful business which is widely considered to be a model social enterprise; it is useful to review the following case study and to decide whether Ben and Jerry's is a 'social enterprise' or is merely an ordinary for-profit business which has very successfully 'commercialised' its 'unique selling point' of doing good while selling ice cream.

2.2 Case studies

Case 2.2.1 Ben and Jerry's – social, commercial or both?

> Welcome to the resistance. Together, Pecan Resist! We honour & stand
> with women, immigrants, people of colour, and the millions of activists
> and allies who are courageously resisting the President's attack on our
> values, humanity & environment. We celebrate the diversity of our glori-
> ous nation and raise our spoons in solidarity for all Americans.

In November 2018, two years after the election of President Trump, Ben
and Jerry's ice cream introduced a new flavour of ice cream called 'Pecan
Resist', and this was the message on the label.

Ben Cohen and Jerry Greenfield started Ben and Jerry's ice cream in a disused garage building in Burlington, a rural town near the Canadian border
in the state of Vermont. Burlington is home to the University of Vermont and
has a long record of social liberalism; in 2014 it became the first city in the
United States to depend entirely on renewable energy.

The new company based its business on the high quality and local content of its ice cream; they accessed their milk and cream from local dairy
farmers, and from the outset they used the titles of their ice cream flavours
to emphasise their originality and commitment to innovation.

The business grew rapidly, but the founding partners maintained the
powerful image of social commitment; in 1985 the board made a formal
commitment to dedicate 7.5 percent of the company's profits to 'community projects'. They also formulated a three-part mission: the company was
to be committed to producing products of the highest quality; it was to be
economically successful for its shareholders, but also for its staff, its suppliers
and its customers; and it was to aim more widely to improve the quality of
life locally, nationally and internationally.

In its early years Ben and Jerry's maintained a relatively egalitarian remuneration policy; the highest paid employee was not to be paid more than
five times the earnings of new entrants. In 1990 this multiple was increased
to seven times, and in 1994 the practice was dropped as the chief executive's
salary reached seventeen times the level of new recruits and the multiple
was thereafter no longer disclosed.

In 1990, 59.6 % of the common stock of the company was owned by Ben
Cohen, 11% by Jerry Greenfield, and the balance was held by a number of
smaller shareholders and some financial institutions.

By the year 2000 the company had grown very substantially. In the first
quarter of that year, the turnover was $54.18 million, and its net profit was
$1.334 million. Later that year the founders decided to sell the company, and
it was acquired by the Anglo-Dutch multinational Unilever group for $326

million. This valuation of over sixty times the company's annual earnings presumably reflected Unilever's belief that Ben and Jerry's earnings would increase substantially in the future.

The purchase was not wholly amicable, in that the joint founders disagreed with Unilever's choice of a chief executive and preferred their own nominee, but they were over-ruled. Ben Cohen ceased to hold any executive position but remained on the board of directors.

Since that time Ben and Jerry's has maintained many aspects of the company's original approach. The annual donation of 7.5 percent of annual profits to the foundation has continued, and as the label on 'Pecan Resist' demonstrates, the company is unusually politically engaged, even when this is highly visible and possibly objectionable to some of its customers.

Ben and Jerry's sales amount to less than one percent of the Unilever Group's total business, and its substantial political and social engagement is probably consistent with the views of many if not most of its customers; the company operates throughout the United States, but its branches are particularly concentrated in New England and California and in university towns and other more 'liberal' areas.

Ben Cohen and Jerry Greenfield are reputed each to be worth about $150 million as a result of the 2000 sale to Unilever, and both continue to be actively engaged in social action. They were both arrested in New York in April 2016 when they participated in a Democracy Awake protest, and Cohen was arrested again in Burlington in Vermont in March 2018 when he drove a truck through the town playing a very loud recording of an F35 jet aircraft, as a protest against the United States Air Force proposal to station the planes nearby (Ben and Jerry's Homemade, Inc. 1999).

This case study poses a large number of important and difficult issues around the general idea of 'what is a social enterprise' or, more specifically, 'is Ben and Jerry's a social enterprise?' and 'are Ben and Jerry social entrepreneurs?' Readers will certainly have many questions of their own, but it may be useful to think about issues such as the following:

1   The overtly political alignment of the 2018 brand Pecan Resist and the accompanying messages are not 'social' in the usual sense of the term, but they are highly political. Does the message imply that the policies and statements of President Trump are less 'social' than Ben and Jerry's customers would prefer them to be? Is the company's use of this message an expression of its founders' genuine convictions which they want to share and to propagate, or is it merely a part of their effort to create a positive 'image' for the company and thus for its ice cream? Approximately half the population of the United States voted against President Trump, and many viscerally disliked his policies, so

is this and the whole edifice of social concern anything more than a brilliant marketing tool to sell more ice cream?

2 Ben and Jerry's is apparently the world's fourth best known brand of ice cream (Zhu 2016). Is this the result of the company's brilliant marketing, or of customers' genuine sense of identification with the company's social message?

3 Ben and Jerry's has long since abandoned its equitable remuneration practice, and its top management's salaries are little or no different from the salaries of others in similar positions; did this change in any way make the company less socially responsible?

4 The two founders of Ben and Jerry's have apparently become immensely wealthy as a result of their work with the company; does their personal financial success in any way reduce the veracity and sincerity of the social messages which they have consistently conveyed in their business careers and their subsequent personal activities?

5 The founders sold the business to the Anglo-Dutch Unilever group, one of the world's largest multinational companies; does its new ownership in any way reduce the importance and impact of the company's social message?

6 Is the 'real' social impact of the company, its raw material sourcing policies, its generous wages and treatment of its staff, its donations to social causes, in any way reduced by the fact that the company makes a big effort to broadcast news of its social efforts as widely as possible and to strengthen their association with the brand?

7 Ben and Jerry's continues to dedicate 7.5 percent of the company's profits to social causes. This represents a far lower percentage of the company's turnover than a typical consumer goods' manufacturer would allocate to its advertising budget; is this policy a relatively low-cost way to create and preserve the company's image of social responsibility, or is it a genuinely sincere and effective gesture?

Our second case study describes a very different type of business; a medium-sized British registered 'charity', or not-for profit enterprise, which in some ways operates like a regular for-profit business, selling its product, or rather its service, in a competitive marketplace, to a wide variety of institutions, including state and private schools, cruise line operators and others.

Case 2.2.2 Kings Active Foundation – a British social enterprise

Kings Active Foundation[2] is a UK registered charity that has worked with more than 3 million children since 1991. The organisation's mission is to get children to be active and to have fun and learn together via the Foundation's own direct programme delivery and via strategic partnerships with organisations that work with children, young people and families.

The Foundation was established by Nigel Floodgate, an entrepreneurial physical education teacher who had worked on summer camps in the United States and saw an opportunity to provide British children with the same positive school-holiday experiences. Driven by his Christian faith, he established the Kings Trust as a Charity, with a board of trustees, based at the Kings Centre Church in Sheffield in the north of England, rather than as a for-profit business.

There was an encouraging initial response from parents in the local area. The founder left the organisation in 1993, but the network of camps grew to accommodate thousands of children and by 1995 the camps operated at around sixty UK locations.

From the start, rather than relying on charitable donations, parents paid for their membership to the Foundation, which covered the cost of their children's attendance at the camps. For low-income families, subsidised fees were made available, and this Supporting Families Programme has provided thousands of financially assisted places. The Foundation has received a number of grants to provide places for children facing hardship, such as a Children in Need grant to enable children leaving hospital to attend a camp as part of their rehabilitation, and another grant from a private trust which enables young carers to have a break and attend a camp. Donations and grants now provide around 10 percent of the Foundation's income.

After making a loss in its first year, the Foundation started to make annual surpluses that enabled it to develop its mission, to donate to several other charities, and to build cash reserves as required by the government's Charity Commission.

Through the 1990s, the sports and activity camps sector became more competitive; many for-profit organisations were set up to provide camps for children of fee-paying families, at prices which made generous profits. Some owners of these businesses even sold their businesses for substantial sums. The Kings Active Foundation is one of a few not-for-profit entities that provide such camps, the others being for-profit businesses.

The Foundation's charitable status provides some modest tax advantages, but the business is generally quite competitive. The Foundation has no shareholders, so its fees are consistently lower than those of the for-profit competitors.

In addition to its camps, the Foundation has also developed other charitable services. In 1997, they set up a trading company to enable it to provide business-to-business services; all the earned profits were covenanted back to the Foundation. The Foundation and the trading company are governed by voluntary board members who guide and support the paid executives' team.

By 2000, the Foundation was providing four distinct services, all linked to its core mission – sports and activity camps for children, work experience and jobs for young people, programmes and equipment for organisations that work with children and families and leadership training to the international development sector.

The Foundation's mission partners include sixty schools and universities that host their sports and activity camps, many leading cruise and resort companies which the Foundation helps to deliver outstanding children's programmes and several international development agencies for whom the foundation equips and inspires their community leaders to use active games to reach children and young people. The Foundation provides training, development and paid work for around a thousand young people every year.

The Foundation has always earned its income from selling charitable services rather than from donations. These services provide value for money to their users, and they also make a surplus to enable the Foundation to be sustainable and to cover its overheads. This model has been successful; annual revenue is almost £3.5 million, or $4.6 million. This has enabled the Foundation to cope with many issues in its thirty years. It has lost money in some years, but its overall financial performance has been satisfactory.

The people who work for the Foundation have ensured that its mission has been maintained for three decades. The trustees are all volunteers, and there are about thirty paid staff, who are paid slightly less than they would be for similar work in a for-profit company. The chief executive manages the other staff and reports to the board of trustees. None of the board members has ever been paid, and there are no shareholders, except one board member and the chief executive, who are the shareholders of the Foundation's trading company. They earn no financial benefit from this.

The Foundation has thus far navigated all its various challenges successfully. It has always satisfied the British government's very strict requirements for charities, or not-for-profit institutions, and for schools. Its record for child welfare and safety is impeccable and has often set the national standard for good governance and safeguarding.

The following figures in Table 2.1 summarise the Foundation's financial performance during 2019.

The 'charitable activities' item represents the money that the Foundation receives from the schools and other institutions which make use of the Foundation's services, and the slightly larger sum that is spent on the provision of the services. The deficit of £118,000, or $150,000, was in part covered by the

Table 2.1 The Kings Active Foundation Income Statement 2019

Income		
Donations	£6,000	$8,000
Charitable activities	£2,420,000	$3,150,000
Trading income	£360,000	$470,000
Total	£2,785,000	$3,628,000
Expenditures		
Fundraising	£228,000	$300,000
Charitable activities	£2,538,000	$3,300,000
Total	£2,766,000	$3,600,000
Surplus	£19,000	$28,000

Note: Figures rounded to nearest 1,000

small number of donations, but mainly by the income received from 'trading', such as sales of activity programmes to cruise companies and other for-profit businesses.

Issues for discussion:

This enterprise, or Foundation, raises a number of interesting issues, including the following:

1   The Foundation was started from a Christian church, and still has strong religious links. Has this made any difference to the way it operates, and to the legal forms under which its management have chosen to operate?
2   What advantages or disadvantages might arise if the Foundation was a regular for-profit business, like its competitors, rather than a foundation?
3   'Donations' make up a small and declining share of the Foundation's income. Is this trend good or bad, and should its management attempt to increase or to eliminate donations?
4   The Foundation is unusual, anywhere, in that it earns nearly all its income from sales, in a competitive market, but is at the same time a registered charity; is this a model which other institutions should consider adopting?

2.3 Follow-up activity

Identify a local 'good cause' such as an old people's home or a facility for disadvantaged young people; try to find its accounts and sources of income on-line, or if that is not possible speak to one of its staff and suggest additional new ways by which it could raise money other than from donations.

Notes

1 Details of the case sourced from (a) Publicly available information from Ben and Jerry's website: "Ben and Jerry's Ice Cream." Accessed November 5, 2020. www.benjerry.com and the publicly available annual report (b) "Ben and Jerry's Homemade, Inc – Annual Report (10-K) PART I." Accessed October 28, 2020. https://sec.edgar-online.com/ben-jerrys-homemade-inc/10-k-annual-report/1999/03/26/section2.aspx.
2 Details of the case and financial statement sourced from (a) Publicly available information from Kings Active Foundation website: "The Kings Active Foundation." Accessed December 19, 2020. www.kingsactive.org/ and (b) Personal communication with the CEO of Kings Active Foundation, Richard Holmes, done by one of the co-authors by email on November 22, 2020.

2.4 References

American Express. 2017. "Redefining the C-Suite: Business the Millennial Way." *American Express Survey*, November 29, 2017. Accessed October 28, 2020. www.americanexpress.com/content/dam/amex/uk/staticassets/pdf/AmexBusinessthe MillennialWay.pdf.

Ben and Jerry's Homemade, Inc. 1999. "Annual Report (10-K) PART I." Accessed October 28, 2020. https://sec.edgar-online.com/ben-jerrys-homemade-inc/10-k-ann ual-report/1999/03/26/section2.aspx.

Ledgerwood, Joanna. 2001. *Microfinance Handbook: An Institutional and Financial Perspective*. Washington, DC: World Bank.

Zhu, Yehong. 2016. "The World's Top-Selling Ice Cream Brands." *Forbes*. Accessed October 28, 2020. www.forbes.com/sites/yehongzhu/2016/06/21/the-worlds-top-selling-ice-cream-brands-2/.

3   PROFITS CAN BE SOCIAL

3.1 Understanding the social dimensions to profit

Traditionally, entrepreneurship has in theory been highly compartmental-ised. Conventionally, if the goal is to 'do good' then the expectation is that the enterprise would be a non-profit and if the goal is to 'do well' then it is assumed to be a for-profit enterprise. More recently, we have come to appreciate that there is a 'middle way', or perhaps that there should be one, between doing good and doing well, and that many people want to do both. We have come to call such institutions 'social enterprises', and to refer to their promoters as 'social entrepreneurs'.

Clearly of course the use of a particular label cannot in itself ensure anything about the reality of the entrepreneur's intentions or their actual performance. Even the entrepreneur her- or himself cannot disentangle the different motives that have prompted the startup of a new enterprise, and people's intentions are in practice almost invariably mixed. The emerging 'middle road' of 'social enterprise', however, reflects the reality that profits can be social in any form of enterprise, and that there is no reason why a for-profit business cannot at the same time 'do good'.

The relatively new recognition of the term, and of the reality, shows that every entrepreneur in some way needs to make 'profits' of some kind, whether monetary or otherwise, in order to survive and to sustain the 'social-ness' of what is being done. In some ways we all need 'profit', in some sense or another, regardless of whether we label what we are doing as a non-profit or a for-profit undertaking.

The preceding statement may make us uncomfortable. It may very well do so, because we traditionally associate the labels 'non-profit' and 'for-profit' with what we believe are the very different realities of entrepreneurs' altruistic as opposed to their opportunistic actions; we prefer our theory and the labels we use to be clear, even if the reality is as always less simple and possibly confusing. This is, after all, the purpose of theory, even though many theories and the so-called 'academics' who propound them serve only to obfuscate and confuse the people who actually do the things which are being labelled by the theoreticians.

DOI: 10.4324/9781003032229-3

If we take a closer look at the practical reasons why entrepreneurs decide to choose a particular label for their enterprise, we may be able to learn from the reality and change our view. In practice, we see many entrepreneurs who operate under a simple for-profit label, despite the fact that their fundamental purpose is entirely social. They believe that if an enterprise is labelled as a 'non-profit' its owners and staff will tend to work inefficiently while they are trying to do good. If the organisational structure and the 'non-profit' label reduce their motivation to be efficient when they are doing good, it is very likely that they will always rely on the profits from someone else's enterprise to sustain their efforts to do good, when it might be perfectly possible for them to make their own enterprise profitable. This may in some ways even encourage them to sustain the very social inequalities which their enterprise is designed to address, in order to sustain their own employment; this will of course defeat the core principles of the not-for-profit mission which they are attempting to implement.

According to the 2017 results of the Edelman Trust Barometer, an annual online survey of people's trust in global institutional systems, non-profit enterprises are caught in a web of distrust because of the many scandals and cases of corruption which have occurred in 'not-for-profit' enterprises and institutions, whose very existence was intended to work against such things (Edelman 2017). Both World Vision and the United Nations Development Programme were accused by Israel of working to support terrorism by Hamas. Cross-border relief operations to Syria were implicated in a corruption probe, Save the Children's staff were accused of being involved in sexual harassment in Haiti, and the previously highly respected Bridge Academies in Uganda had to be closed. Incidents of this kind have created a general climate of suspicion which hangs over programmes of this kind which had traditionally been supported by globally respected international donor organisations and others.

Both investors and donors are coming to appreciate that it may be possible to perceive and to do things in a new way, which will achieve their original individually focused objectives on profit and doing good but can also begin to combine them. They are beginning to move away from the earlier perception of a one-way and unsustainable linear economy towards a sustainable circular economy, where profits and good works can be combined in the same activities and can thus achieve more in both directions than either could on their own.

This new approach is not based on any fundamental mistrust of non-profits and their social missions, but it does demonstrate that people who call themselves social entrepreneurs and label their activities as not-for-profits have a strong obligation to prove that their operations are totally efficient and transparent. The label 'social' can and must not be used as an excuse for sloppy management and inefficiency; on the contrary, a social entrepreneur must be highly efficient.

In a competitive world, where everyone who wants to benefit society in some way is aiming for a share in the limited amount of money which is available for social causes, it is becoming increasingly difficult to operate as a non-profit and to have to wait until the next donor cheque arrives before one can continue to do more good. A social entrepreneur can, at least in theory, focus on her or his enterprise's overall objective, and can at the same time earn more profit, which will also make it possible to do more good; the traditional notion of 'doing good or doing well' need no longer apply. Many people who have started traditional not-for-profit foundations or charities are becoming aware of this new reality, and they are attempting to move towards the status of a social enterprise, because it is now more generally appreciated that it is possible to mix profits and purpose. But as we suggested in Chapter 2, this is not possible for many social causes where the product is not in any obvious way 'marketable', and where the concept of a social enterprise has not worked in practice.

Manoj Kumar Swain is the founder of a small non-profit called SOCH[1] (Society for Children) which works in Odisha, in eastern India, one of the poorest states in the country which itself is home to far more desperately poor people than any other nation in the world. SOCH has a number of teams at busy railway stations, who identify children who have run away from home or have become separated from their families for some reason. Every year, SOCH rescues about one thousand such children and reunites them with their families, or, if that is not possible, the organisation identifies alternative safe homes for them. SOCH also runs a rehabilitation centre for slum children and others who are addicted to drugs or are for some other reason in need of sensitive but concentrated and focused assistance (Harper and Iyer 2013).

SOCH is funded by a small number of loyal personal and corporate donors, but Manoj hopes that it may one day be possible to identify a source of funding that does not depend on the charity of generous individuals but is based strictly on the quality and quantity of the socially valuable work that the organisation performs.

SOCH generates huge social value, and the railway authorities as well as the city administrators who are responsible for the slum areas where SOCH works are very grateful for the services that it provides. In addition to the obvious benefits to the children themselves and to their families, the passengers who use the railways, the police who ensure their security and the general public all benefit; they do not feel threatened by ragged, starving children or potential thieves; if SOCH did not remove these people, the authorities would have to pay some of their own staff to 'clean up' the platforms.

SOCH's railway platform staff also perform a valuable service for the many other groups of people who make their living on the stations. The porters who help passengers with heavy baggage, the numerous vendors of newspapers and food items, the train and station cleaners, even the specialised staff who refill the trains' water tanks are all in one way or another interrupted or otherwise bothered by the quite large numbers of vagrant children who 'infest' major train stations in India. They very much appreciate SOCH's efforts to help these children and thus to remove them from the stations, and they often assist SOCH's staff by helping them to make contact with children. The railway authorities may provide space in the stations for SOCH's rescue staff, and Manoj and his colleagues consider all these people to be an informal but important part of their teams. SOCH's work is therefore not only socially valuable, but it has a definite monetary value.

Nevertheless, Manoj Kumar has not been able to tap this value, and SOCH remains dependent on the generosity of its donors; there does not appear to be a viable model by which the institution could 'capture' the monetary value of its work; SOCH does not appear to have any profit-making potential and is unable to earn any revenue even to cover part of its costs.

Kumar would like very much to transform his non-profit enterprise into a sustainable and income-generating venture. He earlier took a break from his career and took a post-graduate degree from the Tata Institute of Social Science in order to examine the various possible ways by which he might do good but also make a viable independent career for himself. But he was not able to escape from the necessity to attract donor support. He conceptualised a number of hybrid models that might add a self-generating revenue component to his venture, without compromising his primary mission of supporting the runaway children and their families. One possibility was to train railway children to sell bottled water on the stations and trains, but the profit margins on the popular and generally accepted brands were insufficient to provide a surplus to cover the costs of rehabilitating and preparing vagrant children for this work, and other vending possibilities were similarly impractical.

It became clear that if Manoj added a revenue-earning operation to the work of his new institution, it would have to deviate from the actual mission that he and his colleagues really wanted to perform.

Manoj therefore decided to abandon his attempts to make SOCH fit into an inappropriate 'social enterprise' model. He recognised that although this approach might be suitable for many social causes such as his, he could not identify a 'win-win model' which would enable his enterprise to earn its keep directly from its work. He has decided to focus his energy on promoting the social cause, the benefit to the children whom SOCH rescues, and to look for support mainly from people who appreciate this social impact and are willing to support SOCH as a purely social non-profit institution. He accepts what Thomas Jefferson said – "In matters of style, swim with the current; in matters of principle, stand like a rock" – and much as he would like to adopt a social enterprise model, his main task is to promote the mission of SOCH, that is, Society for Children.

But is a determined focus on an institution's central mission necessarily inconsistent with a search for ways to earn income from its day-to-day operations? A non-profit investment institution called 'Slow Money' which is based in Boulder, Colorado, in the United States, has shown that a non-profit investment movement that is based on a common mission and is socially trusted by local communities can be profitable and can attract investors rather than traditional donors (Colpaart 2009). Slow Money[2] aims to encourage and promote the flow of 'patient' capital to local food enterprises and organic farms, and thus to connect investors to the places where they live and to 'bring money back down to earth'. Its 'investors' money is used by local organic farms and food businesses; they pay no interest, and their capital repayments are all re-invested in other similar enterprises rather than being returned to the original investors. Slow Money's long-term objective is for one million people to commit one percent of their assets to local food systems and personally to observe and benefit from the impact of their capital rather than to earn mere financial returns.

Slow Money has also started 'Beetcoin', an online platform which lets individuals invest as little as $25 to help local and organic food enterprises reach their funding goals (Tasch 2015). The loans earn no interest, and every dollar that gets repaid is recycled to future entrepreneurs. In addition, Slow Money offers a service for small food enterprises, called Credibles, which means 'edible credits'. Local communities come together and support their local food shops by pre-purchasing food, and the shops can in turn pass on the advance finance to their farmer suppliers. This expands the concept of community agriculture and shows that small-scale local organic farming can be profitable. Legally, Slow Money is a non-profit, but it achieves its very 'social' objectives by deploying and revolving capital, not by donations.

Enterprises whose founders aim primarily to 'do good' rather than only to make money can assume multiple forms in practice; their labels often fail to capture their social dimensions and the reasons they have adopted their chosen legal forms. These labels generally refer to the operational structures that their founder-entrepreneurs have adopted in order to deal with their internal and external environment; they may reveal or they may inadvertently conceal the fact that any enterprise, irrespective of its label, must earn a surplus to survive, whether this is called a 'profit', a 'margin' or a 'surplus'. The following short case studies should help to demonstrate this, albeit in two totally different contexts.

3.2 Case studies

Case 3.2.1 Micro-finance Credit Rating International (M-CRIL) – inclusive micro-economics

In 1983, Sanjay Sinha[3] together with his British wife, Frances, whom he had met while both were studying at Oxford University in the United Kingdom, set up a small development consultancy business in Lucknow in north India. They both had a passionate interest in development, in a practical sense, and were determined to do something about poverty in India.

They called their new venture EDA, standing for Economic Development Associates, and they set it up as a for-profit limited company. They were both highly qualified and could easily have obtained well-paying jobs in finance, in London or in Mumbai, but they deliberately chose to be self-employed and to start their new venture in Lucknow; this was Sanjay's home city, and is the capital of Uttar Pradesh, India's largest and by several measures among its poorest states.

They were determined from the outset to distance themselves from the powerful 'development industry' which was mainly centred in Delhi, India's capital city, and whose participants were usually NGOs or non-government organisations, registered as such under the 1860 Societies Act, or were branches of similar institutions in Europe or the United States which were often registered as 'charities'. This was one of M-CRIL's founders' reasons for locating their new enterprise in Lucknow, in addition to the fact that they could not afford the costs of living and running a business in the capital city. They chose to register their new enterprise as a normal 'for-profit' company. They wanted to avoid the casual amateurism and occasional arrogance of 'do-gooders' and to organise their activities in a totally business-like and entrepreneurial way.

The business prospered and grew, albeit quite slowly, since the partners were determined to maintain the high professional standards which they felt were often lacking in local development consultancies. In due course they were able to afford to move the business to Delhi, and in 1998 they entered the field of credit rating in response to the emergence of microfinance institutions. Microfinance was a new and unfamiliar field, and financial institutions which were interested in lending to these new enterprises were uncertain how to judge their quality. M-CRIL was set up to rate the quality of microfinance institutions' (MFI) governance, management and financial performance; M-CRIL designed a formal rating system, based on a rigorous desk-based assessment and a standard three-day programme of visits by trained analysts, who call on a sample of branches and interviewed a number of their field staff and their clients. M-CRIL also pioneered a social rating system with similarly rigorous techniques in order to capture the 'social performance' of MFIs; this system is also applicable to other 'double bottom line' and development organisations.

This business also did well, but as time went by and Indian microfinance institutions grew and looked for international recognition, they tended to go to the international rating agencies such as Moody's and Standard and Poor's, or to their Indian affiliates. These agencies knew nothing of microfinance, and their ratings were usually based wholly on a desk-based study of MFI data, with little or no field contact, but the banks, the stock market and other potential investors nevertheless preferred the more familiar rating 'brands'.

M-CRIL responded to this by broadening its range of services and the areas of operation. They introduced a range of training programmes and a variety of related research and consultancy services, and they also expanded internationally. This was initially in neighbouring South Asia, but the business also grew further afield, and M-CRIL established its own offices in Cambodia and Myanmar, together with an office in Patna in Bihar state, east of Lucknow, which focused on assisting farmers' producer enterprises and other rural clients. M-CRIL's international business also included assignments in many other countries in Southeast Asia, China, Africa and elsewhere. The focus continued as before, to engage with organisations working to impact poverty, and to provide the professional services and tools to help them work more effectively.

M-CRIL remained as a limited company throughout; some senior members of the thirty or so staff also received employee stock options but over 90 percent of the shares were owned by the founding couple. The company's salary levels together with variable performance incentives were well in line with the earnings of larger NGOs or local consultancies, although the two owners maintained a comparatively lower salary level and they did not draw any dividends. The non-executive board members, who were recruited from the banking and what is generally known as the 'social sector', received modest fees as well as their expenses, and they regarded their role as being similar to the positions many of them held in not-for-profit and government organisations.

M-CRIL's annual turnover grew steadily, and by 2018 it had reached around $1.5 million and was still growing; profits were maintained at around five percent of sales, or $75,000. The staff were anxious for growth, in order to broaden their own opportunities and to attain the level necessary for stock exchange recognition as a rating agency, and the founders wished gradually to withdraw from active involvement in order eventually to retire; they would need in due course to be able to divest some of their holding, in order to secure the company's future and to ensure a comfortable retirement for themselves.

M-CRIL was at this point fortuitously approached by the Asian Development Bank, a Manila-based international development finance institution, whose management wanted to assist M-CRIL's growth and also to share in its success. The bank eventually took a 25 percent share in M-CRIL, for about $1 million; this money was invested in the business, and could not be withdrawn, but the transaction did set a value on M-CRIL as a whole. This suited the employee shareholders and the two founders.

Like any real-life example, this case study poses a number of interesting questions, and it may be useful to consider issues such as:

1   Is M-CRIL in reality a for-profit business which happens to work in a social field, or has the founders' choice to set it up as a business actually made it more possible for them to achieve their social goals? Regardless of its legal form, is it 'really' a business, or a social enterprise, or a charity?

2   How might M-CRIL have evolved differently if it had been set up as an NGO? Has its simple for-profit business legal form in any way directed or possibly misdirected the founders' goals?

3   It is unlikely that the Asian Development Bank would have acquired a stake in M-CRIL if it had been set up as a 'society' or some other form of non-profit enterprise. Is its part acquisition likely to promote or to erode its social mission?

4   Does the substantial capital gain which potentially may accrue to the founders in any way erode M-CRIL's 'social value'?

5   M-CRIL has a small but highly professional team of staff, whose remuneration is not as high as that paid by the most prestigious financial institutions but is well above the rates paid by many Indian non-profit development enterprises. Is this good for M-CRIL's mission, or not?

6   The founders deliberately set up M-CRIL as a for-profit enterprise because they believed that many traditional charities tend to be 'amateur', unprofessional and badly managed. Was this decision justified?

Eton College in the United Kingdom, a boys' secondary school which is about six hundred years old, provides another very different example. It is a not-for-profit institution, which has provided an excellent education to thousands of young people, from the UK but also throughout the world, large numbers of whom have themselves gone on to make their careers in social enterprises. But it is widely criticised for perpetuating social divisions and inequality.

Case 3.2.2 Eton College

Eton College[4] was founded in 1440 in a small town on the River Thames by King Henry VI of England, with the specific objective of providing free boarding education for seventy poor boys. The king founded King's College at Cambridge University in the following year, and it was intended that the boys who had studied at Eton would then proceed to the college at Cambridge. This was one of the earliest attempts anywhere to bring education to less advantaged people, and it is perhaps significant that this is still an issue in the United Kingdom almost six hundred years later.

The king was only nineteen years old at the time; he had succeeded to the throne when he was only two, and the country had been governed by a Regency Council until 1437; the establishment of Eton may have been one of his earlier attempts to impose his own will on the country.

Henry is said to have been uninterested in politics, but the country he ruled was at this time beset by the so-called Wars of the Roses between the house of York, of which Henry was head, and the House of Lancaster. In 1461 Henry had to flee to France, and the throne was taken over by Edward VI. Edward transferred much of the endowment which his predecessor had granted to the new school at Eton to another establishment across the river in Windsor, but Henry returned to London and to the throne in 1470, and the new school continued.

In addition to the seventy scholars, the poor boys whose costs were covered by the school's initial endowment and for whose education Henry had established Eton, over time the school also admitted a number of local boys, whose families started to pay something towards the costs.

In the twenty-first century, this tradition is in some sense still maintained, in that the so-called 'scholars' live in a separate building, and the 'town boys', or 'oppidans', live in a number of different 'houses' in the town. Some elements of the original fee structure also remain; the basic fee for the 'oppidans', who make up the majority of the students, is £28,300 a year, or about $35,000. The scholars are entitled to a discount of 10 percent on this amount.

Eton College is a registered charity, not a business, and is thus legally treated as a public-interest institution; no taxes are payable on any surplus it may earn, any donations to the school are eligible for tax deductions, and it enjoys a number of other privileges of this kind.

The school is clearly aware of the delicacy of this situation since it is considered as an archetypal bastion of privilege and preserver of social distinction. Nineteen of the fifty-two British prime ministers were educated at Eton, including two of the most recent three holders of the office.

Eton's website demonstrates the institution's concern to create and enhance a reputation for its social contribution. There are five separate sections, of which the second is headed 'public benefit', and it covers a whole range of community activities, awards, bursaries and scholarships. Seventy-three of the present total strength of about thirteen hundred boys pay no fees at all, thus preserving the letter if not the spirit of King Henry's original intention in 1440.

The story of Eton raises many questions:

1   Eton benefits in many ways from its charitable status. It does not make a profit, but any surplus it does make is not subject to tax. It is exempt

from a number of local taxes, and people who give it donations and legacies can thereby avoid taxes themselves. Is this status justified, or should Eton be treated like any other enterprise which sells its services mainly to and for the benefit of wealthy people?

2   Eton reinvests any surplus it may make in its facilities or uses it to subsidise the costs of boys whose families cannot afford the fees. It pays its staff slightly more than teachers in the state system, but nothing close to the earnings of corporate managers, entrepreneurs or even senior civil servants or chief executives of major international charities, and nobody takes any 'dividend' or capital gain from its operations. Is it not therefore reasonable to treat it as a not-for-profit social enterprise?

3   Some people (see for example Green and Kynaston, Engines of Privilege Bloomsbury, London 2019) have argued that Britain's so-called 'public' (and actually rather private) schools such as Eton should be compulsorily reformed so that they become less elitist and more egalitarian, or that they should at least be deprived of their legal not-for-profit status and thus be subject to the same taxes as other businesses which do not claim in any way to be 'social'. Is this a reasonable view?

From the preceding two cases it should be clear that some for-profit businesses can do a great deal of good and some non-profits can do great harm; whatever the aim of an enterprise, it must in some way cover its costs and generate a surplus in order to exist. The word 'surplus' means the same as 'profit', but whatever it is called, it is necessary for any enterprise that wants to develop and grow and not to rely on occasional donations.

The COVID19 'lock-down' panic, which was at its height at the time this book was written, provides further examples. Highly profitable and some would say exploitative on-line delivery providers, such as Alibaba, Instacart and Amazon, made it possible for millions of people to continue to obtain what they need through their non-contact door-to-door home deliveries. The companies also provided employment to large numbers of people who had lost their jobs because their employers were 'locked-down'. These highly commercial for-profit enterprises surely provided a more substantial and dignified social service to millions of people, at no cost to taxpayers or donors, only because their aim was to seize the opportunity, and to maximise their profits. Profits can be social, and there is nothing which is in itself wrong about them.

3.3 Follow-up activity

Identify a social enterprise which has been found to be doing some harm to society, in spite of its mission to do good. This may be from your local knowledge, or it may be a well-known national or international institution about which you know from the media. Try to figure out what went wrong: Did they hire the wrong people? Were their incentives inappropriate? Was there a lack of supervision? Were the staff under-paid or perhaps over-paid? Or Did society expect too much because of the 'social' label?

Notes

1 Details sourced from SOCH website (a) "SOCH-Society for Children" – NGO in India. Accessed November 5, 2020. https://sochforchildren.org/ and (b) email communication with Manoj Kumar, Founder of SOCH by one of the co-authors on November 3, 2020.
2 For more details refer: "Slow Money." Accessed November 5, 2020. https://slow money.org/.
3 Details of the case sourced from M-CRIL website (a) "M-CRIL Inclusive Microeconomics." n.d. Accessed December 28, 2020. www.m-cril.com/ and (b) email communication with Sanjay Sinha, the founder of M-CRIL by one of the co-authors on November 4, 2020.
4 Details of the case sourced from Eton College website "Eton College." Accessed November 5, 2020. www.etoncollege.com/.

3.4 References

Colpaart, Ashley. 2009. "Inquiries into the Nature of Slow Money: Investing as If Food, Farms and Fertility Mattered, by Woody Tasch." *Journal of Hunger & Environmental Nutrition* 4(2): 214–16. https://doi.org/10.1080/19320240902983886.
Edelman. 2017. "Edelman TRUST BAROMETER." Accessed October 30, 2020. www.edelman.com/research/2017-edelman-trust-barometer.
Harper, Malcolm, and Lalitha Iyer. 2013. *Rescuing Railway Children: Reuniting Families from India's Railway Platforms*. India: Sage Publications. www.amazon.com/Rescuing-Railway-Children-Reuniting-Platforms-ebook/dp/B017BZJAWU.
Tasch, Woody. 2015. "Slow Money. From Bitcoin to Beetcoin." Accessed November 5, 2020. https://slowmoney.org/blog/from-bitcoin-to-beetcoin.

4 SOCIAL AIMS AND SOCIAL DEEDS

4.1 Social enterprises: do definitions matter?

Although there appears to be an inevitable conflict between our desire to do good and to do well, there are many institutions that try to do exactly that. They may have different labels and may not have been conceptualised as 'social enterprises' as such, but every one of them has some 'socialness' in it. In fact, it is difficult to imagine an enterprise that does no good at all. A cruel private prison stops some dangerous people from doing more harm, a weapons dealer provides jobs for its employees and even a drug dealer satisfies some desperate people's needs and can be an income for poor farmers for whom any crop other than opium is uneconomic. No enterprises, whatever their aims, can exist without some trade-offs. It may always be necessary to injure or neglect some people in order to help others who seem more deserving.

The value that any enterprise offers must by definition be to fill a gap, to provide a product or service which somebody needs, which the entrepreneur has identified and has addressed through a product or service. It need not be 'new', but it must in some way be useful for someone in a way that was not previously available. The 'four Ps' of marketing are the product, its price, its place and its promotion, and success is said to consist in achieving the right 'marketing mix' of these four ingredients.

Opinions as to what is and what is not 'social' will inevitably differ, but every interaction that involves more than one person is actually 'social'. Everyone's view of what is or is not 'social' in the sense of being 'good' is not the same, and we must avoid allowing our views of the 'socialness' of a given enterprise to be over-influenced by the labels that are used by the entrepreneurs themselves. No enterprise, be it non-profit or social enterprise or for-profit is better or worse than any other in terms of its socialness just by virtue of its label. Academics, like everyone who writes or teaches about human activities rather than actually doing them, want to classify enterprises with labels. We may have unintentionally created the impression that entrepreneurs and their enterprises are necessarily either social or not social or even anti-social. Such over-simplified demarcations are of little value when we wish to assess an organisation's potential to do good in practice; we need

DOI: 10.4324/9781003032229-4

labels for our theories, but in practice, social deeds matter more than social goals, and we must not allow our desire to label things to affect our in-depth and evolving view of what they actually do.

Social goals are self-proclaimed personal intentions which are stated by entrepreneurs. The enterprises which the entrepreneurs have established may or may not be able to operate in accordance with these stated goals, regardless of their founders' intentions. If the over-arching goal is to deliver a marketable product or service, regardless of its social impact on the purchasers or others, so long as it is within the accepted boundaries of the law and morality, then the enterprise becomes a for-profit; if its goals include making a positive social impact or others which are not necessarily profitable, and which may prejudice its profit-making potential, it cannot be a pure 'for profit'. For instance, the stated goal of a microfinance institution could be to 'empower the poor through financial intermediation' and it would be labelled as a 'social enterprise'. It might be labelled as a for-profit or a non-profit social enterprise, if its sources of capital and the way its management use any surpluses differ while they are pursuing the same goals.

The goal of a clearly commercial enterprise such as Walmart might be 'to save people money so they can live better'. These examples of an overtly for-profit commercial business and an obviously social enterprise demonstrate that the goals of very different enterprises all have an element of 'socialness' in them.

It is relatively easy to write and publicise 'social goals' that appear unequivocal, but actual deeds, however 'social' the intentions of those who do them, are less simple to appraise; there are almost always some trade-offs, including the necessity to choose one social need and not another, or to do some minor social damage for the sake of the greater good. Even when institutions report their work as incontestably consistent with their stated social goals, the public interprets such reports through their own particular lens. Hence outsiders' perceptions about what good an enterprise actually does, regardless of whether it is labelled as a for-profit or non-profit entity, are what really matters.

A for-profit social enterprise in microfinance, for instance, is judged by people's perceptions of the results of its services – did it really help poor people to be better off than before, and in the process, did it exploit anyone, or did it actually do little more than to burden them with more debt than before, or compel the women who took the loans to work even longer hours in order to repay loans which their husbands used to buy liquor?

And, in the case of Walmart, or any other mass-market retailer, did it actually enable its customers to save money on decent quality durable goods, or did it encourage them to buy more and waste more, and at the same time exploit both its own employees and those of its suppliers? In either case, what matters is people's perceptions rather than the institutions' statements of their purposes.

In theory we expect social aims and deeds to be aligned, but in practice there will inevitably be contradictions, which can be intentional or unintentional. This is true for all enterprises, whatever the label we give them. So we hope that in this chapter we can help our readers to clarify their own thoughts about labels and the realities they are intended to describe, and about their opinions as to the good or ill that particular enterprises do. It is important to acknowledge the broad variety of social goals and social actions which various entities profess to pursue, and what they actually do, in order to be able to assess the 'socialness' of any particular enterprise. We all have prejudices and stereotypes; it used to be generally accepted that there were some entities which were 'purely' for profit, within or perhaps outside the law, and others which pursued purely social goals. Some of the former did some good, almost incidentally, and some of the latter made some profits, but the two basic categories were clear, in everyday parlance and in law.

More recently, we have come to realise that there is a 'middle' way and that it should be clearly acknowledged. There are some people, some entrepreneurs, who want both, to 'do good' and to 'do well', and there is a need for this duality to be acknowledged, in law, such as for taxation purposes and also in everyday discourse. The term 'social enterprise' has been acknowledged, as have its equivalents in other languages, such as in German, for instance, where a for-profit business is usually called an 'unternehmen', a charity or purely 'for good' entity is called a 'hilfsorganisation', and what in English is known as a social enterprise is a 'sozialunternehmen', following the German passion for new and longer words. It is important for us to clarify our own views on what is and what is not a social enterprise, and thus to improve our ability to use the terminology in a way which we and others can understand.

We must also of course be aware of our prejudices when we use the names which are commonly employed to describe enterprises. Biases are inevitable – we cannot get rid of them – but we should be aware of the role they play when we are trying to judge the 'socialness' of an enterprise.

Our biases about different enterprises may originate from causes of which we ourselves may not be aware. It may be our generalised view of what we understand to be the social goals of an enterprise, and it is important to be clear as to the difference between more 'formal' labels, such as 'charity' or 'business', about whose meaning most people are generally in agreement, and other terms which denote opinions instead of more-or-less accepted facts; the term 'social enterprise;' lies awkwardly between these two.

In order to be aware of our own biases, we can use an example such as the terms 'priest' and 'businessman'; There are some of each who do good, and others who do bad. It is more shocking when the priest does bad things than when the businessman does, and perhaps rather more remarkable when the businessman does good things than when the priest does. But this does not make us want to 're-label' them; the priest and the businessman labels are 'neutral' terms, whereas the 'social enterprise' term is in part normative; to most of us it says something about our views of the goodness or the badness of the enterprise.

This dual meaning may in part arise because the term 'social enterprise' is moving towards a 'neutral' meaning, and there are many legal forms which entrepreneurs can use to show that they want to bridge the gap. Corporate registration regulations in the United States, for instance, are a state matter, not federal, and in some states, entities can register as 'Benefit Corporations'. Italy has a similar system, and other countries may move in that direction.

This trend will continue, but we have to accept that while the meanings of terms such as 'charity' and 'business' are conventionally accepted, 'social enterprise' has not as yet attained that status, legally or in common parlance. The issue can quite easily be tested. Nearly everyone agrees that Walmart is a business and Oxfam[1] is a charity; there might be differences of opinion as to their legal status, but it would not generally be an issue worth discussing. The issue as to whether they are or are not 'social enterprises' would generate a great deal of argument and would mainly depend on what one believed about what these enterprises actually do.

The situation is evolving, but at the time of writing this book, we should accept that 'social enterprise' is still at least partly a normative term and has not reached the more fixed meaning we ascribe to the words 'charity' or 'business'.

It is not the purpose of this book to state what is or is not a 'correct' definition of the term 'social enterprise'. As legal forms proliferate it may be that the term becomes as clear as 'business' or 'charity', but in the meantime it is important to recognise that when any entity is called a 'social enterprise', the intention may be to say one or several things, to say something about its legal status, its founders' intentions, its present activities or even its projected future role in society.

Most people, for example, are clear that Walmart is a for-profit business. But when we consider its social impact on its staff, on its customers and on its suppliers' employees, we have to accept that it is in a sense a very 'social' business.

Similarly, it might seem wrong to consider organisations such as Oxfam or Save the Children[2] as anything other than wholly 'social' enterprises. Recent revelations, however, about the activities of some staff of these organisations when dealing with vulnerable people in Haiti and elsewhere suggest that the high moral tone we usually associate with such institutions may be misplaced, as may the terms by which we refer to them.

We are scandalised, and the institutions have as a result suffered a drop in their incomes, but we should ask ourselves whether we would be equally scandalised if we heard similar stories by the employees of a large multi-national for-profit business such as Walmart or Facebook. We would deplore the behaviour of the individual staff and would expect them to be punished, but we would not hold it against the reputation of their employers in the same way. Is it right to judge 'charities' and their staff by different standards?

Our decisions about the labels which we assign to enterprises can be very complicated; we probably all agree that it is wholly wrong to exploit vulnerable people, but our perception of the activities of an institution itself, and by extension of its staff, can be very different.

We expect a charity whose stated objective is to reduce poverty to do good, and we tend to expect the same of its staff, even in their leisure time, but we do not really expect Walmart to 'do good', except indirectly. We hope that common morality and the laws and expectations of people in the places they work will discourage them from doing harm, but that is about as far as it goes.

Hence, we may ask how much good an entrepreneur and the staff do in the operations of their enterprise, even when there was no compulsion to do so. If the answer is a great deal, then that enterprise might reasonably be termed a 'social enterprise', regardless of its legal status or whatever label is commonly used to describe it. Formal labels may imply good social behaviour, but the reality can be very different. For-profit commercial businesses can do good or bad, and the leaders of non-profit charities are also able to exercise their choice to do good or to do bad, and therefore to deserve or not to deserve to be called social entrepreneurs. We probably agree that a social enterprise should not just be social and 'do good' but should also be operationally sustainable not only or mainly from donations but from the income it earns from its operations.

The following case study describes a little known large, unusual and strongly faith-based charity in southern India called the Shri Kshetra Dharmasthala Rural Development Programme,[3] loosely translated as 'place of holiness', or SKDRDP. It has achieved remarkable results, which are in many respects better not only in social but also in financial terms, than those of other for-profit and not-for-profit enterprises which work in the same field of microfinance. Some aspects of its performance may depend on its unique history and management, but there is much that any social enterprise can learn from its work. Its performance challenges the belief that a non-profit should transform to some sort of hybrid or for-profit form to be sustainable. SKDRDP shows that a 'social enterprise' can assume any form or legal structure based on its founders' belief of what it is to be 'social', whether it is or is not called a 'social enterprise' by others. How the term is used depends on people's perceptions about what the institution actually does. We present the case of SKDRDP to show the extent of social and economic involvement which was needed for an essentially spiritual organisation to bring about the social transformation that its leaders felt was needed in its community.

4.2 Case study

Case 4.2.1 SKDRDP – a faith-based social enterprise in southern India

The Shri Kshetra Dharmasthala temple is located about three hundred kilometres west of Bangalore, in southern India. The land around the temple is of low quality, and only a very small proportion can be farmed. It is suitable for only a limited number of plantation crops, but these can be very profitable, so long as the farmer can afford to invest in planting and can wait as long as seven years for the first harvest.

As a result most small farmers have to plant less profitable crops, for which the land is not suitable, but which can be harvested after six months or one year. Most families in the area live in isolated huts on their own plots, so each village occupies a large geographical area. They farm their own land, or they are employed as daily wage workers on other people's land. The women take care of their families and help on the land. They also roll beedis, hand-made cigarettes.

Until 1974, the situation was different. Most of the land was owned by substantial landowners. Some managed their own land and employed large numbers of agricultural labourers. Others leased their land to share-croppers. In in 1974 the Karnataka Land Reform Act set strict limits on the amount of land that could be owned by one owner. The labourers and tenants now had land of their own, but they could not cultivate their new land because of the high investment that tree crops demanded. This problem was compounded by the fact that many of the farmers were alcoholics.

The Dharmasthala temple was established at some time in the thirteenth century. A local farmer, called Heggade, lived there, and two travelling strangers, who were actually angels, came to his house and asked for hospitality. They were generously received, and after they had gone they reappeared to Heggade in a dream. They thanked him and said that they wished to return in their spiritual form and to live in the place. They asked Heggade to build a small temple for them next to his house, and to offer hospitality in the same way as he had received them.

Heggade did what the angels had told him. He built a small temple and offered food to anybody who came by, and the village soon became a place of pilgrimage. Then the angels sent another messenger, who brought a sacred stone image and installed it in Heggade's temple. This made the temple a place to worship Lord Shiva as well as the original angels and widened its popular appeal. The temple became famous in the area, and its name was changed to Dharmasthala, or the place where service to humankind is the way of life.

Since then, the Heggade family have maintained their position as owners and trustees of the temple and its surrounding area, and as the spiritual rulers of the region. There are a number of similar places in that part of South Karnataka, but Dharmasthala is unique in having been governed by the same family for so long.

The Heggade family are Jains. There are only about 4 million Jains in the world today, most of whom live in India, but they have significantly influenced the religious, spiritual, economic and political life of India for more than two thousand years. Like Hindus and Buddhists, the other two main Dharmic religions, Jains aim to achieve total release from self and desire, or nirvana (Harper, Rao, and Sahu 2008).

Most of the pilgrims are local, and Dharmasthala has never acquired an international reputation. The pilgrims make modest donations and over its long history, the family and the temple have become quite wealthy. This has enabled the family to maintain the temple and, in recent years, to finance and run SKDRDP, their remarkable rural development programme.

Between ten thousand and twenty thousand pilgrims come to Dharmasthala every day. They can stay overnight, and those who cannot afford the cost are accommodated without charge. Nearly every devotee leaves some donation, however small. Many also follow the tradition of having their heads shaved before paying their respects to the God in the Temple; Dharmasthala runs a mass-production barbers' establishment for this purpose, and the mass of hair which is cut from the pilgrims' heads is sold for industrial purposes. Even this raises a substantial sum every year.

The 'Dharmadhikaris', or guardians of the temple, have always been known for their charity, which is paid for by the donations of the thousands of pilgrims who visit the temple every day. Most of these pilgrims are not rich, but the total amounts to a very large income every year. After meeting the establishment and maintenance expenditures of the temple, the balance of the money is given away as charity.

Veerendra Heggade, the present holder of the hereditary position, inherited the position in 1968, when he was twenty years old. As a member of a rich family, he enjoyed modern cars and good architecture. Due to the sudden death of his father, he had to abandon his studies and take on the responsibility of the position of Dharmadhikari. He was worried by the faith which the temple's devotees had for him and he felt he should do something to improve their livelihoods. Could he reduce their dependence on charity without eroding their faith?

Heggade decided to build an institution which went beyond charity and could help the devotees to build sustainable livelihoods, and he slowly transformed the temple's charitable work into a modern rural development institution, which would improve the people's livelihoods but would preserve their faith in the temple.

Heggade disliked the people's dependence on the temple's charity; the money which they had contributed was going back to them in charity; it was not systematically used, and the grants depended on ad hoc responses to individual requests. It was difficult to track their impact, and Heggade wanted to know what was happening to the money he was giving away and to maximise its the long-term benefits, to ensure that it did not merely increase people's dependence on him and on Dharmasthala.

He started two separate development institutions, the Shri Kshetra Dharmasthala Rural Development Project, or SKDRDP, to serve the people in the rural areas around the temple, which was funded and managed by Heggade and the temple, but was intended eventually to be self-sustaining, and the Rural Development and Self Employment Training Institute, or RUDSETI, to offer training and livelihood assistance over a wider area, and was a joint venture between two large national banks which served the district.

The initial task for SKDRDP was to assist the small farmers who had obtained land rights; and it was set up as a temporary project, to provide the farmers with the knowledge as well as the capital they needed in order to make the best use of their holdings.

Four staff were appointed, and Dr. Heggade was in effect the project director. Local village field staff were chosen by the local people. They started in the villages around the temple, where the farmers were struggling to cultivate their land due to their lack of tools, seeds, and fertilisers, and provided them with these things.

The field animators identified needy families and helped them to develop their land with an informal food-for-work programme. The farmers hired labourers when required, and they too were paid by SKDRDP. Every morning all the staff went out with truckloads of rice and cultivation equipment, to work with the farmers, showing them how to clear their land and plant the new tree crops, and paid them for their time with rice, in the same way as the landlords who employed them before. The teams returned to Dharmasthala every evening, but after five years, it was clear this was too short a period in which to make a lasting change.

In 1991 the legal status of SKDRDP changed from its original status as a temporary project, and it was registered as a charitable society, in recognition of the fact that the work would occupy many years.

They also started to work with small groups of farmers who helped one another, and most of the money was under the control of the men; much of it was spent on alcohol. The women and the landless households were being neglected. The interventions had not led to any significant change in the lives of people, although there had been some marginal economic improvement.

In the late 1990s, Dr. Heggade became increasingly dissatisfied because SKDRDP was not growing as he had hoped, in terms of its programmes or its outreach, and he was not himself able to give it the time it needed. The programme had made some improvements, but these were not substantial, and it was probable that they would not survive if SKDRDP's assistance was withdrawn. Basically, it was little more than a continuation of the charitable tradition of the temple.

It became clear that the money from donations to the temple would not cover the expansion or even the continuation of the programmes as they were being run. Since SKDRDP was linked to a temple, which was known to be wealthy and was not seen as being involved in development work, it would be difficult to access conventional development funds.

At this time microfinance self-help groups were becoming popular in other parts of India. These groups were usually promoted and trained by non-government organisations or by banks; the members were usually all women, and they had achieved great success in helping disadvantaged people to save small amounts of money, to receive and to repay small loans and generally to improve their economic and their social position. Dr. Heggade decided that groups of this kind could enable him to reach all the people in the area who needed to improve their position. Dr. L. Manjunath, a veterinary doctor, joined SKDRDP at this time. He introduced a number of radical changes, in order to formalise the institution. Salaries were increased, and a pension scheme was introduced. SKDRDP also started to work with government development programmes. SKDRDP's field staff provided an effective link to the communities where they worked, met every month and carried out all proceedings in Kannada, the language of Karnataka. No English was used in the communication to make sure that everyone understood what they heard rather than being confused, misled or carried away by development jargon and concepts which were alien to the community. In the community, nobody uses the words 'micro-credit' or 'microfinance'; they refer to 'Pragathinidhi', which means a precious and special thing which belongs in part to a deity.

For their initial ten years SKDRDP had worked only with men. When Mrs. Heggade became involved, she introduced the idea that women should be made equal stakeholders; they had always worked on their land, but it was not usually held in their name, and many women earned a little extra income by rolling handmade cigarettes. The SKDRDP groups worked to enable many thousands of women to improve on this very inadequate form of income generation.

The management decided to move SKDRDP away from charity towards a more empowering approach, and to use microfinance to involve the women and landless people who had so far been left out. It was also clear that all their efforts would be in vain unless the problem of drunkenness was dealt with. They also worked actively to prevent alcoholism as since it was clear that whatever good work the institution did was being wiped out by this menace. In 1993, the state government banned the sale of alcohol in the area. This was counter-productive; the sales of illicit liquor more than compensated for the ban.

The ban was lifted in 1994, and the strategy was changed. SKDRDP became centrally involved. They started to run de-addiction camps, which aimed totally to change people's attitudes to liquor. They included health education, counselling, and more fundamental faith-based processes to influence the addicts' basic attitudes. The anti-alcohol movement spread to the whole district, and over two-thirds of the participants stayed away from alcohol permanently.

The SKDRDP groups originated as a way of labour sharing, and they then started small group savings which led to internal lending from the group funds to the members, based on the national self-help group programme which was getting under way at that time.

The groups opened bank accounts and took small one-to-two-year loans. Repayment rates to the banks were maintained at 100 percent; the SKDRDP staff followed up every loan to every group, and no delays were allowed.

These small loans had little long-term impact on members' livelihoods, and the programme did not help SKDRDP itself to become financially sustainable, since the groups usually borrowed directly from their local bank branches, even though SKDRDP had access to the necessary funds to lend to them itself.

The banks were unable to satisfy all the groups' requirements, but SKDRDP was not clear whether they should act as facilitators or as lenders. The links between the credit and savings groups which SKDRDP had promoted and Dharmasthala had weakened, as the banks were now able to lend to them on their own.

SKDRDP itself was also completely dependent on donations from the Dharmasthala Trust, and any expansion would require more money. The temple's resources were limited, and SKDRDP's management decided that this problem could be solved, and the loyalty of the savings and credit groups could be retained if SKDRDP itself started to lend money to the groups when they had outgrown their own savings. This might also eventually make SKDRDP fully sustainable, or even profitable. SKDRDP, with the backing of the temple, was a much better risk than most of the new institutions to which they were being asked to lend.

SKDRDP also decided to extend its entire programme beyond the area around the temple; the banks were happy to lend to SKDRDP, which would itself engage in microfinance, not only as a group promotion institution but as a lender, and that all their development activities would be rolled out to all areas together, including microfinance. SKDRDP rapidly expanded into other districts within the State of Karnataka and was reconstituted as a microfinance institution. The borrowers were all encouraged to engage in livelihood-generation programmes, often in collaboration with government schemes, and they also introduced a very effective insurance scheme. The whole organisation expanded very rapidly, both in the range of its activities and in its geographical coverage, and SKDRDP started to run programmes which cover almost every facet of life that affects the communities in the area, including health and sanitation, education, housing, livelihoods and microfinance. They moved from their exclusive focus on marginal farmers to working with community members of all backgrounds, including women, landless people and young men and women.

SKDRDP's staff believed that their groups provide a base for poor people to be empowered and to escape poverty. SKDRDP provided a full range of livelihood assistance to these groups, based on microfinance. The cost of promoting a group was more than covered by the interest on the loans to the groups, and once a group was firmly established, SKDRDP made a reasonable profit on their loans.

The loans could be used for every conceivable purpose: for consumption, for income generation for farming or non-farm activities, and for housing, toilets, electricity installation and so on. They were funded from group members' savings as well as from SKDRDP or the bulk bank loans it had secured, and members were provided with training on how to use their loans.

SKDRDP's staff trained the group members on how to conduct meetings, how to keep accounts, and how to manage their lending activity in the best interest of the group and of its individual members. Once the group could manage itself, the SKDRDP became their auditor and facilitator.

The groups carried out their transactions in front of a photograph of Dr. Heggade, the Lord Manjunath, or in front of the Bible for Christians or the Qur'an for Muslims. The first loan to a group was usually disbursed in the presence of a village elder or other respected person, and the cheques were all signed by Dr. Heggade and by Mrs. Heggade. Before the recipient took the cheque, a special religious ceremony was held, offering it to God. The banks that lend through SKDRDP also felt that though the loans were unsecured and risky, they were in some way secured by the God of Dharmasthala.

In 1999 SKDRDP made the change from promoting self-help groups for banks to actually financing them. In the following six years the value of loans outstanding to the groups from SKDRDP expanded by about thirty-five times, to over $20 million. Expenses increased by only seven times, to some $4 million, and SKDRDP's earnings from its financial intermediation rose from about $100,000 to over $3 million. The grant from Dr. Heggade's Temple Trust was about doubled, but as a proportion of total expenses it fell from over four-fifths to under a quarter.

SKDRDP expanded the credit limit for loans to groups from four times up to forty times the groups' balance of savings, or two thousand dollars, whichever was less. The four-times limit had been established by the government-owned development bank which started the self-help group movement, and it seemed unwise to commercial bankers. SKDRDP was far more liberal than the banks in many other ways, such as loan terms, and the banks themselves gave very liberal terms for their bulk loans to SKDRDP. Dr. Heggade's status, and bankers' knowledge of the underlying material and spiritual wealth of the temple, contributed to their willingness to do this, even though their loans to SKDRDP were unsecured.

The groups can access funds from three different sources. They can take loans directly from their local banks, they can borrow from SKDRDP, and they can lend from their members' own regular weekly savings. The group members do not take any regular interest on their savings, so the small profit that they make from internal lending becomes an additional source of funds. The groups maintain a single account with their local bank into which all their funds, including loan repayments, are deposited and from which all loans are disbursed. Members who leave their groups can withdraw their savings along with three percent annual interest, so long as they have cleared any outstanding loans.

The members pay their savings and repayments to their groups every week, but the groups repay their loans to SKDRDP on a monthly basis. Unlike most of the several million self-help groups elsewhere in India, the groups promoted by SKDRDP do not make their own decisions on weekly savings amounts, interest charges and so on. These decisions are all made centrally, and the groups do not appear to regret their lack of autonomy. They believe the rules are fair, but they also have the sanctity associated with Dharmasthala and Dr. Heggade.

SKDRDP requires security for loans of over INR 50,000, about $1,000, and whatever assets that are bought with the loan are in any case considered as security. The banks make similar security demands, but the people are reluctant to give them their land title deeds, whereas they are very happy to entrust their most precious assets to SKDRDP.

SKDRDP makes a 'spread' of three or four percent on its loans, which covers most of the running costs of SKDRDP. The groups themselves calculate the interest on loans to their members as a flat percentage of the total amount lent rather than on the outstanding balance. This effectively means that the groups lend at around 20 percent, which enables them to build their own capital.

The groups' costs of funds vary according to the proportions of their own savings, their accumulated surplus, loans from SKDRDP and loans from banks in their pool of money. Groups have to deposit two months' repayment instalments in their accounts before their loans are released. This gives some leeway within which the SKDRDP staff can follow up any problems. These apparently quite onerous conditions are accepted without question by the groups.

Groups can borrow from SKDRDP to finance their lending to their members, which can be used for any legitimate purpose the member wishes, for marriages or personal expenses, for farming, for group activities, in fact, for more or less any purpose a member wants. Loans to women's groups make up well over two-thirds of SKDRDP's total disbursements, although loans to men tend to be for larger sums than those for women. In 2001, the amount lent to women had been negligible.

SKDRDP is one of the largest community development institutions in India, and in spite of its strong Jain and Hindu links, the percentage of Muslims and Christians in the groups is about the same as for the population as a whole in the area.

SKDRDP's growth has been dramatic. Table 4.1 compares the scale of activity in 2001, in 2006 and in 2020.

In 2020 the total amount of loans outstanding to SKDRDP and to banks whose loans are managed by SKDRDP was $1.4 billion. SKDRDP is involved in a wide range of activities, but its 'core' business is microfinance. This is a highly competitive field, and SKDRDP has succeeded not only in its growth and service to large numbers, but also by conventional measures of business success. Many of its Indian competitors are overtly for-profit businesses, often financed with foreign capital, and some have substantially enriched their founders, as well as serving large numbers of clients.

The period from 2008 to 2013 was perhaps the most testing time for Indian microfinance institutions; the field grew very rapidly, but there was a major crisis in Andhra Pradesh, the state with the most competitors, and a number of institutions failed. SKDRDP did not operate in Andhra Pradesh, but SKDRDP stood out during the period in terms of its financial performance.

Out of India's ten most successful large microfinance institutions, SKDRDP had the lowest rate of loan defaults, the second lowest cost of operations as a percentage of its loan portfolio, the only steady return on assets, albeit at

Table 4.1 Scale of SKDRDP Operations

Operation parameters	2001	2006	2020
Staff	230	1,120	21,000
Total groups	4,250	34,000	500,000
Total of active borrowers	21,800	235,000	4,200,000

Source: Figures from SKDRDP website: https://skdrdpindia.org/

a relatively low level, and, perhaps most significantly, by a large margin the lowest yield on its loan portfolio, indicating that its interest rate was the lowest of the ten institutions (Ashta and Parekh 2018).

SKDRDP consistently achieves 100 percent repayment from all its groups. Most borrowers are aware that their groups have in a very real sense been promoted by the God of Dharmasthala. The funds which they have borrowed from SKDRDP are kept in the same bank account as their accumulated savings and surpluses, and any loan from banks, although they are of course accounted for separately, so all the groups' money has a certain sanctity. Defaulters feel that they are cheating God, not just a bank. In 2006 one family came to pray at the temple and then walked across the compound to the SKDRDP office. They handed a small payment to SKDRDP, which, they said, had been owed by their grandfather and had not been repaid when he died some years before. They said that the God had told them to repay it.

The goal of SKDRDP's range of group and community-based programmes is to help thousands of families to improve their standard of living to a decent level. SKDRDP also provides health and life insurance to the communities it serves. This protects them from falling into poverty, but also protects SKDRDP from defaults which may be caused by deaths or ill health. Their insurance covers not only medical costs but also other risks, such as maternity expenses, loss of earnings during convalescence, funeral expenses, losses arising from floods and other natural calamities, damage to housing and standing crops, and accidents.

SKDRDP aims to enable everyone in the region where it works to be self-reliant and to live in harmony with each other. This involves the physical environment as well as the people themselves, since they depend on the land, and water, as well as their known skills. SKDRDP therefore works with small and marginal farmers to adopt sustainable farming practices and to build rural infrastructure.

Everyone is treated the same for the purposes of microfinance, irrespective of their landholdings, but the farmers who own less than a hectare of land are the main targets of the livelihoods programme. They can obtain credit through their groups, but loans alone are not enough to get them out of poverty.

They are helped to prepare five-year farm plans to develop their small-holdings into high-yielding commercial farming businesses. The local conditions are suitable for cash crops such as areca nut, rubber, cashew, vanilla and coconut, and all these have long gestation periods.

The farmers are assisted to prepare individual farm plans, which include fencing, irrigation, dams and terraces, planting trees and short-duration crops, and household assets such as a toilet, improved housing, electrification and so on. The farmers do not regard these plans as an intrusion into their private affairs, since they are worked out together with their colleagues, and they also have some sanctity through being approved by the representative of Dr. Heggade.

Many thousand families have implemented these farm plans, and this has created a big demand for tree seedlings. SKDRDP has therefore financed selected farmers in each village to start tree nurseries. The farmers can use their groups to borrow the money they need to pay for irrigation equipment such as sprinklers and pumps and to dig wells. Over ten million rubber, coconut, areca nut and cashew saplings have been distributed.

The farmers are encouraged to use renewable energy sources such as gas from manure and solar energy. SKDRDP claims to have the largest concentration of solar home lighting systems in any one small geographical area anywhere in the world.

Unlike many NGOs, SKDRDP works closely with government departments, and their field staff ensure that all the official programmes are properly delivered in their villages. SKDRDP's specialised staff provide a link between the farmers and research centres, and they have also taken up watershed management programmes in collaboration with the government of Karnataka.

SKDRDP has also helped women from poorer and often landless households to set up group enterprises, but these businesses often fail to make a profit. SKDRDP has therefore set up a separate entity called SIRI to promote and support its members' group enterprises. The company's role is specifically to provide supply and marketing services to the businesses which SKDRDP's groups had set up.

Well over ten thousand women work in around several thousand small group businesses, producing items such as soap and detergents, pickles, spices and chips, ready-made garments, plastic bags and organic fertilisers and disposable leaf plates. The enterprises are labour intensive, since the aim is to employ as many people as possible. Every group has to contribute to the marketing business's capital, and each has received low-cost long-term loans from a government development bank to finance its operations. SIRI is also the marketing arm for the two thousand groups of women from landless families who have been assisted by SKDRDP. It helps them with designs and quality control, it buys their products, and it has developed a common brand and advertises and promotes it through various channels.

SIRI has appointed local sales representatives and has set up its own retail shops in some nearby towns. The company makes a modest profit, some of which is distributed to the shareholder groups and used for welfare purposes such as the purchase of school uniforms for children whose parents cannot afford them.

SKDRDP started as a charitable activity to help marginal and small farmers to cultivate their fallow land. It has evolved into a multi-purpose business which supports all kinds of income-generating activities and livelihoods with finance and a range of other supporting services. SKDRDP is a banker, a supply and marketing intermediator, or 'middleman', as well as a manager of rural affairs.

The programme started with groups, for small farmers, for poor women and for reformed alcoholics, and these groups have been mobilised and converted into self-help groups, becoming part of the fast-growing national movement but still retaining the special features associated with their origin. Most such groups elsewhere in India have been started, by NGOs, by banks and sometimes by their members themselves, as financial intermediators. Some of them have evolved beyond this, to a whole range of community activities.

The early SKDRDP groups were started for other purposes and moved later into financial intermediation. This has probably made them stronger and has certainly increased their loyalty to SKDRDP and Dharmasthala. SKDRDP has effectively evolved its own model of microfinance, breaking most of the conventional rules, and without compromising its basic goals of supporting life and livelihoods. Under one percent of SKDRDP's loans have had to be written off, and the majority of the groups and their members are regular savers and borrowers.

SKDRDP has worked in the region for some forty years, and its work has moved from simple charity through in-kind donations to a range of sustainable programmes working for integrated rural development in an area with a population of several million people. Having started with agriculture, SKDRDP now covers every aspect of life in the communities it works with: health and sanitation, alcohol de-addiction, education, livelihoods, microfinance with savings and insurance and housing. It has also made a significant if immeasurable contribution to the social empowerment of the previously marginalised people of the region.

Labour sharing has always been fundamental to SKDRDP's approach, and this has enabled the wage labourers who had recently become landowners in theory actually to become landowners in practice. The concept of farmers' labour sharing is central to SKDRDP's success. This is still the unique feature of the whole undertaking and is the principal entry point for most of SKDRDP's programmes. The men still start their proceedings with prayers as they have from the beginning, and the original SKDRDP groups of SKDRDP are the only male-dominated self-help groups in India.

The microfinance programme has been designed to reflect members' needs. There has from the beginning been a demand for larger, longer-term and lower-cost loans than are normal in microfinance, where short, small, high-interest loans are usually the norm. This was necessary because farmers needed such facilities in order to make the best use of their newly acquired land.

Credit is also available from the start for every conceivable purpose, and members do not have to pretend that loans are for 'productive' purposes when what they really need is money for consumption, school fees, medical expenses or family events such as marriage. The programme is in many ways more systematic and standardised than elsewhere. Groups all charge the same rates of interest, unlike most self-help groups, where the members are free to charge what they think fit.

The SKDRDP field workers' focus is on helping the group members to generate sustainable livelihoods. Strong discipline is maintained, partly because of continuous follow-up by the field workers, auditors and others, but also because of the strong sense of shared values and loyalty to Dharmasthala and the person of Dr. Heggade. The SKDRDP staff are seen by the groups as advisers and friends rather than loan recovery agents, which further strengthens the bond between the members, their groups, and SKDRDP and Dharmasthala.

SKDRDP is a viable business in itself through its microfinance programme and SIRI, and its key strength is in its links to Dr. Veerendra Heggade, the Dharmadhikari of the Manjunatha temple. This spiritual link is not incidental but is central to every aspect of SKDRDP's operations.

Dr. Veerendra Heggade is heir to a dynasty of some twenty generations, but he himself started SKDRDP and its development activities in 1982, which is very recent in the context of the temple's existence. He has also set up schools, colleges and hospitals throughout the region which have no formal links to SKDRDP. Dharmasthala is also engaged in other work, such as archaeology, preservation and cultural promotion. Much of the physical development of the temple compound is also quite recent, and Dharmasthala has only become well known outside its own neighbourhood during this Heggade's time. Earlier, it was one of many similar temples, under a local dynastic leader who was somewhat better known than many others because of its Jain-inspired polytheism.

Dr. Heggade's father was a typical wealthy patriarchal figure. Like many such people he had political ambitions, but he lacked a local following and was unsuccessful when he stood for election to the national parliament. Many similar temple trusts in India have been taken over by the government because of misuse, alleged or otherwise, and a legal case was brought against the former Heggade in an attempt to take over the Dharmasthala properties. It was still pending when he died and was later defeated by his son.

Dr. Heggade's work can be seen as a result of divine intervention, as an effective strategy to reverse the decline in his family's and the temple's reputation, and as the result of his genuine concern for the welfare of the people of the surrounding area.

Dr. Heggade is a good leader as well as a good manager. He could see that while SKDRDP initially had to depend on the Temple Trust, not only financially but also in terms of local goodwill, the situation would later be reversed, so that SKDRDP would become a source of strength both for his family and for Dharmasthala as a whole.

Dharmasthala is a Jain temple, and the Heggades are Jains. Many of the better-off people in the area are also Jains, who might have felt threatened by a typically socially activist development NGO. Dharmasthala, like most religious institutions in India and elsewhere, is very much a part of the existing social structure, and none of SKDRDP's programmes have ever appeared to be attacking the local hierarchy. SKDRDP has strengthened the reputation and influence of the family and Dharmasthala, even at a time when many religious institutions are being threatened by the growing secularisation of society.

SKDRDP does not promote any particular religion, or indeed religion as such, at all. It promotes values. The emphasis of Dr. Heggade's is on spirituality and personal values. He has denounced drinking and smoking, and emphasised simple living, health and hygiene. John Wesley, the founder of Methodism, said that cleanliness was next to godliness, and Dharmasthala demonstrates a similar belief. Even the toilets are spotless, which cannot always be said of Indian public places, particularly religious ones.

In addition to SKDRDP, Dr. Heggade set up the Santhi Vana Trust, which promotes value-based living and naturopathy, Ayurveda and yoga. He also set up the Dharmothana Trust to restore temples and places of historic value, as well as a number of educational institutions, including one for orphaned children. He has also established colleges for naturopathic and ayurvedic medicine, as well as a conventional medical school, which can of course be a moneymaking venture as well as an expression of values.

At the level of his own family Dr. Heggade demonstrates the virtues of simplicity. He lives a rather Spartan life, apart from his occasional enjoyment of the collection of vintage cars which he inherited from his father, and he insisted that his only daughter should study in a local school. This was not easy, since his brother's children study in private schools in Bangalore.

He is very much supported in this by his wife, who has emerged from her role as a conventional housewife to play a major part in SKDRDP. She deserves much of the credit for the women's group programme and for the expanding role of women in SKDRDP's work. It might even be said that the only programmes with any claim to be socially radical are those involving women, which Mrs. Heggade has so vigorously promoted.

In addition to their strategic view, their spiritual support and their promotion of certain values, the personal wealth of the Heggades and their institution has of course also been vital to SKDRDP's success. In addition to its initial support, and its continuing subsidy, the Temple Trust has been able to cover the cost of initiatives such as SIRI, which inevitably make heavy losses for some years before they break even.

Fundamentally, SKDRDP has moved out of its charity mode. Most of the earlier charity programmes have been discontinued, except for grants to destitute people. Until 2001 all the costs of SKDRDP's development programmes came from the Temple Trust, but since then funds have come from government schemes and financial institutions. Here again, the reputation and sanctity of the Heggades and their institution have opened many doors.

SKDRDP's values have contributed to its success. They are closely associated with religion, and the need to take a high moral stand in everyday dealings. Everyone in the area, of whatever faith, respects the Dharmasthala shrine, and fears God, whoever they believe God to be. In a very real sense, they believe that SKDRDP's money is God's money. The tradition of associating loan disbursements with a religious ritual, and the fact that cheques carry the signature of God's representative, whom many people regard as a demi-God, means that wilful default is at a minimum.

In the same way, the staff of the banks which have lent large sums to SKDRDP feel that their loans are in some way guaranteed by God, even though they are technically unsecured. After all, who would demand collateral from God?

Respect for divinity has effectively been combined with respect and unity within families and within communities. Labour-sharing and de-addiction treatment are essentially group-based, and these have contributed to SKDRDP's success in community mobilisation of men in a way that few other development institutions anywhere have been able to do. SKDRDP's field staff are treated in what many would consider to be a patronising and old-fashioned way; they can only marry with permission, and any relationships among the staff which go beyond official or collegial ties are forbidden. This leads to some staff turnover, but the local junior staff generally have rather poor formal qualifications and have few other options for employment.

More positively, SKDRDP's field staff have an almost monastic level of loyalty and commitment, and they feel themselves to be very much more than junior field staff of a development institution. SKDRDP in turn has great faith in its local staff and is very loyal to them. Older and senior staff are treated with particular respect and are whenever possible given preference in promotion. The staff are grateful for their jobs, and they feel themselves to be contributing to a higher cause.

The religious values are continually reinforced by Dr. Heggade and his wife. They are in no sense figureheads but are continuously involved in and seen to be involved in management. This behaviour is mirrored by other senior staff, so that all the staff identify completely with the Dharmadhikari, who is the head of the organisation.

SKDRDP's success is clearly very closely related to its links to the Heggades and to Dharmasthala, and these are essentially local in character. The programmes have been successfully expanded beyond the immediate neighbourhood of Dharmasthala in Belthangaddy, within South Canara District and to a lesser extent beyond it. It remains to be seen how durable the programme will be in places which are more distant from Belthangaddy, particularly if it goes to quite different parts of India, as has been envisaged. This question will only be able to be answered by experience.

Many other religious institutions have successfully extended their influence far beyond their place of origin, even to other countries and other continents, but it will clearly require major changes to secure the same loyalty and respect from village people who have had no personal contact with Dharmasthala. Nevertheless, SKDRDP has thus far expanded organically, through gradually extending the frontier of its involvement rather than 'jumping' to more distant locations where funding or other support might be available, and this expansion may continue successfully. It has already been necessary to modify some details of the programme to fit in with practices that already existed in the new areas. In some places, for instance, SKDRDP has had to confine group membership to only one member of each family, as opposed to the more liberal policy adopted in its 'home' area.

The rapid expansion has put strains on SKDRDP's staff. The senior staff team are a major strength but are now growing old and retiring and will have to be replaced. Many younger people with less understanding of the very special organisational culture of the institution have joined and are being promoted to senior positions. SKDRDP still keeps to its policy of recruiting local people at the entry level and then promoting them to higher responsibilities based on their experience and performance, but it is not clear that this can be continued.

A small number of professionals who have had experience in other organisations with different cultures have been recruited. They work in specialist departments, such as training and marketing, but there have been problems, and some have left because they could not 'fit in'.

There are also many issues related to the actual work of SKDRDP. The initial work with small farmers in areas such as Belthangaddy has long been completed, and SKDRDP has changed its emphasis to agro-processing and non-farm activities and to the growth of women's group enterprises. This is more challenging than small farm development, since it involves marketing in competition with well-known brands, and there have been few examples of successful group-owned manufacturing businesses. SKDRDP is taking on a major challenge, and SIRI has to market a wide variety of product lines, which have been introduced because they employ large numbers of more or less un-skilled operatives, not because of market demand. This is a unique achievement.

SKDRDP is an institution that has evolved from a charity and aspires to move towards sustainability. It has already successfully changed course, and thus far the experience has shown that is possible to combine the backing and detailed involvement of a religious trust with professional management.

Numerous questions remain. Southern India as a whole is developing rapidly, and unlike many rural areas, the villages where SKDRDP has worked have not been left behind. There are more employment opportunities than ever before, and people's aspirations are changing. Mangalore has become a big industrial centre in its own right, and Bangalore has become one of the fastest growing cities in the world.

These changes will have a major impact on SKDRDP's client population and on its staff. Most of the village people no longer need the very basic services that were originally so essential, and the brightest and more enterprising young men and women can find work elsewhere; they do not need to work locally for SKDRDP.

SKDRDP is essentially a traditional community-based institution, inspired by a local god, and relying on a local institution and locally recruited staff, to serve local people. Its competence is home-grown rather than professional, and Dr. Heggade has resisted the employment of development 'professionals'. They are more expensive than locally recruited people but, more important, they are often more loyal to their profession than to an institution or still less to one man, even a semi-divine man.

Management succession may also be an issue; Dr. Heggade may be semi-divine, but he is not immortal; in a sense he is a classic social entrepreneur who has used his unique position to create a remarkable social enterprise; he will be hard to replace.

SKDRDP's performance is based on several centuries of tradition, history, family and local performance, and it may appear to be unique, very remarkable but so unusual that others cannot learn from it. There are, however, many faith-based social enterprises and charities worldwide which can gain from some aspects of its management and experience, even if they cannot hope to replicate the whole performance.

In particular, we may consider the following questions:

1 SKDRDP is unique; what, if anything, can other institutions which work in similar fields learn from it?
2 SKDRDP is a profitable business but is also a faith-based social enterprise. To what extent is its success based on its unique association with Dr. Heggade and Dharmasthala, as opposed to its good design and management?

3 SKDRDP was started by Dr. Heggade, albeit on the strong foundation of his own family's centuries-long association. What might be done to ensure that it survives when he is no longer there to direct and inspire it?

4 Nearly every rural and urban area worldwide is home to a number of long-established religious institutions, and also has numerous social problems. How can such religious institutions address the social problems of their surrounding areas and at the same time strengthen their own position, as SKDRDP has done for the Dharmasthala Temple?

4.3 Follow-up activity

List five social enterprises (defined as you will) of whose existence you are aware and make an approximate guess as to their incomes and expenditure. Write down your guesses, and then look up their internet entries and check how right (or wrong) your guesses were.

Notes

1 For details refer: "Oxfam International." Accessed November 5, 2020. www.oxfam.org/en.
2 For details refer: "Humanitarian Aid Organisation for Children | Save the Children." Accessed November 5, 2020. www.savethechildren.org/.
3 Details of the case sourced from the knowledge that one of the authors had about SKDRDP based on a book that he had co-authored on the organisation (a) Harper, Malcolm, D. S. K. Rao, and Ashis Kumar Sahu. 2008. *Development, Divinity, and Dharma: The Role of Religion in Development Institutions and Microfinance.* Rugby, Warwickshire: Practical Action Publishing and (b) publicly available information from SKDRDP website: "SKDRDP." Accessed December 27, 2020. https://skdrdp india.org/.

4.4 References

Ashta, Arvind, and Nadiya Parekh. 2018. "A Hindu Faith Based Microfinance Institution in the Midst of Rising and Falling Market Stars: The Use of Spiritual Capital in Social Entrepreneurship by SKDRDP." *2018 EURAM Conference in Reykjavik (Iceland)*, June 19–22, 2018. https://2018.euramfullpaper.org/programme/show-event.asp?pid=%7BEC6769A2-8F6A-481C-86D1-8EDD47069D00%7D.

Harper, Malcolm, D. S. K. Rao, and Ashis Kumar Sahu. 2008. *Development, Divinity, and Dharma: The Role of Religion in Development Institutions and Microfinance.* Rugby, Warwickshire: Practical Action Publishing.

5 IMPACT INVESTMENT

5.1 The capital to do good

Our topic is 'social enterprise', that is, businesses whose employees, owners and investors intend to 'do good' as well as to make profits. In this chapter we shall attempt to examine one main source of capital for social enterprises, apart from the social entrepreneurs' own investments and their retained earnings, if any.

The most common term which is used to describe this particular type of investment is 'impact investment'. The term itself of course says nothing about the nature of the 'impact' that its investors aim to make, instead of or in addition to the normal return, which is profit. But it has come to mean a positive social impact, beyond that which any successful investment might be expected to achieve. Impact investors aim to enable social entrepreneurs to create and expand social enterprises.

It is not easy to estimate the total volume of impact investment since the various definitions are unclear and there is a large and rapidly growing number of investment funds which focus on achieving social impact as well as financial profit, but it is important to remember that the total figure is still far below the amount invested in traditional funds or businesses, which aim primarily to make a profit.

According to one authoritative source, the Global Impact Investing Network (GIIN), the total value of impact investments in 2017 was $114 billion (GIIN 2017).[1] This is clearly a very large sum of money, but the same source quotes the figure of $61 trillion for the total annual amount invested in all financial markets everywhere. That is, sixty-one thousand billion dollars, meaning that impact investments make up only about 0.2% or around one five-hundredths of the amount invested in all financial markets.

This does not of course mean that the vast majority of all financial investment is in socially 'bad' activities, or that the bulk of investors or managers are not concerned with doing good. As in all human activities, business managers have a wide variety of motives, and these are reflected in the results of the enterprises which they manage. Terms such as 'social' or 'impact' investment may be new, but investors have been pursuing social as well as commercial goals for as long as business has existed.

DOI: 10.4324/9781003032229-5

Like many 'modern' labels, the term 'impact investment' may appear to suggest something very new, but the practice of investing for 'social' as well as monetary returns is actually very old indeed. The earliest traditions, however, are more similar to the admonition in the original Hippocratic oath which is still considered to be the basis for today's medical doctors' behaviour, dating from over two thousand years ago, namely, to 'do no harm'.

This is clearly about what one should not do, rather than the positive approach of doing good which is implied in most contemporary discourse on social enterprise and impact investment, but not doing harm is clearly closely related to doing good. It is perhaps significant that the Google internet search company amended its own statement of purpose as recently as 2015, when it moved from 'don't be evil' to 'do the right thing'. Even this admonition, however, suggests that if the company is faced by a choice between the right and the wrong thing, it should do the right one, rather than it should actively pursue 'doing good' as a corporate goal in itself.

The label may indeed be new, but the notion of looking beyond profit to the other 'impacts' of investments is not new at all. In the biblical tradition, it goes as far back at the books of Exodus and Leviticus. One important component of the Jewish faith, in those days and today, is 'Tzedek'. Like any ancient and traditional word, it can be defined in many different ways, but it refers to equality and justice, and the earlier books of the old testament are replete with practical examples of how business transactions should be informed not only by the search for profit, but also by moral principles which go beyond common sense, caution and decency.

Like many ancient religious rules, these are not always observed or practical today; for example, in every seventh year, or 'shmita', the Jewish people were enjoined to forgive all debts, and to allow everyone to make use of private land irrespective of its ownership (Exodus 23.10–11 n.d.). This is of course not the same as investing for a social purpose, but it is directly contrary to commonsense rules of business. The general principle of Tzedek in traditional Jewish law is about justice and equality and is intended to compensate for the evils which are inherent in nature and indeed human nature also.

Ownership is held to include responsibilities as well as rights, and Jewish law also traditionally forbids charging interest on loans, although it is also believed that this prohibition applies only to financial transactions between Jewish people; this exception may explain the traditional and usually pejorative association of Jewishness with moneylending, as in the behaviour of Shylock in Shakespeare's *The Merchant of Venice*.

There is no specific prohibition of lending at interest in the New Testament, although it appears to be perfectly acceptable in the well-known parable of the talents, where the father rebukes his son for leaving his money idle, and tells him, 'you should have put my money on deposit with the bankers, so that when I returned I would have received it back with interest' (New English Bible, Matthew 25:27 n.d.).

Similarly, and perhaps more clearly and better known, Muslims are forbidden in the Holy Koran from lending at a fixed rate of interest. The issue of the meaning of 'riba', or interest, has been widely debated (Harper and Khan 2017), but it is clear throughout Jewish, Christian and Muslim literature that the problem is with fixed interest; if the lender, or investor, shares the risk as well as the reward, it is completely acceptable.

None of this takes any account of inflation, which is of course by its very nature unknown at the time when the investor hands over the money, but many religions and indeed other institutions have rules which forbid investment in specific types of business which are deemed to be socially damaging.

The holy Qur'an,[2] which was probably written in the sixth century, forbids lending at interest; one alternative interpretation of this suggests that the English word 'usury' is what is forbidden, not interest as such, and this is often interpreted as meaning 'excessive' interest, rather than any fixed rate at all. The debate between these two meanings is endless, and in the strict interpretation the purpose of prohibiting a fixed rate is not about the rate itself but is to avoid the implication that the lender can forecast the future success of the venture. It is argued that only God can make such a prediction, so that an investor must either forgo any interest at all, or that she or he must share the risk and base the return on the actual outcome, not on any forecast.

This argument is of course a recommendation for venture capital and equity investment rather than debt, and Shariah law, as it is nowadays generally practiced, forbids all interest payments. More important for social enterprise, however, it also forbids investments of any kind in entities that produce or sell pork or pork products, alcoholic drinks, the arms industry and any form of gambling.

This prohibition is in a sense a promotion of social or impact investment, in that it forbids investment in activities which are believed to have a negative impact. Islam is of course by no means the only religion or institution which makes prohibitions of this kind. The Church of England, for instance, depends for its income mainly on its extensive investments, and their policy as stated in 2019[3] prohibits the Church from holding investments in businesses which dealt in armaments and weapons, in pornography, tobacco, gambling, extortionate lending, embryo cloning, coal, and oil from tar sands.

They also attempt to limit excessive executive remuneration; they state that the Church will not invest in companies which pay senior executive bonuses which exceed their annual salaries. The Church's own payment policy is remarkably strict; entry level priests and others are only paid about $30,000 a year, which is well below the level of the UK's average wage, and their most senior employee, who is presumably the Archbishop of Canterbury, cannot be paid more than three times this amount. These figures presumably do not exclude the nominal value of the bishops' palaces and other non-monetary rewards, but it is clear that the Church itself, and its investment policies, is strongly influenced by 'social' motives.

The Church has in spite of these self-imposed restrictions succeeded in achieving an annual return of 5 percent or more, after accounting for inflation, on its portfolio of investments which was worth well over $10 billion in 2020. This is not a large sum by comparison with some corporate investment funds, or even some individuals' wealth, but the Church's long-term performance has traditionally been among the best of the major investment funds, in spite, or perhaps because, of its self-imposed ethical or social restrictions. Social investment, or at least investment which is in part directed by social rules, need not be less remunerative than investment which is guided only by the law and the desire to maximise long-term returns.

The Church of England and Islam have been followed by other religions. In the late eighteenth century, the Methodists recommended that their members should avoid investment or involvement in liquor, tobacco, smuggling, gambling and slavery, and a century later the Quakers followed similar rules, and included the management of businesses which manufactured armaments.

This tradition has been followed more recently, so that 'socially responsible investment' has become a major financial class in its own right, with an increasing share of the investment market. In 1928 the Pioneer Fund was started in Boston in the United States, as one of the first non-religious investment funds which was based on social responsibility. Like the faith-based institutions which preceded it, and no doubt partly in response to the investment requirements of people who belonged to these faiths, this fund avoided investments in tobacco, liquor and gambling, although there were presumably few if any legitimate investments in liquor-related businesses during the period from 1920 to 1933 when the production and consumption of alcohol was prohibited.[4]

The Pioneer Fund is still one of the main 'ethical' investment funds in the United States, under the new name of the Amundi Pioneer Fund, with some $300 billion under management, and it still follows the same rules; it claims to have achieved an average rate of return of slightly more than 11 percent during the ninety years between 1928 and 2018, while the stock market as a whole has only achieved a 9.2 percent return during the same period.

The pressure to invest socially, or at least not to invest in activities which are considered anti-social, has strengthened both in the amounts invested and in the range of activities which should be avoided by investors with social pretensions.

During the decade of the 1960s university students in the United States became heavily involved, in part because of their opposition to the Vietnam War, and many universities were compelled by student pressure to divest their endowment funds from any companies which were involved in the manufacture of armaments.

Students worldwide also played a major part in bringing pressure on universities but also on other institutions with large endowment investments to divest their funds from any investments in companies which were based in or had substantial dealings with South Africa. This was to help to bring about the collapse of the apartheid system, which had kept black people and people of Indian descent separate, and inferior, from white people for almost a hundred years, and student pressure became an impetus to force corporations to divest from South African investments. Columbia University students protested against the university's investment in businesses that did business in South Africa, and as a result of this and other protests which the students had inspired, over $600 billion of investments were removed from South Africa by 1993.

It is of course impossible to measure what role these pressures on investment actually had on the United States' governments eventual withdrawal from the war in Vietnam, or the collapse of apartheid in South Africa, but they clearly played some part.

Negative pressure of this kind can of course have very positive effects, in that it publicises the issues and also diverts investments to activities that are presumably more 'social' than the choices which would have been made earlier without the widely publicised public pressure.

The United States and other governments have also played a part, by legally requiring or actually forbidding certain types of investment which may have been profitable but were seen as discriminatory. In 1977, for example, the United States Congress passed the Community Reinvestment Act, which is generally known as the CRA. This forbids discriminatory lending practices in low-income neighborhoods, which have been traditionally known as 'redlining' because some lending institutions marked city plans with red lines to show their staff the areas where the risks were perceived to be higher and where loans should not be approved.

The CRA does not itself include specific regulations, because every district and indeed every loan application is different, but every bank and other property lending institution has to undergo regular checks to ensure that its lending is not discriminatory. Local community organisations also have to play their part, so that very poor areas with little social cohesion are inevitably disadvantaged; the outcomes of the CRA are contested, but the balance of informed opinion is that it has achieved some positive results, and, importantly, that it did not make a significant contribution to the sub-prime mortgage crisis which at least in part precipitated the global 2008 financial downturn.

Similar socially responsible investment funds have emerged more recently, and they too have generally achieved similar or better returns than funds which profess only to aim for long-term profitability. A benchmarking study of the returns of fifty-one funds which claimed to be socially responsible in their choice of investments, compared with the returns achieved by similar funds which claimed only to earn profits, showed that the smaller socially responsible funds achieved a return of 9.5 percent, almost twice the level achieved by funds of similar size with no 'social' claims, and similar funds which invested only in so-called 'emerging markets', earned 15.5 percent, well over the returns of any other funds (Net Impact n.d.).

The rapidly growing share of electricity which was generated by nuclear power and the Russian Chernobyl and United States' Three Mile Island nuclear disasters in the 1980s led to greater concern over the risks of this growth. This in turn fed into the general anxiety about environmental and climate change, which played an important part in the establishment of the United States Sustainable Investment Forum, or USSIF,[5] in 1984.

USSIF itself claimed that by the early 2018 some $12 trillion, or a quarter of all investible funds in the United States, were invested in funds whose stated objectives went beyond profitability. The objectives which these funds address cover a wide variety of issues, which are loosely categorised under the three general headings of social, environmental and governance.

These in turn cover sixteen areas: the environmental heading covers climate, responsible technology, government policies, farming and general 'greenness'; governance includes political contributions, management remuneration, board diversity, board independence and corruption; while the social aspects are workplace safety, labour relations, waste management and recycling, raw material sources and choice, community relations, human rights and product safety.

There is clearly some overlap between many of these concerns, and there is also a possibility for some conflict; some suitable board members may require higher remuneration or may lack independence, and 'green' farming itself requires many compromises. The range, however, is very wide, so it may not be totally surprising that so large and increasing a share of portfolio investment can be said to 'qualify' as socially responsible.

It is perhaps to be expected that the United States, the world's largest and wealthiest economy, should be an international leader in the conceptualisation of this approach to investment, but there has also been global activity. The United Nations Principles for Responsible Investment[6] (UNPRI) were issued in 2006, and the signatory nations together claimed that they had a total of $45 trillion in assets which could be labeled as socially responsible.

Socially responsible investment, however, should clearly go beyond the prohibition of investment in activities which are perceived to be irresponsible or anti-social. It should avoid activities which have a negative impact, however that is defined, but it should also presumably seek out activities which have a clear positive impact, beyond earning profits for the entrepreneurs as well as the investors.

There is a plethora of terms which are used to describe funds which try to invest in businesses which have the dual goals of profit and some sort of social impact – 'responsible', 'impact', 'sustainable', 'ethical', 'value based' and many more – and there is also of course a bewildering range of goals other than profit, not all of which are compatible with each other. Gender, race, environment, equality, and many other causes are pursued, and it is important to consider and analyse goals which may today seem outdated or irrelevant, perhaps because they have been dealt with, such as slavery.

Current concerns, however, may make this issue even more difficult to deal with, since nations, institutions, families and presumably businesses are expected in some way to make amends for earlier investments and activities which they may have ceased many years or even centuries ago, which still played some part in their growth and the establishment of their present position.

It may help to step back in time from such concerns and to recall that multi-purpose impact investments which are intended to achieve non-financial objectives which are agreed at the time to be socially responsible have a long and distinguished history.

One of the best-known and most important 'impact investments' ever made was that made by Queen Isabella and King Ferdinand of Spain, when they financed Christopher Columbus' first voyage across the Atlantic Ocean. Columbus and presumably the investors as well believed that they might discover a new route to India, rather than a new continent; they wanted to open a new trade route to the East, in competition with the Portuguese, who had successfully opened the route around Africa, but they also wanted to explore, to gain new knowledge, and in addition to spread the gospel of Christianity.

Columbus had unsuccessfully tried to raise the necessary investment from Genoa and Venice in Italy and from England, and in the end around half of the total cost was put up by individual Italian investors. They were presumably satisfied with the returns, both financial and 'social', since Columbus went on to raise sufficient additional investments to enable him to make three more voyages to what they saw as the newly discovered Western Hemisphere.

Opinions may differ as to the social and other non-financial outcomes of Columbus' voyages to the Americas, but the example shows that investments have always had many purposes, and also, of course, many unintended consequences.

Another much more recent and perhaps less celebrated socially responsible investment was made by Benjamin Franklin, one of the signatories of the United States Declaration of Independence, who was also an important writer, scientist and builder of the United States, as well as a successful investor with properties in England and France as well as in the nation in whose foundation he played such an important part.

In his will, Franklin bequeathed what was in 1785 the very large sum of one thousand pounds each to the cities of Boston and Philadelphia, which were at that time the principal cities of North America.

The following extracts from the original document of the Franklin's will[7] describe the purpose of these bequests:

> I have considered that, among artisans, good apprentices are most likely to make good citizens, and, having myself been bred to a manual art,

printing, in my native town, and afterwards assisted to set up my business in Philadelphia by kind loans of money from two friends there, which was the foundation of my fortune, and all the utility in life that may be ascribed to me, I wish to be useful even after my death, if possible, in forming and advancing other young men, that may be serviceable to their country in both these towns. To this end, I devote two thousand pounds sterling, of which I give one thousand thereof to the inhabitants of the town of Boston, in Massachusetts, and the other thousand to the inhabitants of the city of Philadelphia, in trust, to and for the uses, intents, and purposes herein after mentioned and declared.

The said sum of one thousand pounds sterling, if accepted by the inhabitants of the town of Boston, shall be managed under the direction of the selectmen, united with the ministers of the oldest Episcopalians, Congregational, and Presbyterian churches in that town, who are to let out the sum upon interest, at five per cent, per annum, to such young married artificers, under the age of twenty-five years, as have served an apprenticeship in the said town, and faithfully fulfilled the duties required in their indentures, . . . so as not to exceed sixty pounds sterling to one person, nor to be less than fifteen pounds. . . . These aids may, therefore, be small at first, but, as the capital increases by the accumulated interest, they will be more ample. And in order to serve as many as possible in their turn, as well as to make the repayment of the principal borrowed more easy, each borrower shall be obliged to pay, with the yearly interest, one tenth part of the principal and interest, so paid in, shall be again let out to fresh borrowers. . . .

If this plan is executed, and succeeds as projected without interruption for one hundred years, the sum will then be 131,000 pounds; of which I would have the managers of the donation to the town of Boston then lay out, at their discretion, 100,000 pounds in public works, which may be judged of most general utility to the inhabitants, such as fortifications, bridges, aqueducts, public buildings, baths, pavements, or whatever may make living in the town more convenient to its people, and render it more agreeable to strangers resorting thither for health or a temporary residence. The remaining thirty-one thousand pounds I would have continued to be let out on interest, in the manner above directed, for another hundred years. . . . At the end of this second term, if no unfortunate accident has prevented the operation, the sum will be 4,061,000 pounds, of which I leave 1,061,000-pounds to the disposition of the inhabitants of the town of Boston, and 3,000,000 pounds to the disposition of the government of the state, not presuming to carry my views farther.

The bequest to the city of Philadelphia was made for the same purpose and on the same terms, and both bequests have been faithfully and usefully carried out. Over two hundred years later, the city of Philadelphia still manages the fund in order to offer loans for higher education to young people from the city, and the city of Boston uses the income to sustain and expand the work of the Franklin Institute.

There are large numbers of more recently initiated social investments which are focused on social housing, which is an obvious candidate for investments which may not qualify for 'mainstream' finance but which are clearly also credit-worthy. Other popular fields of activity are education and health care. Governments are of course heavily involved in financing and supporting these mainstream social services, although the level of public provision differs between countries and even between states and cities. Social investors often play an important role in filling the gaps between the private and the public sectors, and their work demonstrates very clearly the fundamental fact which Benjamin Franklin appreciated when he made these bequests in his will; that many social interventions can and do generate a financial return, and that responsible investors can usually achieve a great deal by lending a given sum of money than by donating it, because it can be 'turned over' indefinitely.

Blue Hub[8] is typical of several hundred social investment institutions of this type which have proliferated recently in the United States and elsewhere. The organisation is based in Boston in the United States, and it operates across the whole country. It is incorporated as a not-for-profit organisation, but it is a lender, not a donor, and it is self-supporting.

During 2019, Blue Hub's average loan portfolio was around $150 million, and it grew by almost 18 percent during that year. It was invested mainly in low-cost housing projects. The organisation earned about $12 million dollars in interest payments during the year, and its cost of funds was just over $5 million, leaving a 'spread' or gross profit of $7 million. The average rate of interest earned on the loan portfolio was about 8 percent; this was well over the national 'prime rate' which in 2019 averaged 5 percent but was much less than the usual rate which was charged for so-called 'sub-prime' loans. Many of the projects which were supported by Blue Hub would not have been financed by regular lenders or would have been subject to intolerably long delays. The function of social impact finance is often to enable construction or other work to start while the slow government appraisal process is taking place.

It can be argued that the present-day social impact investment movement and the rapid growth in the number and scale of specialised funds is a natural outcome of a long period of evolution. Until fairly recently, as typified by traditional families such as the Levers, the Rothschilds or the Cadburys, who were often adherents or members of minority groups such as the Jews or Quakers, wealth was based on local enterprise and tended to be concentrated in local areas where the businesses were based. Such families, and many like them, were not necessarily generous, and the family members themselves often became and remain very wealthy indeed, but they necessarily lived and worked near to the places where they made their money, and their 'good works' tended to be focused on the local area.

More recently, wealth has become more global, and as inequality has increased, so has the 'distance', both social and physical, between wealthy people and those who are not so rich. Wealthy families often set up 'family offices' to manage their investments, as well as their philanthropy. They may live in 'gated' communities, travel in private aeroplanes, and spend time in relatively isolated places where they have little contact with the rest of humanity.

These ultra-wealthy people are not necessarily any less generous, or more selfish, than their predecessors, but they are also business-like; they have made their wealth through wise investments, and many of them want to 'do good', or to 'pay something' back, wisely and efficiently, so that they can maximise the social return in the same way as they, or their parents, maximised their purely financial returns.

Hence, they are responsive to requests from institutions which will help them to 'do good' with their money, but which will do this efficiently, and may also allow them to recover their social investments, possibly also even with a modest return. Global annual inflation has decreased from around seven and six percent in the 1970s and 1980s to around two or even less than one percent in 2020, such that investors do not automatically look for high returns merely to preserve the value of their capital. Hence a social investment which earns no return at all, but preserves the capital sum, tends to be considered acceptable.

As a result of all these developments, socially responsible investment funds have proliferated worldwide, and seem likely to remain as a permanent component of the global investment world, lying between pure philanthropy and pure profit maximisation.

Many commercial banks are unwilling to lend to non-profits or charities, but it is now coming to be understood that there are many occasions when such institutions need finance which can be repaid, and for which they can afford to pay a modest but positive rate of interest. Such money may be needed to cover the period between the start of construction and the date when a facility is completed, and the institution can start to charge a local government or similar body for its services, or to demonstrate competence in a new field. Grants are neither needed nor generally available for such purposes, but there is more than enough investible money in the global financial system to cover all the needs.

Building on this long history, and driven initially by the idea of doing well by doing good, the scope of socially responsible or impact investment has broadened to cover a wider range of fields, and can often generate returns which are competitive with traditional profit maximisation. Rather than merely eliminating investments in products that conflict with social, moral or ethical values, such as weapons, alcohol, tobacco, gambling, social investors now proactively make investments in companies that are creating a positive impact.

They can focus on companies that demonstrate good stewardship of the environment, maintain responsible relationships with customers, employees, suppliers and communities, and exhibit conscientious leadership regarding executive pay, internal controls and shareholder rights, and the results often show that such investments can be as profitable as those which were made with no aim other than profitability.

In the increasingly complex and fragile world, where so many people and indeed whole nations need so much help, 'socialness' appears to be an emerging entrepreneurial opportunity and hence a good field for investors. Entrepreneurs who seize these social opportunities may or may not have the intention to 'do good' but they presumably have a definite wish to 'do well', and to continue to do so, and recent experience shows that this is possible.

The following case study describes the origins and evolution of a prominent social investment fund which is based in India but is also spreading its investments further afield. The institution exemplifies many aspects of contemporary investment vehicles, and it also poses a number of important questions.

5.2 Case study

Case 5.2.1 Aavishkaar

Aavishkaar[9] is a family of Indian investment venture funds which in 2018 had a total of around $800 million invested in a range of what many people would call 'social enterprises', although Vineet Rai, who started the fund in 2001, himself disputes the term. He prefers to say that Aavishkaar invests in ventures which operate in distressed and difficult areas; if they can survive and prosper, they will automatically benefit the poor and disadvantaged people who live there. Vineet Rai was born in Rajasthan in India, and his family moved around a great deal, following his father's assignments as a government hydro-geologist. He had always wanted an adventurous career and initially hoped to join the army, but he failed the officer training entrance three times. He then took a degree at the Indian Institute of Forest Management, and took a job in a paper manufacturing business, where he worked on raw material sourcing in the forests of Odisha, in eastern India.

He spent three years doing this, but by then he was married and his wife was expecting their first child, so he looked for a new position in a more settled location. He took a research position in a project on bio-diversity at the Indian Institute of Management in Ahmedabad, India's most prestigious business school, and was then asked to run the Gujarat Grassroots Augmentation Innovation Network, or GIAN. This was a government-supported organisation which aimed to identify and assist people who had new ideas which could help to improve the efficiency of small farmers' operation and thus improve their incomes.

Vineet spent three years looking for such ideas, but it was not easy to assist the farmers who had developed them to convert them into viable business. He tried to help them to do this, and on one occasion, when he was trying to help a farmer to make a business out of a clever new idea for a modified bullock cart which would cultivate the ground and at the same time also scatter fertiliser, he realised that an entrepreneur is needed to make an innovation into a profitable business, not an inventor. And that person must then have access to risk capital. Clever people, with the right ideas and with capital, can create real wealth, for themselves and for their communities.

Vineet suggested to GIAN that they should change their strategy so that they could provide the vital missing ingredient, but they did not want to change their approach, so he talked to a few potential investors, resigned from GIAN and set about raising capital for a new fund that would change rural India. It proved to be difficult to raise the money. But finally, Vineet was able to present his ideas to a group of well-off non-resident Indians who lived in Singapore. They were impressed by his knowledge of Indian rural realities, and he raised $100,000 and started his new fund under the name Aavishkaar, which means 'invention'.

He was able to start the fund in early 2001, but it took five more years to raise another $700,000; the very idea of using venture capital in rural, low-income markets was very new, and at that time it was not easy even for purely commercial businesses to raise venture capital.

Vineet realised that if they were to grow, rural businesses needed non-financial support, such as research and consultancy, and in 2002 he set up Intellecap to supply these services, with initial capital from his wife's family money. The new activity struggled initially, but it took off in 2005, when the Indian microfinance industry was growing rapidly, and Intellecap complemented Aavishkaar's financial assistance to assist a number of India's more successful microfinance institutions.

They also assisted non-financial enterprises. One of India's better-known social enterprises is FabIndia, which markets authentic Indian clothing and household textiles through an international retail network, and in 2007 Aavishkaar was approached by Rangsutra, which was at the time a not-for-profit artisan collective which supplied FabIndia.

Vineet argued that it would not only facilitate the Aavishkaar investment but would also be more productive for the artisans if Rangsutra became a for-profit business. They agreed, and Aavishkaar invested around $30,000 to buy 25 percent of the new business. Rangsutra used the new money to promote and develop more effective suppliers, and in 2011 Aavishkaar was able to sell its share for almost four times the original investment.

One of Aavishkaar's other successes was Equitas Microfinance, where they invested $1.5 million in 2008 and sold their shares for almost $20 million eight years later. These and other successes made it easier to raise more money, including from international institutions such as the International Finance Corporation, the private enterprise arm of the World Bank, and FMO, Holland's development finance institution. By 2018 Aavishkaar had grown to include six different funds with a total value of almost $600 million and was making investments in Indonesia, Sri Lanka and Bangladesh as well as in India.

On average, the investors in Aavishkaar's funds have about tripled their initial investments; this return does not match the highest returns achieved by 'ordinary' venture capital funds elsewhere, but it is a respectable figure and is sufficient to encourage investors to maintain and increase their commitments. Aavishkaar was born out of the belief that business can reduce the burden on philanthropy with a new kind of capital that is willing to take risks to make a social impact as well as a financial return.

Aavishkaar has maintained its focus on investments in new enterprises in rural and semi-urban areas, and it has almost always been the first institutional investor in the businesses it supports; most are in microfinance, but others include agriculture such as Milk Mantra, health care, education, energy and sanitation.

Vineet Rai dislikes labels such as 'social' or 'impact' investors; he believes that there are good returns to be made from investments in neglected rural areas, and that carefully chosen businesses, run by responsible people, can earn competitive returns for their investors and can at the same time also benefit their employees, their suppliers, their customers and society at large.

Aavishkaar carefully examines the business models of potential investments, as well as their ability to generate livelihoods for people at the margins of the economy. They also appraise the entrepreneurs and their capacity to generate returns from the business. If the business is run by a good entrepreneur, who can start a business that generates urban or rural livelihoods and reduces risk and vulnerability, in fields such as health care, education, insurance or waste management, it will become a good investment. Additionally, they make sure that their investees do not damage the environment, and this is carefully audited by their investors.

Aavishkaar regularly monitors the social impact of the businesses in which it invests. According to their very detailed impact report published at the end of 2018, they had made sixty-one investments; fifty-four of these were in India, and the others were in Bangladesh, Sri Lanka and Indonesia. Aavishkaar had exited from twenty-three of these and was in the process of divesting from another four. Two-thirds of Aavishkaar's funds of $300 million came from development finance institutions, and the balance was from a range of smaller corporate and commercial sources. Aavishkaar was the first institutional investor in nearly all the sixty-one businesses, and other institutions had followed them with investments of over four times what Aavishkaar had put in.

A quarter of the investments were in farm-related businesses, 19 percent were in microfinance and the balance was in a wide range of activities. Three-quarters of the Indian businesses had at least some of their operations in India's poorest states, and Aavishkaar estimated that they had directly generated about forty thousand jobs, and a further quarter of a million livelihoods. Aavishkaar also attempts to assess their contribution to the UN's 'sustainable development goals', and a number of its investees are directly involved in waste collection and recycling.

Aavishkaar has no hard-and-fast rules on the amount of personal reward taken by the entrepreneurs whom it supports. Very few of its investee businesses have generated returns that can create great wealth for their founders, but Aavishkaar puts no curbs on what they can or cannot do. This does not make them the most popular investor, since their need to be profitable ensures that the founders get very low initial salaries; this can change as the businesses grow, and other investors join; Aavishkaar's focus on low salaries relates mainly to the scale of the businesses; it is not a moral bar. But the company claims that it does train the entrepreneurs not to be profligate and to be prudent in their use of any wealth they may create.

Aavishkaar's staff's vision is to keep investing in what they enjoy, and they have no fixed policy on their own future capital gains. The organisation has not made any enormous gains; as Vineet himself puts it, "We are all middle-class people and we have tried to retain middle-class values."

But the partners do have a very clear salary structure. They are required to have twenty or more years of experience or more, and their annual salary is $90,000; this is of course far above average annual earnings in India but is well below what people with their qualifications and experience can expect to earn, in India or elsewhere, and is also much less than many senior NGO managers earn. The partners receive an annual increment of ten percent, irrespective of their performance, and on the rare occasions when do they receive a bonus, it is set at a maximum of thirty percent of their salary; no partners have actually ever received a bonus which is even close to that level.

Aavishkaar has not yet reached the stage where the partners can realise substantial profits, but they do not propose to set any limit on such profits; it is assumed that the partners are not primarily interested in accumulating great personal wealth, and many of them hope to make important social investments in causes or places in which they have a personal interest if and when they do make substantial capital gains.

Aavishkaar is an important example; it has grown and continues to grow very rapidly, and it both exemplifies and calls into question many of the emerging beliefs and tentative assumptions which surround the whole arena. Readers will of course have their own questions, but the following issues may merit consideration.

1   The investment in Rangsutra, the successful supplier of hand-made textiles and garments to FabIndia, earned a 400 percent return for Aavishkaar. Rangsutra's work provides modest but decent livelihoods to large numbers of people who would otherwise be very poor. In general, Aavishkaar triples the values of its investments when they are sold. Such returns are typical for 'ordinary' successful venture capital investors, but do they in any way erode the 'socialness' of Aavishkaar?

2   Aavishkaar's results, and Vineet Rai's own views, may suggest that there is no need for a special category such as 'social' investment, because, as the investment multiples show, the returns can be as high as those achieved by 'normal' investment funds. Have funds such as Aavishkaar demonstrated that there is no 'trade-off', nor any need for specifically social investors?

3   The partners in Aavishkaar can earn annual salaries of up to $90,000. This is far below the remuneration of many who work in finance and venture capital investment in India as well as elsewhere but is many times the earnings of the average middle-class Indian. Are such sala-ries justified for social investors?

5.3 Follow-up activity

Identify a well-known charity or other 'good cause' which you and you hope also your friends would like to support, and design a small and innovative fund-raising campaign for it which does not merely rely on people's generosity but which will also raise money by selling an item, or an experience, which is relevant to the cause and for which people are willing to pay, and which the institution, and you and perhaps your colleagues, would be willing and able to provide. Then do it, and critically appraise the results.

Notes

1 In its 2020 survey, GIIN reports the total market size to have increased to $715 billion. For more details refer: GIIN. 2020. "2020 Annual Impact Investor Survey." *The GIIN*. Accessed December 4, 2020. https://thegiin.org/research/publication/impinv-survey-2020.

2 For more details refer: Tarver, Evan. 2020. "Understanding Islamic Banking." *Investopedia*. Accessed December 22, 2020. www.investopedia.com/terms/i/islamic banking.asp.

3 For more details refer: The Policy of National Investing Bodies of the Church of England and the Advisory Paper of the Ethical Investment Advisory Group of the

Church of England. Accessed December 22, 2020. www.churchofengland.org/sites/default/files/2019-11/Final%20EIAG%20paper_Exec%20Remuneration_Final.pdf.

4 For more details refer: "Amundi Pioneer." *Amundi Hub*. Accessed December 22, 2020. www.amundipioneer.com.

5 For more details refer: "The Forum for Sustainable and Responsible Investment." Accessed December 22, 2020. www.ussif.org/.

6 For more details refer: "PRI." Accessed December 22, 2020. www.unpri.org.

7 Details sourced from: Franklin, Benjamin. n.d. "Last Will and Testament of Benjamin Franklin." *Wikisource*. Accessed December 22, 2020. https://en.wikisource.org/wiki/Last_Will_and_Testament_of_Benjamin_Franklin.

8 For more details refer: "BlueHub Capital." Accessed December 22, 2020. https://bluehubcapital.org/.

9 Details of the case sourced from (a) email interview and communication with Vineet Rai, Founder of Aavishkaar Capital made by one of the co-authors on February 2, 2020 (b) Publicly available information from Aavishkaar website: "Aavishkaar Capital." Accessed December 22, 2020. www.aavishkaarcapital.in/ and the article c) Aavishkaar-Intellecap's Vineet Rai: The Forester Who Turned Financier." *Forbes India*. Accessed December 22, 2020. www.forbesindia.com/article/social-impact-special-2017/aavishkaarintellecaps-vineet-rai-the-forester-who-turned-financier/49127/1.

5.4 References

Exodus 23:10–11. n.d. New International Version Bible. "For Six Years You Are to Sow Your Fields And . . ." Accessed December 22, 2020. www.biblestudytools.com/exodus/passage/?q=exodus+23:10-11.

GIIN. 2017. "2017 Annual Impact Investor Survey." *The GIIN*. Accessed December 4, 2020. https://thegiin.org/assets/GIIN_AnnualImpactInvestorSurvey_2017_Web_Final.pdf.

Harper, Malcolm, and A. A. Khan (eds.). 2017. *Islamic Microfinance: Sharˉiʻah Compliant and Sustainable*. Rugby, UK: Practical Action Publishing.

Net Impact. n.d. "Impact Performance from Impact Investing Benchmark. 2015." Accessed December 28, 2020. www.netimpact.org/careers/impact-investing; Original report available at https://thegiin.org/assets/documents/pub/Introducing_the_Impact_Investing_Benchmark.pdf.

New English Bible, Matthew 25:27. n.d. "Bible Gateway Passage: Matthew 25:27 – New International Version." *Bible Gateway*. Accessed December 22, 2020. www.biblegateway.com/passage/?search=Matthew%2025%3A27&version=NIV.

6 EMERGING MODELS AND CONFUSING SOLUTIONS

6.1 Why is social entrepreneurship popular?

This chapter explores why social entrepreneurship is gaining popularity. Is it because we believe that social entrepreneurs can solve social issues in sustainable ways, or because they can help funding agencies to diversify their portfolios and to address previously unexplored social problems and at the same time identify new commercially lucrative opportunities? There are many different emerging models for social enterprise, and different approaches to financing them, and most people still regard the pursuit of financial profit as being fundamentally separate from the pursuit of social good.

One reason for this is that the basic concept of social enterprises, of doing good and doing well at the same time, has attracted many entrepreneurs who want to do social good, but as might be expected, the only enterprises which can sustain themselves are the ones which are also financially profitable. Is the social entrepreneurship movement being driven by financiers who want to broaden the range of opportunities for investment and at the same time to improve their 'image' in society, or by people who genuinely want to benefit society but are looking for new ways in which this can be done?

The answer is unclear, but in a world where there is a tendency for there to be more finance available for investment than there are profitable opportunities in which to invest it, and where large numbers of wealthy families and institutions are looking for secure, profitable but also 'good' institutions and causes in which to invest, there is a growing demand to broaden the range of investable possibilities. Public-sector and government institutions have clearly failed to solve many social problems, and 'old-fashioned' charities, which give money away and must therefore depend on a continuing in-flow of new donations, cannot solve every problem. There is a need for new types of investment opportunity, and investors are coming to appreciate that traditional for-profit investments are unlikely to do well if the social environment in which they operate is damaged or at risk. If there is insufficient investment in social causes, then the environment and society in which for-profit enterprises must operate will be dysfunctional, and commercial profits will be reduced; steady and secure profits can only be earned in secure societies.

DOI: 10.4324/9781003032229-6

Some short-term social investors may merely be capitalising on new and under-exploited social opportunities, but most long-term investors appreciate that their investment returns depend on social stability; the two are necessarily and inextricably linked. JP Morgan Chase Bank's $200 million investment in Detroit's economic recovery is a classic example of how investments to overcome social gaps and reverse economic inequalities can make financial sense for the future (Valinsky 2019). JP Morgan Chase is the United States' largest and the world's sixth largest bank, with total assets of over $3 trillion. The bank has been doing business in the city of Detroit for about a hundred years; it has twenty-one branches in the city, and over 2 million customers. Detroit is famous as the centre of the American automobile industry, but it has in recent years suffered from a major decline, in part because American companies no longer dominate the industry; the population has gone down, property prices have dropped, and it almost appeared as if the city was stuck in an inevitable cycle of decline.

In 2018 JP Morgan initiated a major programme of investment in affordable housing, small business loans and training and other assistance for local entrepreneurs, together with significant philanthropic donations for a variety of social causes. The bank's staff played a major personal role, by volunteering their time for running training programmes, for family counseling and other services. JP Morgan's investment was planned to reach a total of $200 million by 2022.

By 2020 there had already been some measurable improvement; property prices had risen, the unemployment rate had gone down, and the city's population had stabilised. JP Morgan's investment had attracted a further $270 million from other sources. This was achieved through a combination of social enterprises such as the construction of affordable housing, which would yield a modest long-term profit, small business loans, which were also expected to be repaid including interest at market rates, and philanthropic initiatives, such as training and counselling, much of which was provided at no cost by the bank's own staff.

This initiative in urban renewal appears already to have demonstrated that a major investment of a judicious mix of market-priced products and services, along with some pro bono interventions, can make a very significant contribution to the solution of apparently intractable social problems. JP Morgan is already planning similar initiatives in other depressed urban areas in the United States, and it appears that the Detroit programme will prove to have been a profitable investment for the bank as well as significantly improving the 'image' of the bank and of commercial banks in general. Traditional investments in stocks and shares as well as other long-term assets can deliver their expected average returns only if global market conditions remain more or less as favourable as was expected when the investments were originally made. The average return can deviate considerably from what was predicted, and can be substantially lower, or higher, if local or industry-specific or overall world conditions differ substantially from what was expected at the time of investment.

The whole world is now interconnected, and when local, national or international disasters occur, such as riots, racial conflicts, natural disasters, military conflict, epidemics or strikes in one part of the world, the entire global supply chain of good and services can be affected. The whole international investment climate is negatively affected by individual incidents, wherever they occur, and because we are all inter-connected and inter-dependent; this is woven into the social and environmental fabric of all communities, so that stable returns cannot be guaranteed merely because one small part of the world appears to be secure.

As a result, more and more investors are coming to understand that the more proactive they are in investing in making the world a better place, the better it is for the financial results of their investments. An investor in a wind farm to generate electricity, for instance, may or may not be a genuine socially conscious environmental activist, but the investment makes economic as well as environmental sense in the long run. This very inter-connectedness is part of the impetus behind the movement for social entrepreneurship and for investments in social enterprises. They can be as profitable as more traditional financial investments, but they also contribute to the stability and profitability of all kinds of activity.

Issues such as renewable energy, green investments, and gender and racial inclusiveness have in recent years become important criteria for investors, and major investment bankers are starting to use the so-called 'ESG lens' (environmental, social and governance) when they are making investment decisions and when others are reviewing their investment portfolios. A business may appear to have a strong financial position and a profitable future, but if it fails to achieve environmental, social and governance criteria, it is becoming less likely to qualify for inclusion in an acceptable investment portfolio. Universities and other non-financial institutions were the leaders in using such standards when appraising or building their endowment portfolios, but more conventional investors whose main concern is profitability are coming to appreciate that 'socially responsible' investments make good financial sense; this trend is in a sense self-fulfilling, in that investments which do not satisfy these non-financial standards are become less popular and are thus losing value. The boundary between 'ordinary' and 'responsible' investments is becoming less clear.

The same changes are occurring in private equity and venture capital. Decision makers for such investors have traditionally been less risk averse than those who are responsible for investment policy for colleges, insurance companies and so on, and they too are enthusiastic about the new avenue of social impact investment. These investors are also looking for more investment opportunities in emerging economies and sectors, where more conservative institutions have hesitated to go. Such novel destinations mean that poorer countries are now attracting more capital, which can contribute more to their economic and social improvement than traditional international aid. The recent Global Trends in Renewable Energy Investment report jointly published by the Frankfurt School, the United Nations Environment Program and Bloomberg states that of the more than $2.7 trillion that has been invested in building renewable energy capacity over the past decade, the majority has gone to emerging nations such as China and India rather than to other more 'developed' countries (Krämer 2020). It is clear that in addition to clean energy issues, all the usual social and economic gaps which social investments aim to fill are also more obvious in poorer nations, so that 'doing good' is in these economies the best investment opportunity.

The annual report of Aavishkaar Capital,[1] India, whose operations were discussed in the previous chapter states, "This emerging movement is an initiative by entrepreneurs (impact investors) supporting other entrepreneurs who solve larger problems worth solving for the society." Are these entrepreneurs necessarily social? Vineet Rai, the founder and CEO of Aavishkaar, says "all enterprises generally are social."[2] Based on this notion of the universality of social needs and opportunities, he has created a multi-million-dollar venture fund which invests in sectors and geographies where a conventional commercial investor would have been hesitant to commit its funds. Vineet says, "I want to create businesses in difficult geographies, to take very high risks and support enterprises with my sweat and time and effort and try to generate as close to commercial returns as possible."

This approach of 'doing good and well' at the same time is playing an increasingly important role in emerging models in entrepreneurship. It catalyses creative approaches to innovation, by requiring enterprises and entrepreneurs to be creative and to do both good and well, not just because it is socially acceptable but because it is becoming essential. The case of Milk Mantra,[3] which is presented in the following pages, is a good example of such a win-win investment, where both market and supply gaps in a particular area offer attractive and profitable business opportunities. It explores the mixed meanings that entrepreneurs pursue in the name of creating 'social goods'.

It is followed by a very different example, The Better Meat Company, which operates in Sacramento, California, about as different a location as could be imagined from Odisha State in India. In this case, the social entrepreneur is also working in a cattle-related business, but in a totally different way in that he is attempting to address one of global society's most pressing but least publicised problems: the vast and rapidly growing consumption of meat, which wreaks havoc on the environment, and our health and on the welfare of the animals themselves. The enterprise is clearly 'social', in that the founder's motives are not about making money, but is this initiative genuinely the most effective way in which this particular entrepreneur could address the problem?

The Milk Mantra dairy business may help impoverished small-scale dairy farmers in eastern India to come out of poverty, but it is also enriching wealthy impact investors. While this is exactly what 'social enterprises' should in theory do, by doing well and doing good, in practice there may be an imbalance between the two goals towards either direction. There is not always a trade-off between the two goals, but many social entrepreneurs are faced with difficult choices because of their dual objectives. Do some 'social businesses' start with a theoretical 'win-win' model of doing good and doing well, but eventually turn out to be either purely commercial businesses if they succeed or a non-profit charity if they fail? Should social entrepreneurs start their businesses with a clear idea of the balance they aim to strike between the two sometimes conflicting goals, or should they initiate their businesses with an open mind and allow the balance to emerge as the business grows? Does it matter whether or not society at large or the entrepreneurs themselves consider their business to be what label they give it, so long as it survives and grows and provides some benefit to all parties? And in any case, how can the balance be measured? To what extent should a social entrepreneur limit his or her own earnings or capital gain in order to achieve a social good?

The example of Milk Mantra offers a real-life example through which we can explore the issues of labels, impacts and entrepreneurs' intentions in order to clarify how, if at all, a 'social entrepreneur' should be distinguished from a traditional profit-maximising entrepreneur.

6.2 Case studies

Case 6.2.1 Milk Mantra – a socially conscious dairy business

In November 2009 Sri Kumar[4] and his wife gave up their comfortable jobs in a finance company in London and returned to their native state of Odisha in eastern India. Like many successful expatriate Indians, they wanted to 'give something back', to engage themselves in some kind of activity that would benefit their homeland, and also, they hoped, society as a whole. They did not, however, start a charity or a similar non-commercial activity; they set up a for-profit dairy company, which they called Milk Mantra, which means 'the sacredness of milk'.

They chose the dairy industry because they believed that its existing condition, particularly in Odisha, failed to serve the best interests of the producers, the owners of cows or of the customers, who consumed milk and other dairy products.

India has the world's largest number of dairy cows, with over 40 million animals, or just over 16 percent of the world's cow population. Their average production of milk per animal per year, however, is far below that of many other countries, such that the USA, with only 9 million cows, produces almost twice the volume of milk.[5]

There are many reasons for this low productivity, including the fact that the slaughter of cows is by law forbidden in India, because they are considered to be sacred by Hindus, the majority religious group, but poor rearing practices and inefficient distribution systems also play a major part. Only about a fifth of India's milk is distributed through organised channels, including the well-known Amul[6] group of dairy farmers' cooperatives. The balance is sold locally and is often adulterated with water, which may itself be far from clean, or is spoiled in the hot weather because of the lack of refrigeration facilities or adequate packaging.

The situation in Odisha is even less developed, in that only some ten percent of the milk which is produced in the state is distributed through organised channels. OMFED,[7] the Orissa State Cooperative Milk Producers' Federation, which has apparently kept the state's earlier name, is by far the largest constituent of the formal sector part of the dairy value chain in the state. It has a membership of 5,800 cooperative societies with 260,000 farmer members, which collect 508,000 kilos of milk per day. OMFED, like many state-level dairy farmers' cooperative federations, has some links to Amul, but unlike Amul it is effectively a government-controlled institution and suffers inevitably from many of the problems which effect such entities in India.

The founders of Milk Mantra wanted their new venture to demonstrate what they call 'conscious capitalism'. They summarised their aim by saying that they intended to remove the 'trust deficit' which pervaded every aspect of the dairy industry in Odisha. Consumers could not trust the quality of the milk they bought, the farmers could not trust their own cooperatives or the local retail shops through which their milk was sold, and the system satisfied nobody, not even the cows.

Not surprisingly, it proved difficult to raise the initial capital. The founders' early approaches to institutional investors were generally unsuccessful. Their earlier positions in formal finance meant that they had numerous initial contacts, but traditional investors found it hard to accept that commitments to 'social responsibility' and so on were anything more than cosmetic or even eccentric. It was even harder to persuade them to invest in the dairy industry, which was known to be generally dominated by cooperatives with strong political connections. The location in Odisha, one of India's more backward states, made the project even less attractive.

Eventually, however, some of their personal friends were persuaded to invest a few thousand dollars each in the new venture, and Aavishkaar, a pioneer impact investment fund based in India with some $155 million under management, which was discussed in the previous chapter, made a significant investment. This attracted other institutional and individual investors, and after four rounds of investment and eighteen months of preparation and fund-raising, Milk Mantra was able to start its operations in 2011.

The founders themselves received no remuneration for the first three years of operations, but by 2016 Milk Mantra was turning over about $18 million a year; and the business was covering its costs, before paying interest, taxes or depreciation. This period was not unusually lengthy for an agriculture-based consumer goods company, and by 2019 turnover had reached $3 million a month.

The shares in the company were not publicly listed or traded, but an unofficial valuation suggested that the first investors had multiplied their initial investment by around three and a half times in the first five years of the company's existence; here again, a valuation of this kind is not unusual for a new venture such as Milk Mantra. The founders make the point that Milk Mantra is a socially conscious company which is also able to generate commercial-level returns for its investors.

By 2019 Milk Mantra was buying milk from around sixty thousand farmers, each of whom typically owned one or two milking cows. The milk was collected every day from fifteen thousand collection points, as is necessary in the generally hot climate of Odisha, where there is little or no farm-based refrigeration.

A typical farmer with two cows produces 250–300 litres of milk per month, for which Milk Mantra pays about $110. This is between 10 and 20 percent more than could be earned from local dealers or consumers, but more importantly the farmers are assured of regular payments with no 'leakage' or other losses. Most Indian dairy companies pay their farmers ten days or more after their cows' milk has been collected, and many co-operatives such as the member societies of OMFED delay their payments for much longer. Milk Mantra pays every five days, or six times a month, which makes a significant difference to small-scale farmers who usually operate on a hand-to-mouth basis.

Additionally, the farmers can if necessary obtain finance for new animals from State Bank of India, the largest bank in India with around fifteen thousand branches in rural areas. Milk Mantra has set up a special arrangement with the bank to facilitate such loans, and they can also benefit from the company's extension services; farmers can buy high-quality feed for their cattle and can access advice and training on how to take better care of their animals and the milk which they produce.

Ahalya is a typical Milk Mantra supplier. She and her husband have three children and they have been suppliers to Milk Mantra for six years. She owns two cows, and the family also own a small grocery shop. Ahalya used to sell her milk to local merchants; they often collected her milk too late so that it was spoiled, and they paid very irregularly. Her family's income has significantly increased since they started supplying to Milk Mantra, and she feels financially independent. The family have been able to marry off their daughter without borrowing from a moneylender, and they have also been able to send their son to a technical college.

Ahalya's cows' milk is delivered on the same day that is has been collected from her farm to one of the two dairy plants operated by Milk Mantra, which are equipped with the latest machinery for testing, pasteurising and packaging milk, one near the coast of the Bay of Bengal and the other in the centre of Odisha state. Each plant employs around 150 staff. Milk Mantra produces liquid milk, and a variety of milk-based products such as yogurt, curd and cottage cheese under the trade name 'Milky Moo', and a fruit-flavoured milk-based health product.

The processed milk is packed in a specially developed triple-layered package which keeps it cool but also excludes light, which is itself a major cause of spoilage. This means that liquid milk can be kept unrefrigerated for four days, as opposed to the one-day shelf-life of milk in traditional plastic packets. This is particularly important in the State of Odisha, where there is little refrigeration and where the temperatures can be among the highest in India. Milk Mantra's other products such as cottage cheese last for about ten days rather than the four days which are normal.

The Milky Moo milk and milk products are then distributed throughout most of Odisha state, and also to the cities of Kolkata in neighbouring West Bengal and to Ranchi in Jharkhand state to the north. They are sold through over ten thousand of the ubiquitous 'kirana shops' or small independent groceries which are still the dominant form of retailer in India, as well as through the growing number of retail chain stores. The deliveries take place between 5:30 and 6:00 every morning, to ensure that customers can buy the company's products in the best possible condition.

The retail prices are between 10 and 20 percent higher than the prices of comparable products. Indian consumers are notoriously price conscious, but Milk Mantra's experience shows that they are willing to pay a premium price for items such as milk and dairy products, whose sources are often hard to identify and where quality is not immediately visible.

Is Milk Mantra a 'social enterprise' or is it not? Many readers will no doubt themselves choose the issues on which to base their own answers to this question, and they may have already decided that Milk Mantra is 'social', or have decided that it is not, and will perhaps be puzzled as to why it is included as a case study in a book on social enterprise or be financed by a social investment institution. The following questions are deliberately worded in a sceptical vein, given that Milk Mantra presents itself and is itself presented as being a social business.

1   The customers who consume the milk and other products which are marketed by Milk Mantra pay between 10 and 20 percent over the current market prices; most of these customers are not rich, and the company's products are skilfully and persuasively marketed. Is the company in any way exploiting its customers?

2   The farmers who produce for Milk Mantra are paid a small premium over normal market prices for the milk, but they have to achieve much higher standards, and the margin between what they receive and what final consumers pay is far higher than is usual for dairy products in Odisha. Are they being exploited, like the consumers, in order to enable Milk Mantra and its investors to make large profits?

3   The initial investors more than tripled the sums they initially invested. Is this a genuinely 'social return'?

4   The traditional short distance local value chain for milk and other dairy products minimises transport and environmental costs, whereas much of Milk Mantra's supplies have to be transported over large distances to the processing plants, and thence to the retailers and their customers. Is this environmentally sustainable?

We conclude the chapter with a very different business, which operates in a very different part of the world and is clearly 'social' but in a totally different way from Milk Mantra.

Case 6.2.2 The Better Meat Company – another approach to cattle

There are three good reasons why we should eat less meat, or maybe no meat at all; it is cruel to animals, it is bad for the environment and it is bad for our health.

Paul Shapiro[8] started the Better Meat Company in 2018; he says that his primary motive was to save the planet, but he is also a convinced vegetarian. Before starting the business, he worked for many years for the Humane Society of the United States, which is arguably the world's largest animal welfare organisation, and he is also a well-known and best-selling writer on various aspects of the same subject, including a widely recognised book entitled *Clean Meat*.

Shapiro could easily have found easier and more secure work, and could have earned more money, but he chose to start this new and perhaps slightly eccentric business, because of his passion for society, in its broadest sense.

The Better Meat Company manufactures what are called 'meat enhanc-ers'; they are a blend of vegetarian proteins from a variety of sources including peas, seaweed, bamboo plants and soya. These are sold to pro-ducers of traditional meat products such as sausages, meat balls, meat patties, hamburgers and others, and different varieties of enhancers are also used by manufacturers of crab cakes and other less familiar meat items.

The costs of Better Meat's enhancers are generally well below that of the meat products with which they are blended; typically, they cost between 10 and 15 percent less per kilo, but the main advantage from the consumer's point of view is that they are much healthier. They have no allergens, and much less cholesterol, and they also enable the final product to be 'juicier' and thus to taste better than the 100 percent meat options.

These products are now being bought and blended into new products by major meat product producers in the United States such as Hormel, who advertise their new 'Happy Little Plants' brand and use the word 'Fuse' to stress the mixed origins of the materials. There has been a long tradition of blending plant-based proteins into meat products, but the main ingredient was mushrooms, which are expensive to buy and to process, and which do not contain the same range of proteins which can be obtained from Better Meat.

Paul Shapiro raised the capital of $10 million which was needed to start and grow The Better Meat Company from a variety of sources; the initial investors were generally committed to the same environmental and animal welfare objectives that had motivated him to start the business, but after operations were started these pioneers were joined by a number of more traditional investors; they agreed with and wished to promote the same causes which had motivated Shapiro to start, but their over-rising concern was to protect the value of their investment and to earn a return, whether from a share of the profits or from an eventual sale of their shares.

After about thirty months of operations, he estimated that some 20 per-cent of the total sums invested had come from 'cause'-related investors, while the balance of 80 percent was from those whose motives were mainly financial. At that point, the company employed fifteen people and its annual sales amounted to around three million dollars, but they were growing quite rapidly, and the business was making a modest profit. The main constraint to growth was the shortage of fixed capital for plant and equipment and also working capital to fund the inventory of raw materials and to allow the normal credit conditions to their customers.

Shapiro and his colleagues are passionately committed to what they call 'ecological entrepreneurship'; they want their new business to grow, but they would very much welcome competition from new entrants to the business of plant-based protein additives. They recognise that as of now, Better Meat is making no more than a tiny impact on the enormous and still rapidly growing market for meat in the United States, and further afield internationally the rate of growth is much higher.

They are themselves vegetarians, but they appreciate that it would be impossible to make a major impact on meat consumption by trying to persuade large numbers of people to become vegetarian; meat and meat products make up a fundamental and growing proportion of Americans' diets, and eating more meat is in some ways a worldwide aspiration; it is symbolic of being better off.

The negative effects are nevertheless indisputable; animal production globally leads to more carbon emissions than all forms of transportation combined, and cows in particular produce large quantities of methane, which is a more damaging 'greenhouse gas' than the carbon dioxide which human beings and most animals produce as a by-product of breathing. Animal production also uses more water, which could be used to irrigate large areas of land for growing crops. Meat consumption per head worldwide has almost doubled in the last fifty years while the numbers of people are also increasing at a similar pace.

Something has to change, and Paul Shapiro and his colleagues at The Better Meat Company are doing their best to initiate and to make a difference. They believe that they can and must 'use the power of business to solve social problems'.

As always, this case raises many issues, and some questions from the case for discussion are presented below:

1 Paul Shapiro was earlier a well-known and successful writer and speaker on this whole subject. Might it not have been more productive and have led to more substantive change if he had continued and expanded this aspect of his activities rather than starting a small 'fringe' manufacturing operation?

2 Even if all meat consumers were 'converted' to the merits of blended meat products, there would still be a major global problem of emissions from meat production. Should not Paul Shapiro attempt to address the problem in a more radical way which could lead to more substantial change?

3 Most consumers of The Better Meat Company's products buy them to improve their own health, whereas Shapiro has set up the business in order to improve the environment. Is it right, or sustainable, for the motives of the customers of a social enterprise to be very different from those of the founders of the enterprise?

4 Would you invest in The Better Meat Company?

6.3 Follow-up activity

Think about your own community and identify one or more services which are not presently available and would benefit some local people, but for which these people would not be able to pay the full cost. Approximately what 'mix' of methods would you propose for raising the necessary funds, including selling the services to the proposed beneficiaries or to others, charitable donations, grants from local government authorities, from local businesses or from private donors?

Notes

1 For more details refer: "Aavishkaar Capital." Accessed December 22, 2020. www.aavishkaarcapital.in/.
2 Sourced from email interview and communication with Vineet Rai, Founder of Aavishkaar Capital on December 24, 2017 made by one of co-authors.
3 For more details refer: "Milk Mantra." Accessed December 23, 2020. www.milkmantra.com/index.html.
4 Details of the case sourced from (a) personal interview and communication with Srikumar Misra, founder of Milk Manta, made during the visit to the social enterprise by one of the co-authors on November 4, 2019, and from (b) publicly available information from their website, www.milkmantra.com/index.html.
5 Figures sourced from: "Our Mission Is to End Factory Farming." n.d. Accessed December 23, 2020. www.ciwf.org.uk/.
6 For more details refer: "Amul Dairy." Accessed December 23, 2020. www.amuldairy.com/.
7 For more details refer: "OMFED, Bhubaneswar." Accessed December 23, 2020. http://omfed.com/default.asp?lnk=home.
8 Details of the case sourced from (a) personal interview and communication with Paul Shapiro, Founder of The Better Meat made by one of the co-authors on January 19, 2021 and from (b) publicly available information from their website, "The Better Meat Co. – Plant Protein Ingredients for Better Meat." Accessed February 20, 2021. www.bettermeat.co.

6.4 References

Krämer, Johannes. 2020. "Global Trends in Renewable Energy Investment 2020." *Frankfurt School*. Accessed December 23, 2020. www.fs-unep-centre.org/global-trends-in-renewable-energy-investment-2020/.

Valinsky, Jordan. 2019. "JP Morgan Has Invested $150 Million in Detroit. Now It's Adding $50 Million More." *CNN*. Accessed December 23, 2020. www.cnn.com/2019/06/26/investing/jpmorgan-investment-detroit/index.html.

7 THE NEED FOR INNOVATION

7.1 Innovations in social finance

Innovation has always been the fuel that fosters entrepreneurial ventures. But when entrepreneurs want to achieve financial sustainability, or profits, and at the same time to pursue social goals, to 'do good and to do well' with an enterprise, the need for innovation also has two faces. Innovative enterprise ideas need innovative financiers. Although there is an increasing number of 'impact investors', as people who wish their investments to do well and also to do good have come to be called, and more are joining the movement every year, one major and important criticism of impact investors is that they tend to assume that a positive social impact will be and has been achieved, rather than ensuring that it actually does happen.

The Global Impact Investors Network (GIIN) stated in their Annual Impact Investor Survey for 2020 that most impact investors themselves expect 'impact washing' to be an important challenge facing the market over the next five years (GIIN 2020). Some details of other likely challenges in the field of social impact management, together with an indication of respondents' views of their relative importance are shown in the following Figure 7.1

These concerns were shared by many other authorities, and by investors themselves. Given that impact investing is a relatively new activity, and that there is a broad range of potential objectives, not all of which are necessarily consistent with one another, it is hardly surprising that there should be debate and disagreement as to how to measure impact, and how to compare different investment possibilities.

It is not simple to measure and compare the achievements of different conventional investment funds by the apparently simple standard of financial profitability, since that can be measured over the short or the long term, or by the degree of risk, but 'social impact' is far more complex. It can be stated and defined by a large range of different terms, some of which are quantifiable and some of which are not, and not all of which are mutually consistent.

A social intervention may have a small impact on a large group of people, or it may reach far fewer people but may have a far deeper and long-lasting impact on them, or an environmental intervention may be positive in

DOI: 10.4324/9781003032229-7

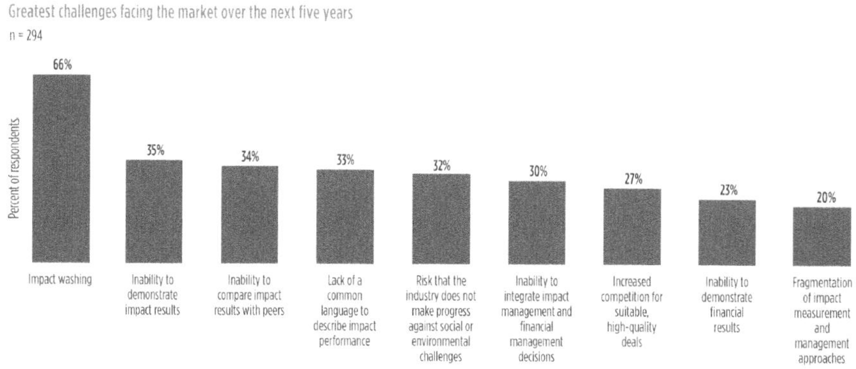

Greatest challenges facing the market over the next five years
n = 294

Figure 7.1 Greatest Challenges Facing the Impact Investment Market

Source: GIIN Annual Report, 2020.

Note: N = 294. Each respondent impact investor selected three challenges. Indicators are ranked in order of the number of respondents that selected each challenge.

its 'green' impact but may at the same time deprive large numbers of needy people of their livelihoods.

The same applies in the field of public health; many of the measures which were introduced in an effort to reduce the number of people who were affected or died from the so-called 'COVID' epidemic resulted in massive losses in education, and in increased sickness and delayed treatment and even deaths for large numbers of other people who were younger or less likely to die from other causes; should the death of an old person be counted as 'costing less' than that of a younger person?

Simple financial profitability does not involve these difficulties, but these problems make it all the more tempting for managers or promoters of social investment funds either to make unfounded claims for the impact of the investments they make or to accept the impact claims of 'their' social entrepreneurs without question.

Given these impact challenges, although on the one hand impact investments are extolled as well-intended innovations which can 'do good and do well', there are also many critics who argue that impact investing is actually no more than camouflaged commercial investment. This criticism is particularly powerful because the majority of investors are 'finance first and impact next' investors whose first demand is that the money they invest should have a positive financial return (Svedova, Cuyegkeng, and Tansey 2014). They also want a social return from any impact investments they make; they may be willing to accept a lower rate of financial profit, but the financial aspect comes first.

Very few investors of any kind are likely to rank the social impact as being more important to them than the financial performance; this is not unreasonable, given that the very term 'investment' implies a positive return or at least the preservation of capital value, but it does lead investors to prefer projects which address market-oriented social problems where there is a good chance of making a positive financial return, such as 'social' or 'affordable' housing. This tends to exclude less 'marketable' and less measurable social causes such as child development, education, youth unemployment, public health and social justice, where the direct returns from success are hard to quantify or are clearly negative. The Global Impact Investors Network states in their Annual Impact Investor Survey 2017 that two out of three investors principally targeted risk-adjusted, market rates of return, but there is widespread acknowledgement of the important role and need for funding for below-market-rate opportunities (GIIN 2017).

'Social Impact Bonds (SIBs)'[1] were introduced as an innovative way to pay for interventions which are designed to address social problems whose successful outcomes are not directly marketable but can save public authorities large sums of money. This money may have been spent on less successful remedies or may be the cost which society has to bear because of the problem, such as crime, or avoidable sickness, but the critical difference between SIBs and more traditional approaches to financing social interventions is that the investments are only profitable to the investors if the intended impact is attained.

SIBs are a type of payment-by-results contract where a charity or other social purpose organisation agrees to deliver a given outcome or impact. Unlike a standard payment-by-results contract, the funding to deliver the project comes from third party investors. If the project achieves the agreed targets, the investors and the charity make money. If these targets are not achieved, the investors may forfeit their whole investment, or a part of it, depending on the details of the agreement; but there is in any case a strong incentive to select a competent implementing agency (Kohli, Besharov, and Costa 2012).

The SIB model has been widely adopted, and by mid-2020 it was stated that 138 bonds had been issued for a total value of over $440 million.[2] This new approach to financing social initiatives has been widely praised because it provides social bodies with freedom to innovate, it allows the development of long-term solutions and early intervention, and it transfers risk away from charities and public commissioners.

One critical aspect of SIBs is that it is essential for the impacts of the interventions which they finance to be rigorously measured and quantified. If this is not done, it will not be possible to calculate whether the social investors should recover their investment, with or without a return, since the expected return from an impact investment is based on the extent to which pre-determined rates of social outcomes, which have been agreed to be satisfactory proxies for success, are achieved. These results must obviously be measurable and independently verifiable by external agencies which are knowledgeable in the particular domain which the intervention aimed to address. The expected social outcome must be measurable so that the financial returns can be calculated and the surplus can be paid to the investors in the bonds. Or, if the outcome was not attained, the investors will forfeit their capital. Without clear measurement and quantifiable results, there is no way of discovering whether or not they did or did not attain the 'impact' which was intended.

This clear, quantifiable and definitive approach can be an effective and innovative way of addressing the issues of mission-drift which are necessarily involved in dual-goal pursuits, and it also helps to avoid the undirected management approach which is often associated with welfare interventions. Social impact investors, unlike many public-sector managers and their political masters, are not willing to accept input-related measures of achievement; it is not sufficient to state that so many people have been hired, or so many have attended training programmes, or more simply that a certain sum has been spent; social impact is about results.

Another innovative side to this form of conditional contracting is that it can help to break down silos and makes conversations possible between all the stakeholders who are addressing a similar social problem but were hitherto working in isolation as they had no incentive to collaborate. A social impact bond can clarify and quantify the incentive that each stakeholder has to 'do good and do well' and can show why a collaborative effort to create a given and quantifiable social outcome can be more profitable and more meaningful for the state and social agencies which are involved. Without such measures, it is all too common for success to be measured by inputs, and for government and social entities to work as 'competitors' rather than collaborators in a common cause.

Through effective collaboration such agencies can look at traditional social problems such as recidivism or homelessness with a new lens that enables them to recognise and re-assess the gaps that have arisen in the respective sectors. They can then design and participate in innovative public-private partnerships and share the different tasks that must be undertaken in order to achieve better results. The core competencies of each player can be recognised, and appropriate financial incentives can be allocated for each player, based on an improved identification and properly respected understanding of exactly what expertise each brings to the table. These pay-for-success or outcome-based bonds were first introduced in the United Kingdom in an effort to reduce recidivism, or re-offending by young prisoners who were serving short-term sentences.

The world's first social income bond was launched by UK-based Social Finance Ltd. in September 2010 to finance a prisoner rehabilitation programme. It forms the basis of the case study which concludes this chapter. Thereafter many Social Impact Bonds have been tried out elsewhere.

One early example which addressed the same problem as the pioneer bond in Peterborough, but had a very different outcome, was the bond which was used to finance an initiative to reduce reoffending by ex-offenders who had been released from the notorious Rikers Island Prison in New York. This initiative did not achieve the expected social returns and Goldman Sachs, who were the main impact investors, were not paid back.

There is however a high risk of failure in situations such as re-offending by short-term prisoners, particularly in the so-called 'carceral state' of the United States, where short- and long-term imprisonment is a recurrent and expected feature of many young people's lives. The Rikers Island bond therefore included a new feature which had not been used before, namely, 'impact guarantors' who would partially cover the risk for the impact investor in case the target impact was missed. In the Rikers Island SIB case,[3] Goldman Sachs paid $9.6 million for the cost of the intervention, on the basis of social impact bond, but Bloomberg Philanthropy, the personal donor institution which was financed from the personal wealth of the mayor of the city, acted as a guarantor. They guaranteed $7.2 million to cover the majority of Goldman Sachs' contribution in case of failure, which of course substantially reduced the investors' risk of loss. The innovative interventions which were financed by the bond failed to reduce recidivism by the expected level of 8.5 percent, but Goldman Sachs' loss was limited to $2.4 million. This commitment presumably made it possible for Goldman Sachs to participate, and it was rather unusual for the mayor of any city, even one as large and wealthy as New York, to be able to establish such a fund from his or her personal wealth, but guarantees of this kind have also been provided for other SIBs, although not usually for such a large amount.

There was also a very substantial upside for Goldman Sachs if the anticipated results had been achieved. If the intervention had been as or more successful than was anticipated, and had reduced recidivism by a percentage between 10 percent and 20 percent, then the New York City Department of Correction would have repaid Goldman Sachs on a sliding scale a sum between $9.6 million and $11.72 million, thus enabling the bank to recoup its investment and, if the results were very positive, to make a reasonable profit. If recidivism had been reduced by anything between 8.5 percent and 10 percent, the city would have repaid a lower amount, down to $4.8 million, thus covering part of Goldman Sachs' investment, and if the improvement had been less than 8.5 percent, which was the actual outcome, then the city did not have to pay anything. Bloomberg Philanthropy's contribution reduced the bank's loss, but it was still substantial.

Hence for a private for-profit institution such as Goldman Sachs, the Social Impact Bond was less costly than a normal Corporate Social Responsibility (CSR) grant, whatever the results, because such a grant would under no circumstances be refunded, in part or in full. Whatever the outcome, their contribution enhanced the bank's positive image as a 'social investor' and gave them an early entry to an unexplored investment domain. The learning and engagement involved in this novel transaction was much more than simply writing a CSR cheque.

Following the trend, many social impact bonds have been put together and are being implemented in various stages across the globe. The most common problem to be covered is re-offending, following the original British innovation in Peterborough; this is of course an obvious problem because of the high financial and social costs it causes, and because results are fairly easily measured. Other issues include homelessness and rough sleeping, also in the United Kingdom, foster care in Australia, children's health in California, single mothers in Mexico and secondary school results in Russia.

More recently, the SIB payment by results concept has been introduced in so-called developing countries, under the label of Development Impact Bonds (DIBs). DIBs finance development programs with money from private investors, who earn a return if the programme is successful, paid by a third-party donor.[4] The first such experiment in a developing nation is being implemented in the State of Rajasthan in India. A DIB is distinct from an SIB in that its outcome funders are philanthropic entities or foundations and not government bodies This pioneering bond addressed the very difficult issue of girls' education in India, and in the state of Rajasthan, where the position of women is particularly bad.

The bond was called Educate Girls and was launched in the year 2015.[5] The Optimus Foundation, which is the 'corporate social responsibility' arm of UBS (the Union Bank of Switzerland) paid $270,000 to finance a three-year initiative whose objective was to increase the numbers of out-of-school teenage girls who return to school, and for them to complete their schooling and to achieve a reasonable level of results. India generally has one of the world's worst records for girls' education; 50 percent of women are illiterate, and the number of girls who do not attend school is double that of boys.

The programme covered Hindi, which is the national language and also the local mother tongue, English and mathematics, and included a number of educational innovations which were unfamiliar in the area, such as individual assessments, group-based learning and holiday tasks, The actual implementation was managed by Indian associates of the Children's Investment Fund Foundation, a United Kingdom–based charity with offices in Delhi and Nairobi, and the results were independently assessed by IDInsight, an international development consultancy.

The three-year programme reached 7,300 girls of school age in 160 schools in 140 villages in Bhilwara district of Rajasthan, and after a slow start the final assessment in 2018 showed that 92 percent of the girls who had started the programme were still in school and their test results were 79 percent better than those achieved by the same cohort of girls who had been attending schools in the same areas but had not been affected by the programme. The UBS Optimus Foundation recovered its initial contribution of $270,000 plus the agreed 15 percent annual return, based on the formula which had been agreed. The total 'profit' for the three years amounted to $144,000, and the Optimus Foundation donated this return and the original capital to finance more similar initiatives.

Partly as a result of this success, The UBS Optimus Foundation launched another similar bond in 2017 in the same state, to address the problems of childbirth, including both mothers' and newborn babies' deaths. The rate of maternal deaths in Rajasthan was nearly 50 percent higher than for India as a whole, and newborn babies' mortality rate was 14 percent worse than for the whole country. The Indian national rates of maternal and child mortality were themselves much worse than most other countries' performance.

This so-called Utkrisht or Excellence Bond[6] was also initially funded by a contribution of $3.5 million from the UBS Optimus Foundation, and USAID, the United States' government donor organisation, and Merck Sharp and Dohme, the multinational drug company, also agreed to cover further costs and the performance payments up to $8 million, to be paid if the targets of the three-year programme were met. The programme was implemented by Population Services International, a large global birth control and maternal health provider, along with local partners. The aim of this bond was to improve the maternal care standards of over four hundred private health care institutions in the same state, and thus to affect over half a million women and their newborn children.

Thus, the apparent advantages of the SIB model have led to its widespread adoption, with over 160 impact bonds across 28 countries, with more than 25 in the United States.[7] In order to understand the operating issues and possible outcomes of this innovative form of bond financing more closely, we discuss the very first SIB in rather more detail.

7.2 Case study

Case 7.2.1 The Peterborough social impact bond – the world's first

On July 27, 2017, it was announced that the seventeen social investors in the Peterborough social impact bond[8] would be repaid in full, together with a 3 percent per annum return. This was the final step in the life of what was the world's first social impact bond.

Peterborough is a prosperous medium-sized cathedral city in the United Kingdom, around a hundred miles north of London. The Peterborough prison was opened in 2005, on the site of a disused diesel engine factory. It is a medium-sized facility with capacity for 480 men and 360 women and is the only prison in the UK which accommodates both men and women, but they are strictly separated in different buildings.

The prison was constructed and is operated by Sodexo Justice Services, which is part of a large international company based in France which provides a wide variety of management and other services to a number of government bodies in the United Kingdom and elsewhere. Sodexo is one of a number of similar companies which are leaders in the controversial but growing field of private provision of public services.

Prison services are traditionally under-funded in the United Kingdom and elsewhere. The 'beneficiaries' are people who have broken the law and have damaged and in some cases physically injured or even killed their fellow-citizens. It is hardly surprising that law-abiding taxpayers and society in general are reluctant to spend money on them; they are seen as deserving punishment, not welfare.

International comparisons, however, suggest that it does not make economic (or human) good sense to under-fund prisons; the following simple table shows the approximate annual cost per prisoner, the numbers of prisoners for every one hundred thousand people in the population and the percentage of prisoners who re-offend and come back to prison within three years in the United States, Norway and the United Kingdom:

Table 7.1 Estimate of Annual Cost Per Prisoner in Different Countries

Country	Prison population per 100,000 population	Re-offending rate within three years	Cost per prisoner per year
Norway	75	20%	$90,000
United States	700	70%	$40,000
United Kingdom	140	50%	$50,000

Source: Statistics on worldwide incarceration rates and criminal recidivism as of 2020[9]

Norway has the world's lowest prison population and lowest rate of re-offending, while the United States lies at the other end of the scale. The United Kingdom has Europe's highest prison population per head and one of the highest rates of re-offending.

The figure for the cost includes only the cost of actually running the prison; it does not cover the costs of the judicial system, nor, of course, the cost of crime to the victims and to society in general. The figures nevertheless show very clearly that money spent on imprisonment can be a good financial investment, irrespective of the intangible human cost of crime.

It can therefore be 'profitable' to spend money on reducing re-offending; the British authorities were anxious to discover new ways of doing this but were reluctant to spend taxpayers' money on remedies which were in any way experimental. Hence, when the prison authorities at Peterborough were offered a new, untried experimental approach to the problem, they were anxious to implement it but reluctant to commit government funding to what might be a failure.

The authorities were approached in 2010 by a consortium known as One Service, which was made up of seven charities and other education and training organisations, including the St. Giles Trust, a London-based charitable organisation, Ormiston Families, Sova, MIND, TTG Training, YMCA and John Laing Training.

The proposal was coordinated by a company called Social Finance Limited, which had been started in London in 2008 with the objective of developing and implementing new approaches to the solution of social problems, and in particular to the numerous issues involved in raising finance for new and untried methods.

The members of this consortium had many years of experience in attempts to reduce re-offending, and many of them were committed to the notion not only of doing good by helping unfortunate people and their families, but also to providing value for money, by delivering programmes whose social and financial benefits were well over their costs.

The St. Giles' Trust, for example, had in 2009 pioneered a programme for prisoners who had sentences of between one and two years, known as Through the Gates. This had been very successful; the total cost was about $1.3 million and at a conservative estimate, it had saved society a total of over ten times that amount. The trust also made extensive use of ex-offenders themselves and other participants to deliver their programmes.

Ormiston Families is a regional institution, originally set up by the family of a young woman who died when she was quite young and had a deep love for children. They work throughout the east of England, and their focus is on building and strengthening troubled families, particularly when a family member is in prison. They support prisoners' families and aim to break the cycle of re-offending.

The other members of the consortium included large national international social welfare institutions such as the YMCA, which provided guidance on healthy living and gymnastic sessions for the offenders when they were still in prison and after their release. John Laing provided on-site training for work in construction, and the consortium also included staff with experience in liaison with property landlords, drug use counsellors, as well as links to services in more distant parts of the United Kingdom when some newly released offenders wished to relocate elsewhere.

The whole criminal justice system, everywhere, needs new and innovative approaches, and the issue of finding money for new and experimental ways of dealing with long-standing problems such as re-offending is particularly difficult. The problem of re-offending by short-sentenced prisoners who are in prison for under twelve months was and still is a major social issue, not only in the United Kingdom but throughout the world. In the UK around 60 percent of these people re-offend within one year of being released, and they may commit as many as five offences within the year.

The national probation services typically devote their very restricted resources to dealing with prisoners who have committed more serious offences and have longer sentences. These prisoners are usually given a small sum of cash, amounting to about sixty dollars, on their release, and they are then on their own. They may or may not have any family which will offer them accommodation, they have no employment and no income, and it is hardly surprising that so many of these people commit crimes and return to prison within a few weeks of their release.

Most of the generally short-term young prisoners in Peterborough prison who were proposed to be covered by the One Service proposal had re-offended before, usually several times. A prison sentence was not in itself an important deterrent; a stay in prison was in a way part of the rhythm of their lives. Most of them suffered from a range of problems; many had mental health difficulties, and many had used and had often also traded in illegal drugs. They tended not to have any permanent place to stay or social group with whom to relate other than young people like themselves, and they had no jobs, no skills to get jobs and in many cases no wish to find permanent employment. The routine of prison, gang life, offending and then prison again was familiar, and they knew nothing else.

The One Service consortium offered a radically new approach to the problem, which involved a high level of contact and one-on-one as well as group remedial attention, both in the prison before the prisoners' release and thereafter when they had been freed. It would necessarily be expensive, because of the large number of highly skilled counselors, supervisors and other specialised practitioners who would be needed, but the consortium members argued that if it worked, it would yield a significant positive economic benefit in addition to the social gains which success would involve.

The programme was estimated to cost a total of £5 million, or $6.5 million, to 'treat' some three thousand ex-offenders over a period of five years, or about $2,000 per person. This was beyond the expected budget of the prison service for post-release aftercare and resettlement, but if it would achieve a significant reduction in re-offending, it would nevertheless be a good investment of government resources in terms of the longer-term savings it would achieve.

The Social Finance UK organisation therefore decided to offer the government a totally new approach to the funding of a social initiative. They put together a group of seventeen British investors which were interested in impact investment and whose management had expressed an interest in supporting initiatives of this kind.

These investors included well-known large donor funds whose management were interested in finding new ways to make more efficient use of their money to fund social initiatives, such as the Rockefeller Foundation and the J Paul Getty Trust, and fifteen other less-well-known institutions such as family trusts and others which were similarly interested in exploring innovative ways of achieving more than could be achieved with one-off and non-returnable grants.

By the year 2010 Social Finance had raised the necessary funds from this group of investors, and they proposed what they called a 'social impact bond'. The One Service organisation, representing the consortium of seven agencies, agreed to provide the package of pre- and post-release services over a period of six years to three thousand newly released prisoners, in three separate groups of about one thousand people in each group.

They agreed that if the percentage of the 'treated' ex-offenders who re-offended within one year was the same or worse than the average re-offending rate of all newly released prisoners in England of the same age and level of offending as the 'treated' Peterborough group, the government would not have to pay. If the rate of re-offending was better than the national average but only by a margin of 7.5 percent or less, the government would partially refund the cost on a sliding scale. If the rate was 7.5 percent or more better than the figure for the 'untreated' prisoners from other prisoners, the government would refund the cost plus a modest percentage of 'profit' on the principal.

The seventeen social investors agreed that they would if necessary bear the loss, but they had sufficient confidence in the quality of what was being proposed to take the risk. They were also accustomed to making grants where there was no question of any recovery, and certainly no possibility of earning a 'profit', so that the downside risk was quite different from that taken by a traditional for-profit investor.

In the event, the overall government policy for managing and financing judicial and penal services was changed two-thirds of the way through the six-year period of the experiment, so that only two thousand rather than three thousand ex-offenders were covered, but the basic principles were unchanged, and the experiment was deemed to have been a success.

The package of services was delivered by the partners as originally planned, in close collaboration with the prison staff and the local and national police services, and it was effectively integrated into the ex-offender support system in Peterborough and the surrounding area.

The 'treatment' was voluntary for the prisoners, and they were not compelled to take part; 70 percent of them participated in the pre-release enrollment and initial service, 80 percent enrolled when they service was offered 'at the prison gate' on their release, but only 20 percent continued to make use of it after three months.

The final evaluation of the intervention nevertheless covered all the prisoners, regardless of whether or for how long they had taken part in the treatment, since such interventions are essentially voluntary and the proportion of the subjects who chose to take part is an important determinant of success. If very few people participate, the programme will fail to achieve significant results, however effective it may be.

The programme was therefore by no means an unqualified success, but it did significantly reduce the rate of re-offending. The rate of re-offending by the two thousand ex-offenders who had been 'treated' under the programme, regardless of how much or how little or for how long they had participated, was nine percent less than the national re-offending rate for the same category of prisoners nationally, and this was considered to be an adequate 'control group' for the purpose of assessing the results of the experiment. The government therefore refunded the seventeen investors' capital investments with an added percentage equivalent to a three percent annual return or profit.

The experiment had been terminated after two rather than three tranches of offenders had been covered, because it was superseded by a new government programme, covering the whole country, which was known as Transforming Rehabilitation. This national programme included some element of payment by results, based in part on the principles and initial results of the pioneering social impact bond. It did not, however, include any means of comparing the contractors' results with those of an equivalent control group, as had been attempted with the Peterborough experiment.

The new programme also evolved very differently, and eventually reverted to employing a small number of large private-sector providers. This was certainly less costly than the Peterborough experiment, but it has not been possible to assess its results in the same way.

David Hutchison, the chief executive of Social Finance, the organisation which had conceived the idea and had put together the consortium, said:

> The Peterborough Social Impact Bond captured people's imagination with the simple premise that it is possible to invest in interventions to tackle difficult social issues. The results today reflect the hard work, commitment and tenacity of all those involved, working with this group of offenders to help them rebuild their lives. I am immensely grateful to all our partners for their commitment over the past seven years. We have learned that impact investment can drive real change and harness

communities and action to rethink how we resolve the challenges our societies face.

This case brings up many important issues: This pioneer social impact bond (SIB) experiment has as we have seen been followed by several hundred similar initiatives, in the United States and Europe and also in Africa, India and other poorer places, and the whole approach raises many fundamental questions. Some of these include:

1   The success of such 'human' interventions depends very much on the personal skills and characters of the people who carry them out; the design details are no more than guidelines and the fact that one group achieves whatever quantitative target was set for the purposes of the bond may mean little for future replications. Hence the results of one experimental programme may not justify its large-scale replication. Are social interventions in any real sense 'replicable'?

2   It is not ethical to put a price on the results of such interventions; human life and happiness is beyond price, and the whole culture of financial reward is inconsistent with the devotion and motivation which are needed to achieve success. Is the move towards SIBs an example of inappropriate 'commercialisation' of the social sphere in general?

3   If the people who implement the programme are aware of the financial implications of achieving certain quantified results, they may be tempted to 'cherry pick', to focus their efforts on the 'easiest' offenders, patients or whoever are being treated, rather than on those who most need their help. May SIBs lead to further marginalisation of the poorest, those who are most difficult to reach and assist?

4   The administrative and management time and cost of putting together the bond, and of monitoring and isolating the inputs and results, may divert management and field staff from the 'real' job of helping the people who need their help. Is the SIB approach more suited for small-scale high-risk experiments than for major social interventions?

5   The results of inputs of this kind may take many years to reveal themselves; in some ways they resemble 'services' such as parenting or education which have lifelong impact. SIBs require a strict timetable which is as short as possible, since the financial results must be measured and the necessary funds transferred within a few months or very few years at most. The timescales are incompatible. Do SIBs move the focus of social interventions away from long-term results towards 'quick fixes' which can more easily and more rapidly be measured?

7.3 Follow-up activity

Select a field in which two or more social enterprises are engaged; this may be local, or it may be national or international, and where the enterprises are providing the same or similar services. Imagine that you are employed in one of the social enterprises, and that you have been asked by a funding agency to suggest how they should decide which one of the social enterprises they should support. Try to identify one or more objectively verifiable indicators of social success which might be used to measure and compare the quality of the work of the different social enterprises which are working for the same cause.

Notes

1 For more details refer: "What Is Pay for Success and Social Impact Bonds?" n.d. *Social Finance*. Accessed December 26, 2020. https://socialfinance.org/what-is-pfs/.
2 Figures sourced from "Social Finance. UK." Accessed July 17, 2020. https://sibdata base.socialfinance.org.uk/.
3 The details are sourced from the publicly available case data sourced from (a) The City of New York Office of The Mayor New York, FACT SHEET: The NYC ABLE Project for Incarcerated Youth www.nyc.gov/html/om/pdf/2012/sib_fact_sheet.pdf and (b) Olson, John, and Andrea Phillips. n.d. "Rikers Island: The First Social Impact Bond in the United States," Accessed December 4, 2020. www.frbsf.org/community-development/files/rikers-island-first-social-impact-bond-united-states.pdf.
4 For more details refer: "Development Impact Bonds." n.d. Center for Global Development. Accessed December 25, 2020. www.cgdev.org/topics/development-impact-bonds.
5 The details are sourced from the publicly available case data sourced from (a) "Educate Girls Development Impact Bond – UBS Optimus, CIFF and Educate Girls." n.d. Accessed December 26, 2020. https://instiglio.org/educategirlsdib/ and (b) Gustafsson-Wright, Izzy Boggild-Jones and Emily. 2018. "World's First Development Impact Bond for Education Shows Successful Achievement of Outcomes in Its Final Year." *Brookings*, July 13, 2018. www.brookings.edu/blog/education-plus-development/2018/07/13/worlds-first-development-impact-bond-for-education-shows-successful-achievement-of-outcomes-in-its-final-year/.
6 For more details refer: "Utkrish-Impact-Bond-Brochure-November 2017." Accessed December 26, 2020. www.usaid.gov/sites/default/files/documents/1864/Utkrish-Impact-Bond-Brochure-November-2017.pdf.
7 Figures sourced from "Social Impact Bond (SIB) Financing: A Pay for Success Strategy." n.d. *Social Finance*. Accessed December 26, 2020. https://socialfinance.org/social-impact-bonds/.
8 The details are sourced from the publicly available case data sourced from (a) "Social Finance UK." n.d. Accessed December 26, 2020. www.socialfinance.org.uk/peterborough-social-impact-bond (b) "Peterborough Social Impact Bond Investors Repaid in Full." n.d. Accessed December 26, 2020. www.civilsociety.co.uk/news/peterborough-social-impact-bond-investors-repaid-in-full.html. and (c) "Peterborough Social Impact Bond Background Information." n.d. Accessed December 26, 2020. https://assets.publishing.service.gov.uk/government/uploads/system/uploads/attachment_data/file/633271/peterborough-social-impact-bond-background-information.pdf.
9 Estimates based on figures sourced from (a) "Incarceration Rates by Country 2020." n.d. Accessed December 25, 2020. https://worldpopulationreview.com/country-rankings/incarceration-rates-by-country. (b) Yukhnenko, Denis, Sridhar Shivpriya,

and Fazel Seena. 2020. "A Systematic Review of Criminal Recidivism Rates Worldwide: 3-Year Update." *Wellcome Open Research* 4(November): 28. https://doi.org/10.12688/wellcomeopenres.14970.3.

7.4 References

GIIN. 2017. "2017 Annual Impact Investor Survey." *The GIIN*. Accessed December 4, 2020. https://thegiin.org/assets/GIIN_AnnualImpactInvestorSurvey_2017_Web_Final.pdf.

GIIN. 2020. "2020 Annual Impact Investor Survey." *The GIIN*. Accessed December 4, 2020. https://thegiin.org/research/publication/impinv-survey-2020.

Kohli, J., D. J. Besharov, and K. Costa. 2012. "What Are Social Impact Bonds? An Innovative New Financing Tool for Social Programs in Social Impact Bonds, Center for American Progress." Accessed December 4, 2020. www.americanprogress.org/issues/general/reports/2012/03/22/11175/what-are- social-impact-bonds/.

Svedova, Jana, Alfonso Cuyegkeng, and James Tansey. 2014. "Demystifying Impact Investing." *ISIS Research Centre*, Sauder School of Business, University of British Columbia. Accessed December 4, 2020. www.sauder.ubc.ca/sites/default/files/2019-02/DemystifyingImpactInvestingFinalVersionApril2014.pdf.

8 IMPACT ASSESSMENT

8.1 Impact: understanding and investing in positive change

Social entrepreneurs want their social enterprises to create positive changes in society, and 'impact' is the term that is generally used to describe this (Brest 2010). There is no standard methodology for measuring this change and every impact investor can use a different technique to measure the impact created by the social entrepreneurs in whose businesses they invest (Robert Wood Johnson Foundation 2011).

To address the complexity of impact measurement, different frameworks are used (Mair and Sharma 2012). Of the diverse models, the Double Bottom Line Report (Clark et al. 2004) presents the Impact Value Chain Model as a research-based framework that maps impact as a change-making process. The model defines impact as the change created by a social enterprise which can transform a social system. This change is visually denoted in Figure 8.1 as the outcome in a society that has happened as a result of the aligned activity of the social venture, above and beyond what would have happened anyway.

In reality, any enterprise can have positive and negative effects on society, in spite of the fact that the desired intent is to make a positive change. The model acknowledges the possibility of the unintended consequences of a social venture operation and can be a useful tool periodically to monitor and align the venture activities with the intended mission of the social enterprise.

This value chain model formed the basis for other frameworks to emerge as it enables all the stakeholders in the impact creation process to reflect and articulate about impact at whatever stage they perceive it to be feasible and useful to do this (Mair and Sharma 2012).

The Global Impact Investors Network (GIIN) Survey 2020 reports that the majority of the models used by impact investors for impact measurement base their output metrics on the United Nations Global Goals, which are known as the Sustainability Development Goals or SDGs. These goals

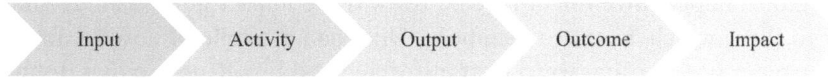

Figure 8.1 Schematic of a Typical Impact Value Chain Model

DOI: 10.4324/9781003032229-8

were adopted by all the United Nations member states in 2015 as a universal call to action to end poverty, to protect the planet and to ensure that all people enjoy peace and prosperity by 2030. The SDGs consists of seventeen principles on which an organisation can report on how it is contributing to the larger global goals, and impact metrics are developed around each SDG principle (United Nations 2015).

An example of an SDG-based framework is the Access Impact Framework, which was designed by Erika Karp, the chief executive of Cornerstone Capital, to measure the impact of the company's investments (Cornerstone Capital Group 2019). Founded in 2013, Cornerstone Capital Group is a financial services firm based in New York, with the mission to enable investors to attain their financial and social goals simultaneously without sacrificing their investments' financial performance. The Access Impact Framework helps investors to create a so-called heat map that they can use to show how the uses of their money measure up to their impact goals, whether it is invested in individual companies, in investment funds or in the portfolio overall. In the map, the concept of 'access' provides a critical link between the Sustainable Development Goals, business activity, and investment opportunity. The framework identifies and uses eleven 'access themes'[1] to draw connections to the social, desired social, economic and environmental outcomes of any investment and uses it as the basis to show how a portfolio investment enhances access to the impact themes that matter most to its investors and contribute to global goals. For instance, investors who want to improve global access to education can use the so-called 'map' to see if their investments are actually achieving what they are aiming for. They can also use it to compare different fund managers to find out, for example, which funds are invested in opportunities that provide access to clean water. These efforts which are focused on investors' global goals help them to align their investments with their preferred SDGs and provide a common language to enable any business, and not only social enterprises, to define the social impacts at which they aim and to think about their impact. In spite of these various efforts, however, the issue of how to compare impact which has been measured by different investors in different ways remains to be addressed.

The Global Impact Investing Network[2] (GIIN), a non-profit advocacy group in the field of impact investing, has attempted to address this impact comparison issue by designing the Impact Reporting and Investment Standards (IRIS+ rating system). IRIS+ serves as a universal taxonomy of social and environmental performance metrics that any impact investor can use and customise according to their needs. Using IRIS+ any organisation investing in a social business can pick the standardised metrics that are widely used in the global impact investment field to track those impact goals that are similar to those which it wants to support. This is an example of how an impact assessment system can start to be transformed and broadened so that it satisfies investors' needs and can enable different investments to be compared.

This tool is not only a way to track the impact of existing enterprises; it also assists investors to carry out their due diligence at the decision stage, before they make investments. It provides standardised metrics for investors' impact goals, which helps them to understand how a particular impact goal can, or cannot, be accomplished through a particular investment and why they should select investment A or B.

GIIN's chief executive, Amit Bouri, claims that IRIS+ is designed to translate impact investing goals such as gender equity, climate change or affordable housing into verifiable numerical results similar to the generally accepted accounting principles used by the Securities and Exchange Commission for assessing financial investments (Sullivan 2019). The IRIS+ website[3] describes the process of quantification of comparable results as follows: Firstly, investors using IRIS+ can identify the impact priorities which are important to them, such as those included in the Sustainable Development Goals or by some other system of categorising impact. If for instance they select Education, then they can retrieve their impact profile by selecting the 'Investment Themes and Strategic Goals' that best match their approach to education. If their goal is to 'Improve access to education for children in crisis and conflict-affected environments' then IRIS+ will come up with a curated set of results that can be used to track this specific impact goal. The results will include a short list of generally accepted impact indicators for this goal, research and evidence on what has worked in other similar endeavours, risk factors and best-in-class resources relevant to the impact profile. This helps impact investors to pick comparable metrics for their investments.

Yet another impact assessment measurement system that enables investors to compare investments in different fields is from B Labs,[4] an American non-profit organisation that strives to redefine business success and uses its so-called B Corporation certification to provide what they hope is an objective measure of non-financial performance. The B Corporation certification rates companies using social and environmental metrics as they relate to their business and employees, and then awards them a score of between zero and two hundred points. A company needs a score of at least eighty to receive the B Corp designation, and companies can use their scores to help them to compare their performance with other businesses and to identify immediate and longer-term impact possibilities. B Labs has also designed an associated impact investment rating system which is known as the Global Impact Investment Rating System[5] (GIIRS), which enables them to compare different impact investments which are made by venture capital and private equity funds. The rating for funds is a composite weighted score of all the companies in which they are invested. This weighted average is then translated into a medal and star rating. In addition to overall ratings, the fund which is being rated can receive more detailed ratings at specific impact area levels that include community, customers, environment, workers and governance. These scores help to motivate companies' management to improve their non-financial impact, but they do not differentiate between impact sectors and industries whose efforts to create change are very different and therefore need different standards for assessment.

To address this issue, the Sustainability Accounting Standards Board[6] (SASB) came up with a framework on the lines of the system used by the Financial Accounting Standards Board (FASB). In the same way that FASB establishes financial accounting and reporting standards for public and private companies and not-for-profit organisations that follow Generally Accepted Accounting Principles (GAAP), the SASB creates standards for sustainable investing. The SASB's standards provide a framework for analysing 77 industries along a consistent range of environmental, social and governance metrics; and it is gaining traction in the business community. Unlike the rating frameworks from GIIN and B Labs, SASB attempts to provide measurable and comparable standards. SASB's CEO Bryan Esterly states:

> We don't produce ratings. Our view is, the ratings could be more accurate and robust if there was a market standard out there. General financial information for most companies is available online, but the same cannot be said for a company's approach to using environmental, social and governance measurements. Even companies that provide their own sustainability reports do not do so in a standardised way as they do with accounting measures. What we produce are standards.
>
> (Sullivan 2019)

The standards and metrics which are surveyed previously are promising in their apparent ability to capture the various dimensions of impact, but they still fail fully to address the problem of measuring impact creation when the goal is to pursue social goals and make a profit simultaneously. Impact can be unique for each social cause and for each different location. This means that it is not as yet possible to quantify or even usefully to compare impacts of different kinds or in different places; it is unlikely ever to be possible to design a measurement method which is universally applicable and widely accepted, but it is important to strive towards this goal in order to make different impact investments more comparable with each other, and less dependent on personal preferences. More and more investors and others are interested and indeed financially involved in impact investment, but a great deal remains to be done before this becomes as acceptable as the search for purely financial returns. The challenges of 'doing well and doing good' are still little understood.

Acumen,[7] a non-profit impact investment fund that raises charitable donations to make equity investments in social enterprises, illustrates how not-for-profit enterprises are also turning towards impact-based and sustainable investments. They use their Best Available Charitable Option, or BACO, model to explain how they are attempting to compare the social impact of different charitable institutions which attempt to achieve similar charitable causes. It is important to understand that both the social impact and the financial performance of investments are critical in portfolio decision-making. The BACO tool can be used to answer the question: For every dollar invested, how much social output does the investment generate compared to other social enterprises or charitable institutions that address the same social cause? If a given social investment appears to be more cost-effective than a traditional charity, it may be right to support that particular cause regardless of whether the enterprise is profitable or not (Acumen 2007).

Acumen uses the example of investment in long-lasting anti-malarial bed nets to show how BACO works (Ebrahim and Kasturi Rangan 2011). If an investment in a bed net manufacturing company in Tanzania and the projected number of people who will be reached and will thus be protected from malaria shows that this is a more cost-effective way of protecting people from malaria than by a traditional donation to a charity which also gives away bed nets in the same region, then this provides Acumen with a quantitative justification for a social investment in a company rather than a donation to a charity. The BACO technique is not yet fully tested or accepted, but the very fact that it is being developed and tested shows how investors even in non-profit institutions are looking for quantitative financial justifications for their work and may be using market-based sustainability approaches to solve social problems that have traditionally been addressed by charities.

The following case study describes the workings of an investment fund that supports social enterprises and non-profit causes by investing in social businesses which address traditionally charitable causes. The example poses many important questions, such as the identification of the real impact of this fund.

8.2 Case study

Case 8.2.1 The Not for Profit Finance Fund (NFF)

The Not for Profit Finance Fund (NFF) began life in 1980 in New York City in the United States as a highly specialised source of assistance to help non-profit organisations to cope with their rapidly increasing energy costs. After forty years, in 2020 the Fund had extended its activities to a very broad range of social issues and had invested about $1 billion in 623 organisations, of various different types, promoting and working for all manner of good causes.

The fund is now one of many similar investing institutions, some of which are much bigger, and its history and activities provide a useful picture of what is one of humanity's most exciting and positive fields of activity. It is not a new field; indeed, as we have already seen, there have been social investors as long as there have been investors of any kind; what is new is that social investing has come to be recognised as a separate activity, with its own rules, laws and institutional culture.

NFF's first chief executive was Clara Miller. In 2001 she was picked by President Clinton for an important position in the United States government; she was replaced by Antony Biggs Levine, who had worked with the Rockefeller Foundation and elsewhere and was a leading advocate of what has come to be called 'outcomes-based' financing as opposed to the 'results-based' approach. The difference can best be illustrated by a simple example; an institution which works to improve the position of troubled homeless people can measure its achievements by the direct output, that is the number of people it accommodates in its shelters and for how many nights. Or it can use the longer-term but far more significant measure of how many people it helps to escape from homelessness and to be self-supporting members of their communities.

Clara Miller gave an interview about the fund[8] and its work, and here are a few extracts from what she said which in many ways summarise what the fund tries to do, and how it does it.

Q: What is the Non-profit Finance Fund?

We are a community-development financial institution focused on connecting finance with non-profit success. We have provided flexible debt financing to non-profits for twenty-five years, and now, increasingly, equity-type financing for non-profits, which we're in the process of inventing. Our goal is to meet the non-profit sector's 'whole enterprise' financial needs.

We also speak, write and advocate for improved financing and funding practices for the sector. That is a little bit different from what most people would currently think of as good non-profit financial practices, which largely focus on compliance and comportment. We look at how to fix the underlying business model – how to help people understand what their commercial proposition is, and to get the tools they need to be able to thrive.

Q: How is social return on investment measured and how is it explained to equity investors?

I think this is a multi-layered question. When every organisation tries to take on every layer, it can get expensive and dysfunctional. The people doing the work aren't the ones to do big social return on investment studies. For them it should be simple: did the people we serve get what we supply? Yes. Okay, check. Did something simple – in our band of control – change? Yes, people can now (let's say) read at a first-grade level.

But there's what people call 'transformation', which includes second and third order effects – i.e., 'being literate means you pay more taxes'. And measuring that requires long-term, longitudinal, econometric studies. With those studies it's not so much change that's measured. And it's not just production, although I think that's also worth measuring. It's also things that don't happen as a result of doing what we're doing. It's the avoided taxpayer costs for the next 45 years of not having a kid who is in foster care. That can be wonderful in a big econometric sense. Even though it's very easy to demonstrate you have a reduction in expense, it's not in real time. It's much farther down the line. And that's the other piece of this non-profit/for-profit puzzle, that non-profit achievements with great social payoffs require long-term investment. Real change and the real transformation take time.

In the financial markets it's sometimes like a gigantic commercial fire sale out there. You're either hitting your numbers or you're gone. But if we translate that over into the non-profit sector, that can't be good, because it means we don't invest in anything that takes time – like providing a great education or finding a cure for cancer. So, it could mean that we don't invest in things that take a while. That's another piece of the social return on investment that has to be very carefully crafted; we don't want to be measuring long-term payoff with short-term instruments.

Q: Are people from the private sector entering philanthropy, trying to apply the business world models, and running into problems?

There are some people who can really be helpful. And there are some folks who imagine that they can advise when they can't. Very enthusiastic, smart folks who don't really understand the different set of commercial assumptions, may try to solve for the wrong set of variables.

I was talking to a VC one day who was excited about bringing the venture capital model to the non-profit sector, and so I said, "Okay, you've put money in to build the capacity of a programme that prevents child abuse. Everyone has decided that rationally the programme will be overstressed if it serves more than 100 children this year." Then the executive director takes in 10 more kids, saying, "They were going to be beaten up. I just couldn't say no." I asked the VC, "What do you do?" And he said, "Same thing I'd do with a venture capital start-up, just 'put my foot on their throat' until they change."

With non-profits the proposition is different. It's not just about profitability. It's about service to the world. In many cases, especially in health and social services, the greatest risk is actually borne by the people being served. So, there are moments where you have to figure out how to manage around risk to a small child. And that's not the same as risk to a stockholder.

But non-profits do need to understand how the world of commerce and money works. Right now, in the non-profit world it's very common to have capital campaigns. And to some extent a capital campaign is like an equity campaign, except that in most cases the non-profit sector has the funny habit of cordoning off asset classes: these funds are only for bricks and mortar, and these are for endowment. In a period of growth, that's disastrous, because it restricts cash. And cash is the primary hedge against risk.

That's something that the current non-profit setup can take from the venture capital side of this, the notion that you need tangible, accessible cash to fund growth itself. Part of the NFF Capital Partners and equity capital idea is to help non-profit managers understand the whole range of resources that are needed for growth.

There's a lot of talk about for-profits and non-profits and hybrids and for-profits that do social good and all this type of stuff. Sometimes we think that's cutting-edge work. But if the fundamentals aren't there, we're only tinkering with tax status, and that doesn't change an untenable business proposition. So, we do a lot of kidding around about, "Oh, yeah, there's another 'duh moment' for our sector. It's cutting edge, but it's also back to basics at the same time."

A few examples can give some idea of the nature, scale and variety of NFF's more recent investments in the United States.

In the urban area of Los Angeles they have invested half a million dollars in a $1.5 million predevelopment loan to initiate the construction of 120 affordable homes and adjacent space for community services, and they have supported the Skid Row Housing Trust in its efforts to provide almost two thousand low-cost supported homes for people who have experienced homelessness, extreme poverty, poor health, disabilities, mental illness and addiction to lead safe and stable lives. Elsewhere in the Los Angeles area they have provided a $2 million credit line to complete the building of schools which will educate over a thousand children from disadvantaged neighbourhoods.

Elsewhere in the United States, NFF has assisted a similarly wide variety of social projects. These include programmes to enhance family stability in Ohio and in Connecticut, to assist newly released offenders to obtain accommodation and to reduce re-offending in Utah, to prepare newly arrived immigrants for employment in Massachusetts, to establish effective nurse-family relationships for needy families in South Carolina and to assist troubled young people in Virginia to find and keep secure employment.

All these programmes have been financed on the basis of payment for success, with carefully designed and monitored metrics which measure not only the direct outputs, such as homes constructed or numbers of participants and their attendance, but the longer-term outcomes, such as families resettled for an extended period or sustained periods of non-offending. The design and monitoring of these metrics are not simple, but NFF and its partner institutions believe that the investment is worthwhile both for the success of the individual project but also for future projects in similar fields.

The following figures in Table 8.1 and 8.2 show the financial performance of NFF during 2019, and its financial position at the end of that year.

Table 8.1 Income Statement NFF 2019

Income

Interest on loans	11,325,000
Grants	5,784,000
Loan management fees	2,292,000
Programme fees	1,490,000
Donated services	273,000
Investment Income	20,000
Total	21,184,000

Expenses

Interest on loans	5,942,000
Salaries	9,373,000
Benefits	2,374,000
Consultancy	386,000
Professional services	751,000
Travel and incidentals	1,182,000
Rent and occupancy	1,333,000
Depreciation	371,000
Provision for loan losses	3,798,000
Total	25,510,000
Loss	4,316,000

Source: NFF 2019 Accounts https://nff.org/page/financials

Note: Figures in US dollars rounded to nearest $1,000

Table 8.2 Balance Sheet NFF as on December 31, 2019

Assets/Uses of Funds		Liabilities/Sources of funds	
Cash	20,671,000	Accounts payable	4,336,000
Restricted cash	9,240,000	Deferred revenue	9,364,000
Accounts receivable	4,959,000	Loans payable	133,947,000
Grants receivable	4,517,000	Capital	21,273,000
Investments	1,101,000	Loan loss reserve	4,404,000
Loans receivable, net of loan	149,580,000	Programme fund	6,200,000
loss allowance $3,506,000		Grant Fund	795,000
Property and equipment	2,192,000	Loan fund capital	11,941,000
Total	192,260,000		192,260,000

Source: NFF 2019 Accounts https://nff.org/page/financials

Note: Figures in US dollars rounded to nearest $1000

The loans receivable are virtually all secured against the borrowing institutions' real estate or bank accounts, and the grants receivable are to be received from a mix of foundations, government bodies and corporations. The restricted cash is reserved for certain beneficiary institutions which have been chosen in the same way as earlier recipients. The loans to beneficiary institutions carry annual interest rates of between 2 percent and 7.5 percent.

On the liabilities side, the loans payable are owed to eighteen different banks, with maturities running out as far as 2030, although most are due in the forthcoming five years. The interest rates are positive, and at around the same levels as rates for loans to high-grade commercial businesses.

Questions and issues for discussion:

1   NFF has almost $200 million of assets deployed in various ways. Are the amounts in each type of asset appropriate? Could NFF achieve more social 'good' if its funds were deployed in other ways?

2   NFF could in theory invest its $200 million in reasonably secure and profitable investment assets and could use the interest and dividends as grants to support social and charitable causes. Would this be a more 'socially responsible' approach? Would it achieve more good with less administrative 'hassle' if it adopted this approach?

3   What is the average 'spread' between the cost of NFF's funds and the interest it receives on its investments? Is this adequate, in view of the risks and inevitable losses involved, or is it excessive?

4   In some European and other countries local and national governments perform many of the social enterprise functions which NFF assists in the United States, and support of the type which NFF provides would not be necessary. Is NFF in any way 'crowding out' government, and, more generally, are social enterprises performing functions, and relying on financial support, for which the public sector should take total responsibility?

5   Investors whose objective is to maximise their long-term profits within the boundaries of the law and morality need only compare the financial position and future potential of prospective investees in order to decide in which projects to invest. Social investors such as NFF, however, must compare 'apples with oranges'; what criteria should they use when deciding between a number of different investment possibilities?

6   Assuming that the amounts of money, the timescale and the apparent experience and competence of the staff were similar, should NFF support a project which will help one hundred severely handicapped children to obtain marketable skills and to support themselves, or one which will help one thousand disabled old people to live in decent accommodation? How can an institution such as NFF ensure that decisions of this kind are reasonably consistent with one another?

7 In general, should an institution such as NFF choose to focus its investment on specific types of social enterprise, such as education, or housing, or recidivism, or health care, or on particular locations, such as cities, states or regions, or should they be willing to look at any type of intervention?

8.3 Follow-up activity

Undertake a brief survey of the 'charitable' activities of a sample of your friends, and of your own. Ask them (and yourself) approximately how much money, or time, they give, and to which causes; ask them and again yourself whether you prefer to donate your cash or your time or whether you would prefer to assist by buying some goods or services from them, even at a slightly higher cost or less convenience. How do your friends, and you yourself, assess the impact of your generosity? Do you need better indicators, and if so what might they be?

Notes

1 For more details on the eleven themes refer: "Access Impact Framework – Sustainable Investing Fund | Cornerstone Capital Group." Accessed December 6, 2020. https://cornerstonecapinc.com/access-impact-framework/.
2 For more details refer: "The GIIN." Accessed December 4, 2020. https://thegiin.org/.
3 For more details refer: "IRIS+ System | the Generally Accepted System for Impact Investors to Measure, Manage, and Optimize Their Impact." Accessed December 4, 2020. https://iris.thegiin.org/.
4 For more details refer: "Certified B Corporation." Accessed December 4, 2020. https://bcorporation.net/.
5 For more details refer: "GIIRS Fund Rating Methodology | B Analytics." Accessed December 4, 2020. https://b-analytics.net/content/giirs-fund-rating-methodology.
6 For more details refer: "SASB." Accessed December 4, 2020. www.sasb.org/.
7 For more details refer: "Acumen." Accessed December 4, 2020. http://acumen.org/about/.
8 Details sourced from the publicly available interview: "How Should We Fund Non-profits?" 2008. Yale Insights. Accessed May 8, 2020. https://insights.som.yale.edu/insights/how-should-we-fund-nonprofits.

8.4 References

Acumen. 2007. "BACO to Help Acumen Rate Investments." *Alliance Magazine* (blog). Accessed December 4, 2020. www.alliancemagazine.org/news/baco-to-help-acumen-rate-investments/.

Brest, Paul. 2010. "The Power of Theories of Change (SSIR)." *Stanford Social Innovation Review*. Spring. Accessed December 4, 2020. https://ssir.org/articles/entry/the_power_of_theories_of_change.

Clark, Cathy, William Rosenzweig, David Long, and Sara Olsen. 2004. "Double Bottom Line Project Report: Assessing Social Impact in Double Bottom Line Ventures.

Methods Catalog." *CASE*. Accessed February 2, 2021. https://centers.fuqua.duke.edu/case/knowledge_items/double-bottom-line-project-report-assessing-social-impact-in-double-bottom-line-ventures/.

Cornerstone Capital Group. 2019. "Access Impact Framework – Sustainable Investing Fund: How Can Investors Drive Progress Toward Achieving the UN Sustainable Development Goals?" Accessed December 6, 2020. https://cornerstonecapinc.com/access-impact-framework/.

Ebrahim, Alnoor, and V. Kasturi Rangan. September 2009. (Revised May, 2011) "Acumen Fund: Measurement in Impact Investing (A)." *Harvard Business School Case* 310–011. Accessed December 25, 2020. https://store.hbr.org/product/acumen-fund-measurement-in-impact-investing-a/310011?sku=310011-PDF-ENG.

GIIN. 2020. "2020 Annual Impact Investor Survey." *The GIIN*. Accessed December 4, 2020. https://thegiin.org/research/publication/impinv-survey-2020.

Mair, Johanna, and Shuchi Sharma. 2012. "Performance Measurement and Social Entrepreneurship." In *Social Entrepreneurship and Social Business: An Introduction and Discussion with Case Studies*, edited by Christine K. Volkmann, Kim Oliver Tokarski, and Kati Ernst, 175–89. Wiesbaden: Gabler Verlag. https://doi.org/10.1007/978-3-8349-7093-0_9.

Robert Wood Johnson Foundation. 2011. "Impact Capital Measurement, Approaches to Measuring the Social Impact of Program-Related Investments." 67. Accessed December 4, 2020. www.issuelab.org/resources/12984/12984.pdf.

Sullivan, Paul. 2019. "Investing for Social Impact Is Complicated. Here Are 4 Ways to Simplify It." *The New York Times*, May 3, 2019, sec. Your Money. www.nytimes.com/2019/05/03/your-money/impact-investing-standards.html.

United Nations. 2015. Resolution adopted by the General Assembly on 25 September 2015, "Transforming Our World: The 2030 Agenda for Sustainable Development | Department of Economic and Social Affairs." Accessed December 20, 2020. www.un.org/ga/search/view_doc.asp?symbol=A/RES/70/1&Lang=E.

9 LEGAL STRUCTURE CHOICES

9.1 Incorporation of social enterprises

This book does not claim to be a legal guide or to show our readers what legal form they should choose to incorporate any proposed social enterprise. As should be clear, there is a wide range of possibilities, and they differ quite radically between countries or between states of the United States or India or even between the far smaller four nations of the United Kingdom. The social entrepreneur's intentions and methods of operation are much more important than legal niceties.

As we have tried to show, there is a slow or perhaps not so slow international trend to break down the barriers between doing well and doing good, to expect new and even existing businesses to attempt to maximise both their social and their financial value. Aspiring social entrepreneurs may have to decide whether to adopt some kind of dual approach, under which the 'social' operations of their businesses can be incorporated as such, and may thus be qualified to benefit from the tax concessions and other privileges of so-called charities, or foundations, as well as from the 'softer' image which this form of enterprise may have, which can make it easier to attract supporters whose main objective is to 'do good' rather than to make a profit.

But there are many different approaches, and a wide variety of legal forms. The following exercise is designed to expose readers to some of the options which are available.

Read these brief descriptions of four very different social enterprises. Imagine that you are the social entrepreneurs who have conceived each of them. The four examples are followed by notes which outline the alternative legal forms of association which are available for social enterprises in the United States, the United Kingdom and India. Depending on which country interests you most and is most appropriate for your own situation, try to decide which legal form is the right one for each of the social enterprises; it may also be possible to set up two linked entities for a given enterprise, one to engage in trading with any profits going to the other which has purely charitable status, but this is of course more complex than having one single entity. If you yourself have an idea for a social enterprise, use the options to make your own selection.

DOI: 10.4324/9781003032229-9

The following issues among others should be considered when choosing the most suitable legal form, and it is important to recognise that it may be difficult to change a legal form once an enterprise has started its operations.

- What are the most suitable sources for the financial investment which will be needed, what risks should they be prepared to bear, and what security and return will the providers of the initial and any later finance demand?
- What are the official regulations which apply to each legal form, and how will they affect the initial formation and the subsequent development of the social enterprise?

What form of governance will be most suitable for the social enterprise; what kinds of people will be most likely to sympathise with its objectives?

- What financial or other risks are relevant for the social enterprise, and what will be the liability of the management for such risks?
- What impact will the legal form have on the willingness of prospective beneficiaries and clients, staff, funders and society in general to collaborate with the enterprise?
- How will the chosen legal form affect the ability of the social enterprise to distribute its profits, if there are any?
- Will the chosen legal form make it easier, or harder, to report its results in ways which will make it easier for it to pursue its social goals?
- What will be the local and national taxation implications of the chosen legal form?
- How will the chosen legal form affect the ownership and transferability of any assets which the enterprise may need?

Social enterprise A – the Loving Dogs' Home

There are hundreds or perhaps thousands of stray dogs roaming about in Caninianville, the local capital of a low-income area of the nation which is growing rapidly. Very few of the inhabitants of the city are at all bothered by the dogs; the better off people live in well fenced and guarded homes and travel around the city in private cars or taxis, and the poverty-stricken majority have always been used to living with such animals, and they have far more important things to worry about than the welfare of the dogs or the slight danger that may arise from being bitten by dogs. Some people even argue that the dogs are a good thing; they eat rats, and they make life even more uncomfortable for the large numbers of beggars and others who have to sleep on the streets.

When the dogs get too numerous or there are instances of rabies or other issues, the police go out and round up as many dogs as they can find and take them to a rubbish ground where they are shot and buried. Many of the dogs are ill or injured and most of them are malnourished, but the majority of the population of the city are generally unconcerned; dogs, whether they are well or sick, injured or in good condition, are a normal part of the background of life in the city.

Recently, however, a number of people from other parts of the country, and also some foreigners, have come to live in the city, and many people from Caninianville have been educated and have lived elsewhere in cities where just about the only dogs to be seen are well-fed and well-cared-for pet dogs, and where there are many institutions which have been set up to take care of stray dogs. In some cities the police collect up the few stray dogs that there are as they do in Caninianville, but the dogs are then treated by veterinarians for any health problems and people take them as pets, even paying quite substantial sums for each dog to enable the institutions to continue their work.

A number of these more recent residents are very bothered by the dog problem, as they see it. Some of them have complained to the police and to other local authorities; the police have undertaken a few more 'dog hunts', as they call the round-ups, but nothing more has been done.

Finally, half a dozen women who had recently moved to Caninianville got together and agreed that something must be done about the problem; they all love dogs and have their own pets, and they hate to see dogs being mistreated. Some of their children have seen a 'dog hunt' and have been very distressed, and their mothers have told their husbands that they want to move away unless something can be done.

They decided to start an organisation to deal with the problem. They agreed that it would be necessary to make regular 'sweeps' though the city, to pick up stray dogs, and then to cure them of any diseases, to accommodate them for some weeks and then to find new owners who would take good care of them. They decided to buy two small trucks and to hire drivers and two or three specially trained people to do the work, as well as one properly trained and qualified veterinarian, and they also needed to rent suitable premises and to construct accommodation for the dogs. In due course they hoped that it might be possible to expand the service to other similar cities in the area which had the same problem, and perhaps even to expand to other cities in neighbouring countries where there were similar problems.

The founding group could not afford to pay all the money themselves, although they could between them contribute around a third of the $100,000 they estimated they needed to start the new institution. They reckoned that it would cost about the same amount each year to run it in Caninianville, and they hoped that it would after a few years be possible to raise a proportion of the costs from dog lovers who would 'buy' rescued dogs as their own pets, but it was not possible to estimate the income from this source at the beginning.

They decided to call their new institution The Loving Dogs' Home, and they then had to decide under what legal form they should register it.

Social enterprise B – mobile meals for the elderly folks

Joe is an entrepreneur at heart; he loves to start things and to see them succeed and grow, and he has made a reasonable amount of money out of his six business ventures. He has sold off his shares in four of them, he enjoys building the other two to the level where he can also sell them, and he has enough money to live on, but he wants to do more, and if possible to make a socially useful contribution as well as to build his personal fortune.

Joe comes from a very modest background, and his parents are retired and no longer earning, but Joe is able to take care of them as well as his own family. His parents have many friends of their age who are not so fortunate, however, and some of them cannot even afford to buy decent meals. Joe has occasionally helped his parents to buy food for such people, but he has decided to address the problem properly and to start a business to do it.

Most of the older poor people who are not being properly fed can afford to pay something for their food, although some are almost destitute; they lack physical access as much as money, and many live alone and need assistance in establishing a routine, in planning and in simple cooking. The local government authorities are aware of the problem, and they do run old folks' homes for people who cannot take care of themselves; these homes are costly to run and are full to capacity, but the government has no alternative remedy for the problem of poverty-stricken old people.

Joe has experience in running a restaurant and catering business, and he has estimated that he could provide decent simple meals for old people, and could deliver them, for about two dollars a person a day, so long as his business could achieve a reasonable scale. This is of course much less than the cost of accommodating someone in an old folks' home; some old people or their families could afford to pay the full cost, or even enough to provide a small profit; others could pay part of the cost while others would not be able to pay anything.

There are therefore many possible sources of income; Joe does not particularly want to make a lot of money out of the new business, but he wants it to be able to cover its costs as well as to attract volunteers and others who may be willing to work for nothing or for much lower salaries than they could earn elsewhere. He dislikes the notion of 'charity', and he believes that many of the eventual clients of the business are proud of their independence and would themselves be reluctant to be beneficiaries; they want to pay their way.

Joe has decided to call his new venture Mobile Meals; now he has to choose a suitable legal form which will help him to raise the capital he needs and to enable the business to achieve its objectives and to cover its costs.

Social enterprise C – keep them outside

In many countries the majority of people who are sent to prison re-offend within a year of being released; a prison sentence may appear to be a good way of discouraging crime, but it actually seems to have the opposite effect; prisons are sometimes considered to be places where people learn to commit more crimes, rather than being a way of stopping it.

This worldwide phenomenon is known as recidivism; prison is expensive; although it is not too difficult to prevent people from escaping, it appears to be very difficult to 'reform' them, so that they do not come back to prison and continue to burden society still further.

Maria was herself an example of this problem; she had an unsettled childhood and was already into drugs in her early teens. She soon became involved in trading drugs, in order to maintain her habit, and when she was seventeen she was arrested and sent to a special school for young offenders.

The school, like most such institutions, struggled to prevent its inmates from re-offending almost as soon as they were released, and generally failed, but Maria was an exception. She was fortunate enough to meet Simon, a newly qualified social worker who had come to the school on a study visit. They had a short conversation, but both recognised that they had a lot in common; Simon had also had a difficult upbringing but had been fortunate enough to be guided by an excellent schoolteacher. When Maria was released, they renewed their contact, and Maria eventually qualified as a social worker and joined Simon in the same team.

They worked for some years for the various government agencies which were responsible for the different components of the prison and social welfare system, but they were both frustrated by the system; young offenders were assisted and advised by a range of different workers, and the couple could see from their own experience that a more focused approach was needed. This might or might not be more costly than the existing system, but the economic value of a significant reduction in recidivism would be enormous.

Maria and Simon had developed and had themselves informally tested a more focused system, which required sustained one-on-one counselling by the same counsellor, and they eventually decided to resign from the government system and to set up a new institution to apply the methods they had evolved.

They had no other source of income, so they would have to earn a living for themselves from their new venture, but they also wanted people to realise that their main motivation was to help young people to rebuild their lives; they hoped that their passion and insights into helping other people could also yield enough money to pay them more or less what they used to earn as social workers, but would also do a lot more good to society.

They both had good connections with the authorities, and they realised that there was certainly a need and a 'market' for the service they wanted to offer, but it would probably take some months or possibly over a year before they could prove its value by showing clear results. They hoped to be able to train others to offer the same service, so that in time their venture could make a real impact, but initially they needed to raise sufficient money to keep them both for about a year, and to undertake some publicity.

They estimated that they would need about $100,000 before they could realistically expect to earn any income; they decided that they should demonstrate their seriousness by registering their venture under a suitable legal form; it would have to send the right signals to the community in general and to the decision makers who controlled the access to offenders, and would also have to allow them to earn an income for themselves and to grow their enterprise so that it could make a genuine contribution. They did not themselves particularly want to make a lot of money, but they hoped to build something of national and perhaps international importance; it did not concern them whether this happened because others copied them or their own enterprise grew; what mattered was the results to society.

They wondered what legal institutional form would best suit their ambitions.

Social enterprise D – better books for children

Marian and Alice love books and they love children. Their families are now grown up, and they are looking forward to having grandchildren. They appreciate that many aspects of children's upbringing have evolved and improved a great deal since they themselves were children and when they raised their own families, but one aspect which they believe has not got better, and which they are sure has got worse, is the quality of children's books.

They had themselves written and illustrated one children's book, which their own children and grandchildren enjoyed, but they were unable to find a publisher who would publish it. They approached several well-known firms, but they all said that the book was too old-fashioned, that children wanted exciting modern stories with some fighting and violence; simple old-fashioned stories about children in the countryside or similar traditional themes did not sell anymore, they claimed.

Marian and Alice are determined to do something about the situation. Some of their friends have written books similar to their own effort, and they know that many other parents and also some schoolteachers agree that there is a need for something better. They have time on their hands, and their respective partners have well-paid jobs. They are also willing and able to invest some of their savings if this will help to make better children's books more widely available.

One of their friends has some experience in publishing, and he has told them that he would like to join in their efforts to improve children's reading material. He is also willing if necessary to provide a modest amount of capital if they can be reasonably sure that the money will not be lost and that it will earn a modest return.

Alice and Marian are determined to improve the situation, for the sake of their own grandchildren and for society in general; better children's books are their passion, and they believe that there is a genuine need. They know that they have the passion which will be necessary to succeed, and they feel a real sense of responsibility, given that they have the necessary resources and expertise.

They want to devote all their efforts to make better books for children, and they believe that better reading material can make a real difference to children's education and to their behaviour as adult members of society. They now have to find a suitable legal form under which to register their enterprise, and then they can start in a small way to improve the world.

These four examples are loosely based on the experience of real-life entrepreneurs who were very anxious to pursue the social goals which they had chosen, and each of them wanted to choose a legal form which would enable them to pursue their visions.

Try to imagine that you have been asked to advise them. Some readers may be familiar with the legal options which are available for social enterprises in their respective countries, and they should feel free to ignore the following material in Section 9.2, which briefly summarises the possible forms of incorporation which are available in the United States, the United Kingdom and in India.

Alternatively, readers may choose to use some or all of the three summaries of the forms of incorporation which are available for social enterprises in the United States, in India and in the United Kingdom as a basis for deciding what form is most suitable for each of the three proposed social enterprises in each of the three countries, or in one country of their choice. This material is drawn from published sources in each of the three countries, and is necessarily only indicative of the possible options, rather than being complete and definitive.

There are no uniform laws or legal forms for social enterprises, either globally or nationally, so social entrepreneurs such as those described in the case studies have to choose from a variety of possibilities, depending on the nation or as in the United States on the state in which they propose to locate their enterprises. No form is ideal, but the entrepreneurs should try to answer the following questions, as well as the more general issues we mentioned earlier, and then to choose what appears to be the best option.

- How much money will be required to set up and then to run the enterprise?
- Who will benefit from the services of the enterprise?
- Will the enterprise be able to sell its services, and if so to whom? What will they be willing and able to pay for the services? What proportion of the cost might be raised from such sales?
- Will local or other government bodies benefit from the services of the enterprise, and how if at all might it be possible to get them to pay some or all of the cost?
- Are there any institutions, private or public, which might be persuaded to donate some part of the start-up or running costs, either in money or in kind, such as the provision of premises?
- Are there any wealthy individuals or institutions who might be willing to donate some part or all of the start-up costs and/or to contribute to the running costs, in return for the resulting good publicity?

Table 9.1 Suggestions for Legal Structure Choices for Social Enterprises

Social Enterprises	United States	United Kingdom	India
The Loving Dogs' Home – stray dogs	L3C or 501C	Community Interest Company	For-profit small enterprise
Mobile Meals for elderly folks – meals for old people	B-Corporation	Community interest company	Hybrid – for profit and society
Keep Them Outside – youth re-offending	Non-profit	Charity	Society
Better Books for Children	Regular for-profit company	Regular for-profit limited company	For profit private limited company

Source: Created by the authors based on legal structure choices in the US, UK and India

There are no completely right or wrong answers, which is why many or even most entrepreneurs of all kinds, social or otherwise, spend large sums of money on lawyers to advise t hem on such issues, but the following table (Table 9.1) makes some workable suggestions as to appropriate forms of incorporation for each of the four proposed social enterprises in the three countries. The decision in the United States is of course complicated by the fact that some forms of incorporation are only available in a small number of states.

9.2 Forms of incorporation: the United States, United Kingdom and India

The incorporation options for social enterprises in the United States, United Kingdom and India are presented in the following heads A, B and C, respectively.

A) USA social enterprise incorporation guidelines

The following summary of the available options for USA is based on 'Social Enterprise: Choice of Legal Entity' from 'Start-up Garage' a mentoring service provider in the US (Jensen 2012).

The main options are:

Non-Profit: A non-profit is the most common legal entity chosen by social enterprises. However, a non-profit that has attained 501(c)(3) or 501(c)(4) status with the Internal Revenue Service, or IRS, the government body which administers taxation, faces a lot of limitations as to how profits can be re-invested into the company and how they can raise investment capital by offering outside investors a reasonable return on their investment. Therefore, a non-profit is not the ideal structure for a social enterprise that seeks to re-invest its profits and pay competitive salaries to its employees.

L3C (Low Profit Limited Liability Company): This option, which is considered to be suitable for a for-profit enterprise with a socially beneficial mission, is available in nine states and pending in ten more. The purpose of the L3C is to simplify the use of programme-related investments (PRIs) from private foundations. Foundations must direct 5 percent of their assets to a charitable purpose, and an L3C can be a recipient of an investment that satisfies the criteria of this requirement which are used by the IRS.

Benefit Corporation: A benefit corporation is an entity type in California and seven other states that is required to have a public benefit purpose for its Articles of Incorporation; the requirement is audited by a third-party standard. The most well-known third-party standard developer is known as B-Lab, which certifies complying companies as 'Certified B Corporations'. Different states have different requirements for incorporation as a benefit corporation.

Flexible Purpose Corporation: Unique to California, a flexible purpose corporation is another entity type that is allowed to pursue certain special purposes and relies on shareholders to oversee the fulfilment of the special purposes through minimum voting requirements and required disclosures.

It is also possible to choose an LLC or a corporation as an entity form for a social enterprise, and companies in some states may be required to do this for a lack of alternative options. Both an LLC and a corporation offer personal liability protection for the owners but differ in their tax benefits and corporate formalities. To determine the best entity choice for a new enterprise, it is best if possible to consult a lawyer.

There is no perfect business structure for success in a social enterprise: the model that will ultimately be the best depends on the good or service being delivered, the market being served, the ability to obtain funds for growth, and the political, social and cultural context of the regions in which the social entrepreneur plans to operate.

B) UK social enterprise incorporation guidelines

The available options for UK are from the article titled 'How Do I Set up a Social Enterprise?' from 'Informi' a business mentoring service provider in the UK (Informi n.d.)

The main options are:

Sole traders and partnerships: Social enterprises can be sole traders (individual self-employed people) or partnerships (where two or more people come together) who decide to donate the majority of their profits to a good cause.

Limited company: A limited company has a legal identity that is separate from its members and directors; therefore, individuals' personal liabilities are limited. Companies are governed by a board of directors (which can be just a single person) and must comply with the requirements of Companies House, the official entity that regulates registration in the UK, including filing annual returns and accounts. A limited company may also be a charity or a so-called 'Charitable Incorporated Organisation'.

Unincorporated or incorporated registered charity: To become registered, a charity has to meet one of the Charities Commission's defined objectives, and to be run by a voluntary board of trustees. An incorporated charity is one that is also registered with Companies House; that is, it is a charity but is also incorporated like a company. Many charities seek incorporation in order to mitigate personal liability for their trustees and members.

Charitable incorporated organisation (CIO): This is a relatively new type of legal status that has been designed to enable charities to have the benefits of incorporation while only needing to comply with charity regulation, that is, they do not have to also comply with company law.

Community Interest Company (CIC): Unlike other types of limited company, a CIC has to have a social mission. A CIC has to pass a community interest test imposed by a regulator, which examines the motivation of the company – including whom it will help and how – and what it will do with any profit or surplus.

Industrial and Provident Society: These are in essence co-operatives that are run by and for their members, but which can also operate for the benefit of the wider community. They have to register with the UK Government's Financial Services Authority (FSA) and also must meet specific FSA conditions.

C) Indian social enterprise incorporation guidelines

These guidelines on the available options for India are from the report titled 'Social Entrepreneurship in India Unveiling: The Unlimited Opportunities' from Swissnex India. The section in the report titled 'Legal Set-Up' is the basis for the discussion on legal options in India (Swissnex India Consulate General of Switzerland 2015).

There are a number of reasons and implications for choosing the right legal structure, such as: how the social enterprise gets funded, how the profits (if any) should be distributed, the governance structure, reporting responsibilities, tax liabilities, and ownership pattern. The law in India, unlike in many other countries – such as the USA and the UK – does not offer much flexibility in terms of legally structuring a social enterprise. India has the following three types of legal structures from which a social entrepreneur can choose:

Non-Profit or Public Charitable Organisation: A non-profit is legally structured in India as a charitable Trust (under the Indian Trusts Act, 1882), a non-government organisation (under the Companies Act, 1956) or a Society (as is laid down by the societies Registration requirements of each state). The non-profit has to use no less than 80 percent of its funds as charity for public good and 20 percent of its funds for operational and internal organisation costs, although these percentages can be quite liberally interpreted. Non-profits are assumed mainly to be dependent on grants, but they can earn some revenue so long as it is only used for direct charitable purposes.

The biggest benefit of registering as a non-profit is the eligibility to get tax benefits under the Income Tax Act of 1961; non-profits can also accept foreign donations under the Foreign Contribution (Regulation) Act, so long as they can conform to the requirements for registration; experience suggests that this may be a long, drawn-out and complicated process. One of the problems with this model is that it may be difficult to hire top-class staff or to invest in the latest technology and infrastructure. One advantage is that non-profits can focus solely on creating social impact without the pressure of having to earn a financial return, but a major disadvantage is that there is a constant need to raise funds.

The For-Profit Social Enterprise: A social enterprise is legally structured as a for-profit or business entity which has a clearly defined social impact goal. In India, there are five options to set up a for-profit social enterprise: sole proprietorship, partnership, limited liability partnership, private firm and as a co-operative, but 80 percent of Indian social enterprises are structured as for-profit private limited companies. This type of legal structure is perhaps best suited for social enterprises that aim both to grow and to be profitable. The business model is based on the social impact their founders want to make or the social problem they are trying to solve. Some key features of social enterprises are the fact that those who benefit from their impact and its target customers who pay for the product or service may or may not be the same. The enterprise can be structured for impact investments and can accept debt or equity financing, and it has to report its profits as well as its social impact. A social enterprise has to function internally like any other commercial business in terms of its management, its operations, its people and its resources.

These companies can attract funding from venture capital companies; they can usually afford to pay for the best staff and can invest in the highest quality technology and infrastructure. On the other hand, they have to focus on earning profits, and this can lead to a mission drift, which may be unacceptable to the original shareholders and stakeholders.

The Hybrid Model: With the evolution of the concept of social entrepreneurship, new models which allow the enterprise to sustain itself from earned income have emerged. The hybrid model brings a non-profit entity and a for-profit business together to solve a social problem. The non-profit entity is able to raise grants from benefactors and at the same time, it can charge for its services or products through its business entity in order to earn revenue. The hybrid model helps organisations which aim to achieve high social impact by offering them cross-subsidy options that strike a balance between earning revenue from customers and providing access to high quality services to benefactors. This approach can be the best of both worlds, as it allows a social enterprise to separate its social and revenue-generating activities. The model allows social enterprises both to attract donations and grants and still to be able to have access to social venture funding. It may however be difficult for management to focus on both types of entity, and it is hard to build a common culture.

It is clearly difficult to choose a suitable legal structure as many dynamic factors have to be considered at the time of incorporation, when the founders know that there are many uncertainties and that changes may be necessary as the enterprise evolves. The following case study of BASIX, a pioneer microfinance and livelihoods business in India, illustrates some of the institutional options which are available to an enterprise whose promoters want to 'do good' and at the same time to earn a profit and thus be 'sustainable'. We then present the case of Rang De, a pioneer peer-to-peer lending model which entered the same India microfinance space as BASIX with the principal objective of reducing interest rates for the poor. Rang De was the first institution in India to offer peer-to-peer lending and was therefore operating in an environment where there were no available legal structures which were specifically suitable for their business. Later, as the regulatory authorities came to appreciate the intricacies of social lending on-line, the founders had to go through a number of business models in order to address the legal structure changes with which they had to comply, and the sustainability issues that were involved.

9.3 Case studies

Case 9.3.1 BASIX – for profit and for good – together?

Vijay Mahajan, the founder of BASIX,[1] was born in 1954. He took his first degree in Electrical Engineering, and after working for a few years, he attended the Indian Institute of Management in Ahmedabad, India's most prestigious business school, whose graduates typically move on to high-paying jobs in the private sector. Vijay worked for a few years in marketing for Philips, the multinational electrical business, but he then decided to use his management education and experience in the field of economic and social development.

In 1982 he therefore co-founded PRADAN, a not-for-profit development institution; the Hindi word means 'giving back what is owed', and the acronym also stands for 'Professional Assistance for Development Action'.

Vijay and his colleagues built PRADAN's activities in several areas, including rural development, livelihoods and education, but he came to believe that economic development could best be achieved by institutions which were run like businesses and which were indeed themselves businesses. It might be necessary for some activities to be heavily subsidised early on, but it should be possible for any institution whose aim was to improve poorer people's incomes to earn an income for itself.

He therefore left PRADAN, and in 1996 he moved to Hyderabad in the southern state of Andhra Pradesh and set up BASIX, a livelihoods development institution which would offer microfinance, that is the delivery of financial services to unbanked populations, but would also provide livelihood development assistance, such as training, and would in addition help disadvantaged rural people to build their own robust institutions.

The new institution was financed by a combination of equity and loans; the initial support came from the Tata Trust, who were closely followed by the Swiss Development Corporation and the Delhi office of the Ford Foundation, and a number of development finance institutions in the Netherlands and the United States. Microfinance was at that time beginning to take off in India, and BASIX was the first significant lender to Self Help Groups, the peculiarly Indian approach which has since been taken up on a large scale by India's commercial banks; by 2020 almost 10 million such groups, with well over 100 million women members, had taken loans from banks and other financial institutions.

Indian microfinance was led by the country's nationalised banks, which were later joined by numbers of specialist non-bank microfinance institutions, most of which used the by then well-tested Grameen approach which had been pioneered in neighbouring Bangladesh. Many of these institutions started life as not-for-profit 'societies', which were registered under an 1860 Act or similar rules, but most eventually converted themselves to for-profit companies.

They did not have banking licenses and were thus not permitted to take their clients' savings beyond small amounts of security for loans, but the management of small cash savings accounts can never be a highly profitable business. Mass market money lending, on the other hand, at rates of interest which are much higher than such institutions' cost of funds, but well below the rates charged by traditional local moneylenders, proved to be highly profitable.

BASIX did eventually receive a banking license under a new regulation, which permitted the group to open a small full-service bank called Krishna

Bharti Samruddhi Local Area Bank, or KBSLAB, in two districts of Andhra Pradesh and one in neighbouring Karnataka, but the bulk of its financial services business continued to be in lending, with the addition of life, livestock and crop insurance.

In spite of the relative simplicity and profitability of microfinance, however, and the enthusiasm of some of BASIX' investors, Mahajan and his colleagues were clear that BASIX was not merely a microfinance institution; its role was to promote and improve its clients' livelihoods, through credit but also through skills training and the development of their own local institutions.

It was possible to earn some revenue from these latter functions, but they could certainly not be as rapidly and highly profitable as moneylending on its own. Mahajan therefore decided that the microfinance operation should be incorporated as a for-profit business, which was called Bhartiya Samruddhi Finance Limited, or BSFL, meaning 'national prosperity', whereas the livelihoods development and other traditionally not-for-profit activities would, as they had been in PRADAN, be undertaken by a not-for-profit institution. This was called Indian Grameen Services, or IGS, using the same word 'Grameen', meaning village, which was used by Professor Muhammad Yunus'[2] Grameen Bank in Bangladesh.

The overall direction of these different entities was controlled by the BASIX Group's main board of directors, which included representatives of social investors from the USA, and of the voluntary sector, some of whom had also served PRADAN, and, as well as people from for-profit institutions, such as the international accountants and consultants PWC, and a British management school.

The board meetings were not always easy, since the more 'socially' oriented members were less familiar with the demands and language of financial investors. The representatives of for-profit institutions were generally less involved in the work of IGS, particularly as BSFL was growing rapidly and did not appear to need any assistance from IGS, and they had no financial interest in IGS either. BSFL rapidly moved into new areas where IGS was not operating, and some board members felt that IGS might be irrelevant to the main mission.

In 2003 BASIX undertook a study of the impact of BSFL's moneylending on their customers; it was found that the impact was limited and of short duration, that some borrowers were substantially worse off after they had taken loans, and that the poorer clients generally benefitted the least. It seemed to be clear that borrowing money on its own was not enough to enable people to escape from poverty; the operation was profitable, and people wanted to borrow, but its 'development' impact was questionable at best.

As a result of this finding, it was concluded that BSFL should itself offer non-financial services to its borrowers, rather than depending on IGS to 'catch up' with its rapidly growing loan business. IGS transferred many of its staff to BSFL, and they were based with and managed by BSFL's regional offices.

This inevitably increased BSFL's costs, and some of the board members who represented foreign financial interests, even though they were nominally social rather than 'pure' for profit investors, argued that BSFL was a remarkable example of a profitable institution which served the poor. Its profitability should not be eroded by the costs of services which were not directly related to its core business of lending money.

The Swiss Development Agency, which had supported BASIX from the outset, made a substantial grant to BSFL in an effort to mitigate the impact of the non-financial services on BSFL's profitability, but this was only a temporary palliative. The scale and profitability of India's microfinance institutions was rapidly increasing; BASIX had been one of the main pioneers, but its size and profits had been eclipsed by other relatively younger competitors, and many people both from inside and outside the BASIX group, including senior management as well as investors, believed that BASIX should regain and retain its leadership, in its volume as well as its approach.

The earlier decision to combine the financial as well as the non-financial operations was therefore reversed in 2008, and the non-financial development role was reassigned to IGS. BSFL grew rapidly, and by September 2010 its valuation had by some estimates reached around half a billion US dollars. Mahajan and other early investors were even concerned that should they wish to realise their investment it might not be easy to avoid making personal fortunes out of their efforts to build a viable social development institution. This would have been inconsistent with their own ambitions, and it might also send the wrong signals to other 'social entrepreneurs'.

In the event, however, their fears were unjustified. In October 2010 the 'bubble' burst, thanks to the competing microfinance institutions' reckless drive for growth, the adverse publicity arising from the suicides of some indebted farmers and clumsy intervention by the state government of Andhra Pradesh, which even forbade clients to repay their loans.

The majority of BASIX' and most of its competitors' outstanding loans were in the state, and BASIX, along with most of its competitors, was forced to write off the bulk of its loan portfolio. Some of the institutions went out of business, while others such as BASIX were unable to repay the loans from banking institutions which had financed most of their business.

BASIX had by this time generated a small constellation of related businesses, which were separately managed, with various different shareholders. These included Sub-K, a for-profit company which facilitates web-based financial transactions for unbanked people; B-Able, a for-profit livelihoods development and training business which obtains most of it work from the government's National Skills Development Corporation; KBSLAB, the full-service bank which they had been licensed to start in the year 2000: and Indian Grameen Services (IGS), the not-for-profit entity which had originally provided the group's non-banking businesses.

Like most microfinance institutions, BSFL withdrew altogether from the state of Andhra Pradesh and did not return. The KBSLAB bank continued to operate in its permitted two districts in the state; its borrowers knew very well that it was allied to BSFL, but the repayment performance was very little affected by the October 2010 crisis. This may have been because its customers knew that it was not covered by the state government's prohibition of repayments to microfinance institutions, but their behaviour was also influenced by the fact that they knew the bank as a place where they could safely keep their savings, as well as a moneylending institution. The bank was eventually sold to other investors, but it continued to operate and to serve the same low-income clientele. Sub-K and B-Able continued to be successful members of the BASIX Group, and IGS retained its not-for-profit status and continued to operate in various locations.

BSFL, the main lender, continued to operate profitably in a number of states outside Andhra Pradesh, including Odisha, Tamil Nadu, Karnataka, Jharkhand, Madhya Pradesh and Rajasthan. Although the Andhra Pradesh crisis removed what had been the financial core of the BASIX group, its constituent entities have survived and continue to serve the same sections of the population. By 2019, Sub-K had grown to reach some 3 million customers, acting as the facilitating agent for ten of the country's largest banks, including both public-sector and private institutions. Sixty percent of its customers were women, and their accumulated savings amounted to almost $30 million. The loan portfolio was some $15 million.

Sub-K is thus facilitating the provision of full-service banking, rather than moneylending alone, and makes it possible for previously unbanked people to access other financial services such as individual bank accounts, and savings and remittances, all of which are badly needed by lower-income households in rural and urban areas. Sub-K also plans to build a digital platform to allow people to access services such as input suppliers, extension services and produce buyers.

The other BASIX enterprises also continue to promote livelihoods and at the same time to be modestly profitable. BASIX Krishi Samruddhi Limited works with some forty thousand farmers through four hundred producer companies by providing linkages with input suppliers, extension services and output buyers. BASIX CTRAN Consulting Limited works on carbon transactions and climate change adaptation and mitigation, and BASIX Consulting and Technology Services Limited uses BASIX' experience to advise other organisations such as the World Bank and United Nations agencies.

BASIX Municipal Waste Ventures Limited works with urban waste pickers and helped to make the city of Indore the cleanest city of India, while the vocational skills training company BASIX Academy for Building Lifelong Employability (B-Able) is a leading skills provider; they trained over 200,000 young people between 2009 and 2019, of whom about 20,000 are self-employed; this includes over 5,000 rural opticians. B-Able lost money for some years but has since 2015 made a profit of between 10 and 15 percent on its annual turnover of around one million dollars.

This case study clearly covers a wide range of issues, and the institutional choices which were made by BASIX were clearly in part a function of the Indian regulatory framework.

What general lessons can be learned from it?

1 In particular, did BASIX make the optimum choices of institutional forms for its various activities and locations? Would the different activities have been more successful had they been more closely linked or, alternatively, if they had been more separate, or had been undertaken by quite different organisations?

2 The 'core' activity of micro-lending in Andhra Pradesh collapsed, for a number of reasons, leaving very substantial unpaid debts to several banks. Was there any way in which management might have avoided this, and to what extent did the institutional structure exacerbate or mitigate the damage which was caused?

Case 9.3.2 Rang De – from non-profit to for-profit

Ram NK[3] is a well-qualified and experienced engineer from Secunderbad, India. He was married in 2004 and like many of his peers he was in 2004 invited by his employers to work abroad for a period. His wife, Smita, is qualified in social work but she too was happy to accept the invitation. The couple settled in Kidlington, a rural village near Oxford. They enjoyed living in the English countryside, within easy reach of their work. Smita had a good job with a local government authority, Ram was well paid, and he enjoyed his work; his initial contract was extended, and they might have remained in England for many years.

Both Ram and Smita come from well-off middle-class families, and they could have continued on the same fortunate and comfortable path for many years or even throughout their careers. But they were dissatisfied; they both felt that they should do something for their country, and in particular for their fellow Indians who did not share their good fortune. Both of them had spent time as volunteers in poorer communities before their marriage, and in 2008 they returned to India, determined to do something for the Indian poor.

The couple first decided to live in a village; Ram decided to continue to undertake assignments in information technology. This remained an idea. They still wanted to do something for the Indian poor, however, and they continued to look for opportunities. In 2006 they had read about the award of the Nobel Prize to Professor Muhammad Yunus, in recognition of his pioneering work with Grameen Bank in Bangladesh; this was a business, not a traditional charity, and it appeared able to benefit millions of poor people in a way which preserved and even enhanced their self-respect, and which could also be 'sustainable', in that it did not necessarily depend on donations. Ram and Smita shared the belief that handouts and gifts were not a long-term solution to poverty; poor people needed opportunities to be able to earn a living for themselves and their families.

The couple had already heard about microfinance, and they knew that Yunus' idea had inspired similar initiatives in India. But they had also learned about the problems which had arisen, particularly in the state of Andhra Pradesh. Indian microfinance had initially been pioneered by charities, but many of these were not well operated; they remained very small and local, and they were not well managed. At the same time there were a number of government-run loan schemes, but these tended to be very political and to base their lending, and in particular their policy on loan write-offs, on political rather than welfare grounds.

It seemed to be clear that a more business-like approach was needed, and several experienced entrepreneurs entered the field, some of whom had worked in finance overseas; Indian microfinance grew very rapidly, mainly in the southern state of Andhra Pradesh, where the chief minister offered an enthusiastic welcome. Ram and Smita thought that microfinance might be a field where they could use their experience in business and in social work to make a positive difference in India, but then they came across an article which described how some borrowers from microfinance institutions in Andhra Pradesh were committing suicide because of their indebtedness to microfinance institutions, which was in part due to high interest rates.

This issue had been taken up by the local media and by politicians, and the head of the local government had apparently issued an order stating that borrowers need not repay their loans from microfinance institutions in the region. It was clear that such orders could result in the collapse of microfinance, in Andhra Pradesh and even throughout India. The local government officials appreciated the risk, but they argued that the high interest rates which were charged by some of the microfinance institutions were not acceptable. Ram remembered an official being quoted in a published article:

"I understand what Professor Yunus is doing in Bangladesh but please help me understand what is happening in India?" It did not seem right for some Indian microfinance institutions to charge as much as 50 percent interest, while Yunus had shown that an interest rate of between 9 and 12 percent was enough to sustain the operation.

Smita and Ram both believed that they should try to do something about India's poverty, and that affordable credit could be a useful tool to help poor people. These people needed education, housing and jobs, but these would take time; if they could access affordable credit, on a business-like basis, this would give them the self-respect they needed to obtain other things for themselves. They made some enquiries and found that the true annual cost of microcredit was generally between 36 percent to 45 percent. The general view seemed to be that this was lower than local moneylenders and that the fact that poor people were willing to borrow at this rate showed that they could afford it.

They felt that this was a false argument; people's willingness to pay for an over-priced but necessary product did not necessarily mean that the price was fair. They looked around the world for examples of institutions which were providing poor people with credit at a reasonable cost, and they identified a California-based institution called Kiva.

Kiva is a peer-to-peer online lending platform, or P2P, which uses the power of the internet to enable better-off individuals to lend directly to poorer people. The lenders can choose their borrowers from a wide range who are shown on Kiva's website, and they can lend as little as twenty-five dollars. The loans are facilitated and managed by local microfinance institutions, which charge the borrowers their usual interest, but the individual lender bears the risk of non-repayment of the principal and does not usually receive any interest; the interest fee is used by the local institution to cover its costs.

Kiva has a very limited presence in India, and lenders have to make their loans in US dollars; Ram and Smita believed that there was a good potential for a similar institution but based in India, which could work in Indian rupees and therefore be able to enable Indian individuals as well as non-Indians to lend to less-well-off Indian borrowers.

Ram had at one time designed an online giving platform for a charitable organisation for which he used to volunteer. The platform was never actually used, but Smita and Ram believed that they could design and build a lending platform. They wrote some funding proposals to finance their proposed venture, but they were all rejected; they realised that they would have to be able to show prospective funders something more than an idea; they would have to have a working prototype of the system, and designing and building this would require a team effort.

They decided at this point that they must commit themselves to the idea; they had saved some eight thousand dollars for a vacation in Switzerland, and they decided instead to spend it on building the first prototype. They told themselves that this was their limit; if they could get something that worked for this amount, they would proceed, but if not, they would forget the whole idea.

Ram and Smita made enquiries from various well-qualified groups as to the cost of developing a robust system; initially, several groups expressed an interest in helping them, but it soon became clear that it would cost far more money than the modest sum which they had allocated for the work; it seemed that a robust system would cost four or five times as much.

They persisted with their efforts and appealed to people's patriotism; they explained that they were leaving their well-remunerated work in Europe in order to bring affordable credit to disadvantaged people in India, but the response was always the same; people wanted to help but they needed also to be paid the market rate. Ram told them that they could only afford a tenth of what they were asking; the IT consultants were impressed by the idea, but they insisted that they had to be properly paid.

After a few weeks of such disappointment, the situation suddenly changed; several of the groups whom the couple had approached came back to them; one very well qualified group who had not even replied to their request sent them a message whose first sentence was 'transfer 3,000 GBP immediately'. They realised this was the moment when they had to make a real commitment. Ram and Smita responded at once, and in a few days, they had put together a team which could provide a world-class solution and was able to guarantee all the security checks that were needed for on-line lending.

In 2007 they finally left their life and work in England behind. Various people who had worked successfully in microfinance in India agreed that the time was right for an on-line social microfinance platform. They took a stall at the new Microfinance India conference in Delhi and the concept was an immediate success. The couple had decided to name their start-up Rang De, meaning 'Colour' and 'Share'. Their idea was well timed; Professor Muhammad Yunus' Grameen Bank had been awarded a Nobel Peace Prize the previous year, and although there were many initiatives in India, the NGO community in particular felt that the whole issue of interest rates was being neglected; the Rang De concept appealed to many investors and Ram and Smita had three offers of private equity finance.

They politely refused, as they wanted to take time to be sure what they wanted to do before accepting any capital. They wanted 'capital with a conscience', which meant that they needed investors who would be patient and would allow the new model time to evolve rather than immediately to go for scale.

They eventually shortlisted four NGO partners with whom they would work to connect on-line lenders to the right borrowers. They visited each of them to ensure that they were suitable, and that their village contacts included the truly marginalised people Rang De was intended to reach. In order to save money, and to meet other social entrepreneurs, they based themselves in the new business incubator workspace at the Indian Institute of Management in Bangalore and started to train their proposed partners on the use of their Rang De technology platform. Smita also investigated the various legal options for their organisation in order to choose the right form before going live. They chose to register it as a trust, which is the Indian equivalent of a British charity or the United States 501(c), so that people would realise it was more than just an idea.

They wanted to be sure that they had the right legal form, because on-line lending was a novel concept, and there was no precedent for such an operation in India. They approached some recognised law firms, but they had a similar experience as with the possible investment partners. They were quoted fees of a million rupees, or about $12,500, which was way beyond what they could afford, so they decided to go ahead and launch their operations as a trust.

They had decided to go live on January 26, 2008, India's Republic Day, and in the Microfinance summit they had announced it as their launch date. However, with their lack of legal clarity they deferred their launch date and informed everyone who had registered interest in their idea.

They also wrote an email to thought leaders in Indian microfinance seeking their help on resolving their legal dilemma. One response was from Dr. Nachiket Mor, who was then the head of the newly founded ICICI (Industrial Credit and Investment Corporation of India) Foundation for Inclusive Growth. He offered to provide them with whatever help they needed, and ICICI Bank's legal team offered to give them legal advice free of charge as this was an idea that would serve the country. Nachiket asked Ram and Smita to launch their platform as planned on January 26, 2008, and to meet the legal team in India in December.

Ram and Smita had nearly used up the money that they had set aside to turn their dream into reality. Ram changed his visa status so that he could maintain his consultancy practice, and they moved to a less costly apartment in order to reduce their rent. The rent saving was used for funding the start-up idea and for the couple to travel back and forth from UK to India to execute the idea.

They now had about fifty thousand dollars to fund their new business, and Ram still had a well-paid job. He went back to the lawyers who had asked for their normal fees and paid what they had asked. They recommended an escrow agency structure, whereby Rang De would contract a broker to set up an account in which funds could be held while a transaction was being negotiated and would either pass them on or return them. This allowed Rang De to lend on-line without liability to the lender in case some personal or natural disaster occurred before the loan had been finalised.

Smita was the CEO of the trust. They hired their first employee and started their operations in 2008 in a village in Vidarbha district of Maharashtra, about five hundred kilometers east of Mumbai. They slowly built a team of people who had worked with the main technology companies in India, and the business grew steadily. Ram worked as Head of Technology for the ICICI Foundation and Rang De was also based in their offices.

Their aim was to reduce the cost of borrowing for poor people in India, and they believed that they achieved this by combining the power of technology and of social lending. The borrowers paid a maximum of 8.5 percent a year on their loans, which was the equivalent of 17.9 percent cent on the declining balance or 17.9 percent APR. A maximum of 5 percent went to the field partners for their work in identifying the borrowers, 2 percent to the social investor who lent the money, 1 percent to Rang De and 0.5 percent for contingencies.

In 2010, however, two years after Rang De had started, there was a major crisis in microfinance in India, centred in the state of Andhra Pradesh. The initial problem was caused by a number of suicides by over-indebted borrowers; this had been caused by over-lending from private for-profit microfinance institutions, and the issue was exacerbated by clumsy local government officials and sensationalised reporting by the press.

As a result of this the government set a maximum limit of 26 percent on microfinance interest rates; Ram and Smita were proud that Rang De's interest rate had never exceeded 17 percent, but their business was not yet profitable. It was doing good, but it was not yet doing well. On-line lending has high fixed costs, and the key to profitability is volume; individual loans can be as low as twenty-five dollars, so long as there are enough of them.

The business continued to grow steadily and had passed its break-even point and had started to earn a modest profit. In 2017, however, the Reserve Bank of India extended it regulations to peer-to-peer lending. By that time Rang De had raised and lent over $12 million; this had been lent by fifteen thousand social investors, and they had lent to a total of 65,000 borrowers, in eighteen states of India.

Until that time Rang De had operated as a public charitable trust, but as a result of the new regulations, Rang De had to be reconstituted as a private limited company and to apply to the Central Bank for a non-bank finance company peer-to-peer lending license. This meant that the business had to have a paid-up capital of almost $300,000. To their surprise, Ram and Smita were able to raise this quite rapidly from twenty-three social investors who had been lending through Rang De for some years. The finance was therefore not an issue, but they feared that the new legal structure would lead to changes in structures, systems and, most importantly, in mindsets. They had always wanted to remain as a trust as they believed it would protect their social mission, and they were worried that their uncompromising mission of providing credit at affordable interest rates might be impacted by the change to a private limited company.

Rang De had in any case to stop its operations for over a year in 2018 and 2019 in order to make the change, but the company was able to survive through grants from Tata Trusts and Friends of Women's World Banking, or FWWB, both of which had also assisted the company when it was starting up eight years earlier. Finally, in September 2019 Rang De was approved as a private limited company and could start its operations again.

The new equity investors advised Ram and Smita that they should plan for the long-term sustainability of Rang De without compromising its social mission. The previous model had never turned a profit, and this time the regulatory change made them think hard about 'doing good and well' at the same time. In the new form Ram adopted a platform model which runs on membership. Even in this model the poor borrowers pay interests ranging between 0 percent and 10 percent flat per annum for their collateral-free loans. Thus, Ram and Smita made sure that they did not deviate from their mission.

Ram believes that as long as the founders have not lost focus on their mission, change in legal structure does not matter. The forced regulatory norms made him realise this. He says that an enterprise can be a 'social enterprise' whether it is for-profit or non-profit, whether it is donor funded or not, but the most important thing is that its social mission should be audacious to begin with. It should be bold and have the potential positively to impact a sizeable population and thereby attract multiple stakeholders to partner with it. In that case it is bound eventually to be sustainable, and all the owners will collaborate to build its impact. Ram says that social entrepreneurship is about solving social problems at scale with collaborative effort, be it with or without grant funds. But in their new for-profit structure Ram and Smita were forced to think about sustainability at once rather than later and to expand the social mission to scale its impact more than ever before. However, they did not want to do this by charging more interest from borrowers or by lending them massive loans.

The founders then did a lot of research and design thinking and came up with a new business model which would have zero reliance or dependency on the interest the borrower would pay on Rang De's sustainability or profitability. Ram calls it the 'Recurring Revenue Model'.

In this model, Rang De was repositioned not just as a peer-to-peer lending model that allows the poor to get credit at lower interest rates but as a platform that also provides two other groups with a world-class experience in social finance: (1) social investors can lend to the remotest Indian villages with a click of a button and (2) third-party field partner NGOs and community institutions can raise money through Rang De at a low cost.

If these two users were charged a nominal fee, this would provide recurring revenue for Rang De. It was like an Amazon Prime membership model in the social space. Social investors could for a fee access and invest in India's rural communities with a click of a mouse through trusted field partners which Rang De had curated, and social lenders could if they preferred avoid the fees by opting for a free plan, but if they chose a paid plan for which they would have to pay one dollar a month, then they would have access to more borrower profiles and exclusive access to other features on the platform. The domino effect of one dollar from a million investors will provide Rang De with recurring revenue for Rang De and will enable the investors to invest in any state in India without any limitations for a month, through Rang De's due diligence.

Another stream of revenue would come from the third-party NGO partners and community institutions that can raise money through the Rang De platform. Rang De solves a very critical problem for them, by providing their communities with timely and affordable access to credit. These partners were donor funded and previously had always to depend on occasional grants.

In the new model these partners are asked to use their grants to pay a one-time setup fee and a recurring annual fee which will help them efficiently to raise funds at a lower cost than from banks. The fees will not be related to the amount of money these partners can raise through Rang De, and Rang De guarantees that any borrower listed on their platform will get funded.

The borrowers can decide on the interest rate based on what they can afford, and the rate can range from zero percent to ten percent flat per annum. The new platform also lets the social investors choose their preferred rate of return, which in turn is used to determine the interest rate paid by the borrower. The lender can also if he or she wishes lend at zero interest for a loan which is listed at four percent. Rang De and its social investors have never in their twelve years of operations experienced a wilful default from the poor in India. For poor people, repayment is about self-esteem.

The Rang De revenue model provides and protects that self-esteem, and it enables the operation to achieve sustainability without diluting its social mission. Ram and Smita aim to build Rang De and to list it in India's first social stock exchange in years to come and to prove that social enterprises can grow and create a major social impact with the support of social capital markets. The equity investors who have funded the new business believe that the model they are trying out is perfect to balance the 'doing good and well' philosophy in a social enterprise. It is worth trying out, regardless of whether it will result in financial success for Rang De or not. The number of individual equity investors has increased from 23 to 77 and by January 2021 they had invested a total of almost eight million dollars in the business. Ram concludes:

> There is no money at the bottom of the pyramid and if it were there it would have been tapped long back by commercial businesses. We work with below the bottom of the pyramid communities in India and Rang De was not set up to make money from the poor. It provides a missing infrastructure that enables the poor to participate in India's growth story and for Indians across the globe to contribute to that development.

The Rang De case poses a number of questions. These include but also go beyond legal structure options and show how a social entrepreneur's background and ability to adapt to changes in the regulatory environment can play a role in the sustainability of a social enterprise.

1   Ram and Smita suffered a number of setbacks over some years in their efforts to set up Rang De, and they were remarkably patient and persistent over a long period. Their personal skills and employment history enabled them to persevere and eventually to succeed, but does their experience imply that genuine innovation must necessarily involve sacrifice and patience of this kind? Or might they have achieved the same or similar results more quickly if they had chosen different methods?
2   The couple deliberately chose a relatively informal type of incorporation, and they only converted to a more formal type of corporate identity when they were compelled to do so. After the event, they concluded that this change had actually benefitted the organisation. In general, should social entrepreneurs start informally, and then formalise as they grow? Should they adopt what they believe will be their 'final' legal form from the beginning, or should they attempt to remain informal and to keep their activities free from legal constraints for as long as possible?
3   Rang De's successful evolution depended on an unusual and in some ways fortuitous set of circumstances, but the technology which makes peer-to-peer lending possible had been available for some years, as had the legal forms which made it possible, and the concept of 'removing the middleman' (and middle woman) was not new. Must genuine innovation depends on 'good luck' of this kind, or might

international peer-to-peer lending between wealthy and poor individuals and nations have emerged anyway on a commercial basis in a few years?

4   One or a number of the many existing microfinance organisations might have been expected to grasp the opportunity to introduce peer-to-peer lending to microfinance, given that they already had contacts in Indian villages and had sources of finance. In the event, however, the 'disruptive innovation' came from outsiders. Why is it that new methods so often originate with relatively unqualified and under-financed entrepreneurs, rather than with the organisations which are already familiar with the field and have the necessary finance, contacts and experience?

9.4 Follow-up activity

Identify a local 'good cause' such as an old people's home; try to find its accounts and sources of income on-line, or if that is not possible speak to one of its staff and suggest additional new ways by which it could raise money other than from donations. Will this change its legal structure and if so how?

Notes

1 Details of the case sourced from: (a) Personal interview and communication with Vijay Mahajan, Founder of BASIX by one of the co-authors (b) Publicly available information from BASIX website www.basixindia.com/ and publicly available articles (c) "Corporate Social Focus." April 2019. Accessed December 27, 2020. www.corporate socialfocus.com/the-magazine.asp; "The Curious Case of a Clean Clean Indore-Business News." July 2017. Accessed December 27, 2020. www.businesstoday.in/ magazine/columns/the-curious-case-of-a-clean-clean-indore/story/254144.html.; Singh, Abha. 2018. "B-ABLE – Locally-Relevant Skills Delivery with DomesteQ and Eye Mitra." https://doi.org/10.13140/RG.2.2.24506.44489. Accessed December 27, 2020.

2 Professor Muhammad Yunus established the Grameen Bank in Bangladesh in 1983. He won the Nobel Peace Prize in 2006 for the work done by the Grameen Bank to create economic and social development for the poor through small loans on easy terms – so-called micro-credit. For more details refer: "The Nobel Peace Prize 2006." *NobelPrize.Org.* Accessed December 26, 2020. www.nobelprize.org/prizes/ peace/2006/yunus/biographical/.

3 Details of the case sourced from: (a) Personal Interview with Ram, Co-Founder & CEO, Rang De on September 30, 2013, and January 19, 2021, (b) Personal Interview with Smita, Co-Founder & CEO, Rang De, and Aseem, Manager, Rang De on February 10, 2021 (c) Publicly available information from BASIX website "Rang De. Our Story." Accessed January 28, 2021. https://rangde.in/about/our-story and publicly available article (d) Kashyapp, Sindhu. 2019. "How Rang De Pivoted from a Social Grant Platform to a P2P NBFC." Accessed January 28, 2021. https://your story.com/2019/12/rangde-pivot-social-grant-p2p-lending-startup.

9.5 References

Informi. n.d. "How Do I Set Up a Social Enterprise?" *Informi*. Accessed August 13, 2020. https://informi.co.uk/business-administration/how-do-i-set-up-social-enterprise.

Jensen, Tyler. 2012. "Social Enterprise: Choice of Legal Entity." *The Start-up Garage*, October 24, 2012. https://thestartupgarage.com/social-enterprise-choice-legal-entity/. Accessed August 17, 2020.

Swissnex India Consulate General of Switzerland. 2015. "Social Entrepreneurship in India Unveiling the Unlimited Opportunities." *Swissnex India*. Accessed August 23, 2020. www.indembassybern.gov.in/docs/Social-Entreprenuership-Report.pdf.

10 THE SOCIAL ENTERPRISE LIFE CYCLE

10.1 The nature of change and its inevitability

Social entrepreneurship is considered to be distinct from entrepreneurship because it is based on the contention that it is possible to pursue the dual goals of 'doing good and doing well' through a new type of entity known as a 'social enterprise'. But just like whatever every entrepreneur envisages for the future of an enterprise – whether it is commercial or charitable – a social enterprise changes as it moves from its original conception into its reality.

As time passes; enterprises grow bigger, or they shrink; they may absorb other businesses or be absorbed; the founders may leave, other staff may change; or the founders may merely grow older and the businesses may cease to exist.

Just like other entrepreneurs, before they aspire to expand their businesses, social entrepreneurs must check that there is a valid market for whatever product or service their business is proposed to provide. A social entrepreneur should from the outset aim to start a business which will be financially sustainable and should also create the 'impact' that he or she intends to make, whether it is social, environmental or ecological, so that it contributes positively to the world's development in a sustainable manner (Mueller, Brahm, and Neck 2015). As some social entrepreneurs began explicitly to claim that their businesses could create value along all three dimensions, the report of the 2005 World Summit on Social Development recognised the three components of society, the economy and the environment, and thus created a basis for judging business performance on all three dimensions, rather than considering profit as the central aim with the planet and people merely as side issues (United Nations General Assembly 2005).

Figure 10.1 illustrates this trans-disciplinary approach and the potential for this blend of values which exists in every business.

Some more progressive investors are starting to consider enterprises that contribute to all domains to be more sustainable than traditional businesses, where profit is the dominating goal and the other aspects are considered more as fortunate by-products. They thus attempt to evaluate prospective investments by considering their performance across all the three axes of value (Clark, Emerson, and Thornley 2015) as shown in Figure 10.2.

DOI: 10.4324/9781003032229-10

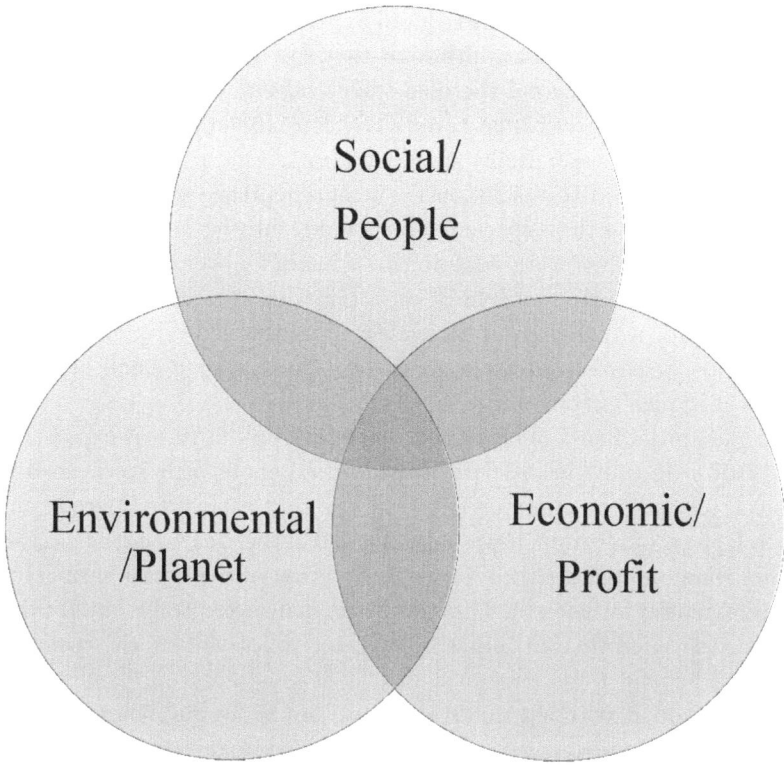

Figure 10.1 Inter-disciplinary Nature of Value

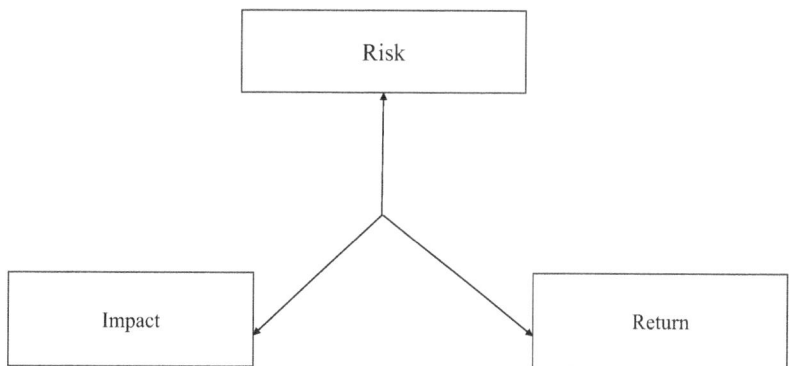

Figure 10.2 Three Value Dimensions for an Enterprise

Although every type of entrepreneur contributes directly or indirectly to all these three dimensions of value, either positively or negatively, a social entrepreneur, right from the inception of the enterprise, will claim that the very motivation and existence for her or his social venture is to strive for impact along all three dimensions, using market-based forces rather than merely to maximise profits alone (Zahra et al. 2009).

This claim is inspiring, but first-hand experience[1] shows that most promising social enterprise ideas, although they are well intended, will probably fail to develop beyond the idea stage and will probably die at a very early stage or perhaps change completely into something that is very different from what was initially conceptualised. One of the co-authors of this book attempted to teach social entrepreneurship to young people in order to give them the experience of conceptualising and planning social enterprises while they were pursuing an academic programme. Most of the students were able to conceive of an interesting idea, and many of them even attempted actually to put their ideas into effect, but like all enterprises of all kinds, regardless of their promoters' aims, only a small proportion were ever implemented.

For example, when a microfinance enterprise initiative was explored in a tribal region in India in order to provide the people with access to formal financial services, the community's response to it was very different. In the research phase of ideation, it was hoped was that the idea would be welcomed by the community and that it would itself grow into a social business with a huge potential for growth. Though the idea attracted some initial funding support, the microfinance initiative was not welcomed by the community for whose benefit it had been designed. It proposed a group lending model which did not fit with the cultural beliefs and economic behaviour of the people it was intended to assist. They considered finance to be a completely private aspect of their lives, which should not be undertaken in groups, and they preferred a completely different solution, with village grain banks and an individual insurance system rather than group loans (Guha, Patel, and Parekh 2017).

Social enterprises which are well intended by the social entrepreneurs who introduce them and have been approved by prospective funders, and which appear to be scalable or to have worked well in other locations and with different people, may not always find a market in a different community. There can be many different solutions for the same social problems because each community and its circumstances are different.

When would-be social entrepreneurs are generating ideas, they often forget this because they want to be the 'changemakers' who fix problems and propose solutions; they often forget that they must keep an open mind and respond to the needs of each specific situation and be willing to modify or even to discard their own ideas when they are confronted by the reality of the problem itself (Barney et al. 2015). Social entrepreneurs have to come up with business models that work for the community and whose products or services have a market potential so that they can also be viable businesses. These entrepreneurs have to think beyond their own ideas and to fall in love with the problem so that their enterprises provide their customers with what they genuinely need rather than the particular solution they may have had in their minds (MovingWorlds n.d.).

Growth: dilemmas and trade-offs

Social entrepreneurs must, as is suggested previously, be aware of the problems they may face when they first attempt to put their ideas into practice. Their next big challenge is to understand what 'growth' really means for their unique dual-goal businesses. Social entrepreneurs have to distinguish themselves from conventional commercial business founders on the one hand and from charitable people who only want to do good on the other hand; they must themselves understand and then make others realise that they are in the business of creating social value that is making a positive social impact, and that at the same time they intend to do this by implementing a market-oriented model that creates financial value, so that the business can be sustainable and can survive and perhaps grow and thus continue to create both financial and social value. Once the enterprise has actually been started, the social entrepreneur then has to confront a critical challenge; can it survive, and grow, and at the same time maintain and expand the social impact which was the main motive for its establishment? It is not easy to set up any business, whatever its aims, but at this point, once the enterprise has been successfully established and when the enterprise starts to grow, the entrepreneur has to show that her or his initial plan to achieve both goals can be implemented in the real world.

Brock and Steiner, in their important 2009 paper, entitled 'Social Entrepreneurship Education: Is it Achieving the Desired Aims?' suggest that the biggest challenge in training people to be social entrepreneurs is to help them to learn how to scale a social enterprise. There are several approaches to teaching people how to start building such an enterprise (Brock and Steiner 2009).

It is not easy to build any enterprise, whether it is a for-profit business or a charity or a hybrid which we are calling a social enterprise. But it is even harder to build a social enterprise, and to strengthen or even merely to maintain its 'social' aspect. The enterprise may appear to survive, and even to grow, but all too often its growth is accompanied by a slow or even a rapid drop in its 'socialness', as the realities of markets and finance and staffing make it harder than ever to maintain its hybrid quality. Almost inevitably, the two goals start to appear to conflict with each other, and it is clearly hard for a social entrepreneur to compromise the very survival of the business in order to retain its socialness. It seems to be obvious that it is worth forgoing the social goals for a short period rather than to risk losing everything, but then it becomes very difficult, and sometimes appears even to be impossible to recover them.

It becomes difficult to pursue the dual goals of social impact and financial sustainability when an enterprise starts to expand and opportunities for growth appear directly or indirectly to require the entrepreneur to make a choice between impact and sustainability. In general, social entrepreneurs seem to be motivated to pursue growth rather than social impact when external threats have to be confronted or opportunities must be pursued (Tyk-kyläinen Saila 2019).

Entrepreneurs want to grow their businesses for two fundamental reasons: to make them bigger and therefore stronger in order to avoid threats and dangers, and to make them more able to profit from the gains offered by perceived opportunities. In general, the first reason, to avoid the risk of financial losses, is taken more seriously than the desire to profit from new opportunities. Ormiston and Seymour (2011) find that social entrepreneurs look for goals and metrics which relate to organisational growth as indicators of their success; most often these are quantitative financial performance metrics relating to scale and surplus. Social impact is by its very nature qualitative and hard to measure, and we often assume that impact will automatically grow when an organisation grows,[2] even though impact is the primary goal, and its pursuit is what social entrepreneurs claim makes their enterprises different from others.

In practice, of course, social entrepreneurs hypothesise that their enterprises will make a positive social impact when they are planning and deigning their businesses, and there is a natural tendency to assume that the social impact will continue to be achieved as the enterprise grows. They may try to monitor and measure it, but generally they assume that their enterprise's social impact will follow the implementation of the activities that they have designed in order to attain it (Clark et al. 2004).

To take social and economic inequality as an example, social entrepreneurs such as those who start microfinance businesses naturally assume that if their activities reach large numbers of people, then there will be less inequality. The more people they reach, the greater will be the impact on inequality. Some of the early pioneers in microfinance, however, achieved very different and indeed quite contradictory outcomes.

There would seem to be an obvious, definite and positive social impact when a microfinance institution makes small and affordable loans to poor people who are economically disadvantaged, financially excluded and from the marginalised segments of society. This helps them to be part of the mainstream financial system, and it seems fair to assume that if more of it is done, then the social impact will be better, even though the dynamics of the impact may be different when a microfinance institution grows and lends more money to more people. But events have shown that when a microfinance institution grows, the assumption that the more loans it makes and the more poor people it reaches, the greater will be the positive social impact may turn out to be wrong. It becomes hard to monitor and control the social impact when the institution is driven by the desire to grow.

Impact by its very nature is multi-layered and is a kind of ladder with assumptions ingrained at each step. In the case of microfinance, loans made is rung one, loans made to women is rung two, loans made to women and repaid is rung three and loans made to women with the hope that it will be used by the women to benefit themselves and their families is rung four.

Impact measurement in microfinance usually goes no further than rung three as it has to be if the main concern is with the survival and sustainability of the loan programme. If the social entrepreneurs who run the microfinance business try to use a more effective measurement method, it will cost money, which will reduce the sustainability of the whole enterprise, and the very effort that is needed to achieve and to measure the highest standard of social impact will in itself cost more money, and will thus reduce the institution's ability to reach more people. But when the microfinance institution grows even larger and more successful, as judged by the common measures of numbers reached, loans repaid and costs well covered, it becomes even more able to reach out to even more people, but it becomes even more driven by numbers and by the need for ever greater 'sustainability', meaning profits. And then its management almost inevitably lose their ground-level perspective of the fourth rung, which relates to the extent to which the loans are genuinely enhancing their customers' overall well-being, however that may be defined or measured (Bull 2007).

The very rapid growth and subsequent problems of the microfinance 'bubble' in the Indian state of Andhra Pradesh in 2008 exemplify this problem. The assumption that 'more loans would automatically mean more women's social empowerment' had unintended outcomes and consequences throughout India and even further afield. Many investors supported the rapid growth because lending to poor people was well regarded and it also helped financial institutions to achieve their targets for so-called 'priority sector' lending which were required by the government of India; additionally, it also appeared that this unexplored market might be very profitable. A number of banks and, in particular, many of the new specialist microfinance institutions that had been set up in response to the government's pressure and in an effort to replicate the success of the Grameen Bank in neighbouring Bangladesh entered the market, particularly in the southern state of Andhra Pradesh, which at the time had a population of between 80 and 90 million people. This resulted in serious over-lending, with a high level of defaults and borrower stress, even leading to borrower suicides. This of course negated the impact thesis of the microfinance institutions which had claimed that social transformation and economic empowerment of women would follow their financial inclusion (Marakkath, Olivares-Polanco, and Ramanan 2012).

The case of microfinance in Andhra Pradesh shows that growth alone can mislead social entrepreneurs who believe that if their social enterprises do indeed 'do good' at one stage in their growth, this will necessarily continue as they grow.

Growth: diverse viewpoints and strategies

The realities of growth for social enterprises highlight the tensions that can arise when dual goals are pursued and when the primary goal of impact can suffer. Growth can lead to contradictions and can increase the likelihood of mission drift or financial losses (Battilana and Dorado 2010; Battilana and Lee 2014; Smith, Gonin, and Besharov 2013).

This means that it can be a major challenge for social entrepreneurs to expand their enterprises and at the same time to avoid 'mission drift' and to maintain or if possible increase their positive social impact as they grow (Tyk-kyläinen Saila 2019; Battilana and Lee 2014; Smith et al. 2013). This means that growing a social enterprise is almost certain to be difficult. It is not easy to expand any business, but social entrepreneurs have to understand that if they provide more of their product or service, it will not automatically trans-late into an equivalent or even any growth in their social impact, and growth may even damage or destroy the social impact which they were able to deliver when their business was smaller.

Lewis (2017) in his article entitled 'The Dirty Secret of Social Entrepre-neurship' argues that scale is over-rated in the social entrepreneurship sector. He suggests that social entrepreneurs should avoid scaling up and should not automatically believe that their business ideas have to be very large in order to prove the 'reality' of their original ideas. What they should do is continually to check that the achievement of their social goals is not being prejudiced by the process of growth. Any social entrepreneur should feel free to abandon his or her explicitly social goals and to expand their enterprise either as a 'pure' for profit business, or as a 'pure' charity which depends on donations for its survival and growth. There is nothing fundamentally 'wrong' with a for-profit business so long as its practices do not break the law or transgress the principles of common decency, nor is it in any way 'wrong' for a social entrepreneur to abandon the dual objectives which are implied by the concept of a social enterprise.

But if a social entrepreneur wants to maintain the hybrid reality which is inherent in the notion of a social enterprise, he or she has to manage the process of growth in such a way that both aims continue to be achieved. And if as is quite frequent it begins to appear that it will be impossible to continue to maintain both goals, then it may be necessary to sacrifice growth in order to continue to achieve the social ambitions, albeit on a smaller scale than had been originally anticipated.

What is important is to be sure that the business is progressing towards the social goals which motivated the founder to be a social entrepreneur in the first place. Success is not necessarily about the size of the organisation, or its geographic coverage or its budget; it is not possible to serve everyone, to 'save the world', however many people there may be who need whatever ser-vice or assistance the social enterprise aims to provide. Social entrepreneurs should perhaps remember that 'less is more', that it is often better for a social enterprise to aim for and achieve a relatively modest impact, on a few people. This may be to connect with a quite small number of people, perhaps in one community, and to make a significant positive impact on their well-being, rather than to have a far broader outreach which may be less important and less durable. Scale is not everything, but numbers are by their very nature measurable, and this leads many social entrepreneurs to try to do too much and actually to do little or nothing. Scale may be an adequate measure when the main or only concern is profit, or growth in revenue, but the quality of impact can be far more significant.

There are also some social enterprises whose growth actually deepens their impact as well as enabling them to reach more people. For example, SKDRDP microfinance, which was discussed in Chapter 4, initially deepened their impact by focusing their operations in one area where the founding family's temple had substantial influence in the community. Later on, they spread operations to other adjacent districts within the State of Karnataka, where the founders and management were well known and had some presence in the community. SKDRDP provided microcredit to an increasing number of people in the region and thus grew horizontally, but at the same time they also grew vertically, by addressing many other social issues that prevailed in the region, including alcoholism, general healthcare, sanitation and training for self-employment. Their staff and management soon found that all these issues were interconnected; there was an urgent need to empower the whole community in that part of Karnataka State of India so that they could confront and deal with their multi-faceted social problems.

The work of the Rural Development and Self Employment Training Institute (RUDSETI) that was set up by the same faith-based group that had established the microfinance institution demonstrated to the community that the Dharmasthala temple organisation cared not only for lending money and recovering the loans but was also willing to help the people to ensure that the loans they received from SKDRDP would enable them to become more self-reliant so that they would no longer depend on charity or moneylenders. The management of SKDRDP also worked with the government and with the local banks rather than to consider them as competitors and thus to do everything possible to help the people to transform their own livelihoods; this of course also created a more sustainable market for the banks. Additionally, the fact that their field staff were employed from the same community which SKDRDP wanted to assist helped the management to make the organisation's leadership and inclusive vision a shared responsibility.

This meant that their staff had been brought up in the same area and knew its people because they were themselves from the same groups also helped, as did SKDRDP's holistic ambition to help in the development of the whole areas and its people, not merely to make a profit from lending them money. This also paid off financially for SKDRDP, as their repayments and profitability were unaffected by the national crisis in microfinance which led to severe losses and even to bankruptcy for several specialised microfinance institutions which operated in other parts of the state and in particular in the neighbouring state of Andhra Pradesh.

As we saw in Chapter 4, when compared with India's ten most successful large microfinance institutions at the time, SKDRDP had the lowest rate of loan defaults, the second lowest cost of operations as a percentage of its loan portfolio, the only steady return on assets, albeit at a relatively low level, and, perhaps most significantly, by a large margin the lowest yield on its loan portfolio, indicating that its interest rate was the lowest of the ten institutions. SKDRDP if of course a very special case, in that it was set up and directed by a unique seven-hundred-year-old religious institution, with enormously strong and well-established links to the local community. There are also, some other examples from the same field of microfinance, such as BASIX, whose case is discussed in Chapter 9. They had to move beyond the area in the state where they were originally set up, because this appeared to be the best way to grow when the local situation and the external regulations became a constraint. These regulatory issues were in part a cause but were also a result of the crisis in their original region of operations when one of their competitors expanded too rapidly, partly because they had been over-financed.

Although BASIX did not share the long-standing community links which gave SKDRDP such an enormous advantage, they did have a holistic outlook on development, and its management appreciated that microfinance, which is fundamentally indebtedness, could not on its own 'develop' disadvantaged communities. BASIX's interventions included a wide range of other services, such as training and skill development along with the provision of loans. This helped BASIX to diversify and sustain their growth despite having to face very restrictive regulations which had challenged their very existence in their original region of operations and had effectively derailed their growth plans in that area.

BASIX and the banks and other financial institutions which had financed its operations there suffered very substantial losses, since large sums which had been borrowed from both public sector and private banks had to be written off. In spite of these blows, however, which effectively destroyed a number of competitive microfinance institutions that had operated in the same areas, BASIX demonstrated that it was indeed a social enterprise and that its aims were broader than the simple pursuit of profitability.

The survival of most of the various companies and not-for-profit entities which made up component parts of the BASIX group showed that if it is adaptable, and continually evolves with a broad outlook to development issues, a social enterprise can always survive and find its place despite a dynamic operating environment.

As is discussed in the case study, the management of BASIX had to reposition its value proposition and experiment with different legal structures. These problems arose in part from the way management allowed its mission to drift as they confronted a variety of problems at the micro level, and in part because of the unintended consequences which arose because the staff and promoters of BASIX itself and of many other microfinance institutions pursued growth without proper consideration of other factors. Several other promoters of microfinance institutions in Andhra Pradesh that were faced with the same problems of government hostility and an over-crowded market successfully disengaged themselves and abandoned their colleagues and clients and sometimes also their creditors without loss to themselves or even with substantial personal profits.

The founder of BASIX also had substantially to 'downsize' the institution, mainly by closing its operations in the worst affected state of Andhra Pradesh, which meant that several thousand of the staff lost their jobs, and a number of banks had to write off large sums which they had lent to the organisation to finance its rapid growth. He did not abandon the fundamental social mission, however; a number of what had been peripheral businesses survived. They had operated as different legal entities for a number of reasons, but they were therefore fortuitously shielded from the financial problems of the central moneylending operation.

The circumstances in this particular state of India were of course unusual, in that there was a 'bubble' of microfinance which was followed by a 'crash'; some of the leaders of BASIX' competitors allowed their institutions to fail, or could not prevent them from doing so, and some of them also successfully protected their own personal wealth which they had acquired during the period of rapid growth.

The founder of BASIX chose to move its focus from the state of Andhra Pradesh, where both government's and customers' reactions to the gross overlending had effectively destroyed the market, to other neighbouring states where BASIX had already initiated some activities through one or more of its numerous affiliates.

The founder suffered a substantial personal loss but he understood that his social enterprise was more than a large and institutionalised village moneylender, and he moved the focus of the BASIX group beyond microcredit to encompass a wide range of livelihood services which addressed more than the need for finance.

BASIX had always been a holistic livelihoods promotion organisation, rather than a mere moneylender, and in the second decade of the twenty-first century they built on and further evolved the wide range of other services which had already been initiated. These were and indeed continue to be delivered by some eight different and more or less independent entities, which fill a number of the gaps which had in part precipitated the collapse in Andhra Pradesh. These include the provision of on-line financial service facilities, a variety of links to businesses which service livelihoods, wholesale finance and international consultancy. They are all fully or partly owned by the BASIX Group; most are profitable, and their survival and growth have in some sense demonstrated that a group of social enterprises which have been designed to fill a gap and improve disadvantaged people's livelihoods, rather than to make short-term profits by delivering debt, can actually be more profitable and sustainable than a simple money-lending operation which had few pretentions.

BASIX was a large and resilient organisation whose objectives went beyond profits or even mere sustainability, and many small-sized microfinance institutions had to shut down operations forever as a result of the crisis in Andhra Pradesh. Paradoxically, a social enterprise such as BASIX, whose objectives went beyond the traditional measure of profit maximisation, proved to be more durable and sustainable in a strictly financial sense than many of its counterparts, whose objectives were purely financial (Panwar 2011).

Mergers, whether they are planned or unplanned, are a major turn of events in the life cycle of any business, but this is particularly true for a social enterprise, whose 'socialness' may appear to be a constraint to other partners in the merger. The idealism that drives a social entrepreneur may be confronted by a completely different set of motives when a social enterprise is sold for its monetary value and its leadership and culture has to undergo change. As we saw in Chapter 2, the people who started and for some years managed the Ben and Jerry's ice cream business were driven at least in part by strong 'social' motives; this enabled them to achieve very substantial financial success, which benefitted all the stakeholders. When Ben and Jerry's was acquired by the Anglo-Dutch multinational Unilever group, the dynamics changed more towards its profitability than its social sustainability. Of course, this increased the range of Ben and Jerry's operations, both as to the places in which they operated and the variety of their products, but the founders' presence diminished, as did their influence, and Ben and Jerry's 'socialness', however that might have been defined, was substantially reduced. It could be argued, of course, that the sum total of the 'good' that the company provided was much greater, although it was diluted. Given that there is no quantitative measure of the 'social goodness' that an enterprise can provide, it is impossible to make a clear comparison between the 'value' of the wider geographic availability of its ice cream and the other aspects of its presence and their more concentrated presence when the business was still controlled by its founders. The argument on that issue can be made in either direction.

When a social entrepreneur starts a business, she or he is usually a strong believer in the social goals it is intended to achieve and in the feasibility of combining these goals with a viable business. When the founders confront the reality of being in business and having to cover all their costs, including the expenses they have to incur to pay for their own livelihoods, does this seriously erode their initial idealism and their conviction that both aims can be achieved? If this is what happens, should social enterprises be so-called just because their founders claim that they would achieve a positive social impact when they were starting the enterprise?

Can an enterprise reasonably be called 'social' when it is starting and or in its early stages but not later, or might it be acceptable to give it that label at any stage in its life cycle, so long as the management at the time can present sufficient evidence to justify the claim? Can we reasonably use the term 'social enterprise' to describe any enterprise, at any stage of its life, so long as its operations merit the label? Is it more useful to use the label of 'social' as an expression of the founders' or present management's intentions, regardless of whether or not they are realised, or should we reserve it for enterprises which are actually being 'social' at a particular time? Should the term be an expression of intent or should it be applied only when an enterprise is being actively social; given that is it not and is unlikely to become a legal term or even a fairly rigid one, do these questions matter? What in fact does the British experience as described in our first chapter tell us about the value or lack of value in using 'social enterprise' as a rather firm definition?

Transformation paths: hybrids, corporates and charities

In this chapter, we have discussed social enterprises which started with a strong commitment to being social and successfully achieved a measure of financial sustainability at the same time, but which then appeared at least partly to move away from socialness as they adopted different strategies as they grew in order to sustain their operations. In the process some of them were transformed into different types of business; some became more social, some altered the balance between being social and being profitable, while the management of others appeared almost to abandon their social ambitions, either because this seemed to be unavoidable in order to maintain their growth or even to survive. Given that the extent of an enterprise's socialness is not strictly measurable, it is not easy to analyse such apparent transformations, but it is clear that they do take place, and that in some cases their socialness is more or less forgotten.

Some microfinance businesses in India, for example, which had been started following the example of Grameen Bank in neighbouring Bangladesh, seem to have had completely different dynamics when they were replicated and taken to scale in the very different environment of India. During their growth stages, the social impact and financial performance of these microfinance institutions took very different directions, in part because they were operating in an environment where there were no clear regulations for mass moneylending of this type, They grew very rapidly, and within a fairly short period, in part because of some bad publicity in the local press which led to very adverse public opinion, and because of the clumsy over-reaction of some local government officials and others, but also because of their own reckless expansion, some local officials over-reacted and even went to the extent of ordering people not to repay their loans.

One particular microfinance business that had grown even more rapidly than its competitors very briefly achieved a high stock market valuation, and its founder was able to make a very substantial capital gain and then to leave the business. This, and the hardships of some borrowers and the harsh behaviour of staff who were told to recover loans at all costs, discredited the whole microfinance industry. BASIX, on the other hand, as we have seen, extricated itself at some cost to its staff and shareholders and effectively ceased to operate in Andhra Pradesh.

Even ten years later the millions of people in the state who were too poor to be properly served by regular banks were still not able to satisfy their need for short-term and affordable credit such as had been provided by microfinance institutions, which had effectively been banned from the state (Roy 2019). The whole debacle demonstrates that even the deeply committed leaders of a social enterprise can be prevented from fulfilling their social ambitions if the environment prevents them. Microfinance in the state of Andhra Pradesh started very much as a social industry, but it was prevented from achieving its social goals by the unfortunate combination of clumsy government and greedy competitors. The BASIX business survives but is unable to reach and work for the very needy people for whose benefit it was originally set up because of issues which were largely beyond the control of its management.

Such crises and contradictions have led many social entrepreneurs to explore more hybrid prototypes where the need to balance the tensions between social and financial goals can be addressed more at the initial design stage than when the enterprise has started its operations and is moving into its growth phase. Battilana et al. (2012) describe hybrid entities such as Hot Bread Kitchen, where a social enterprise has both its social and its financial goals fully integrated in (or perhaps baked into) the business model. Hot Bread Kitchen is a New York–based immigrant baking collective, where women with diverse histories can come together to hone their skills and secure meaningful careers in what is generally a male-dominated food industry in New York City.

With this vision they employ low-income immigrant women, who bake bread whose recipes have been inspired by their regions of origin. This enables them to learn skills that can lead them to good jobs and sometimes also to management roles in the food industry. Hot Bread Kitchen earns the money they need to support the work they do to achieve their social goals with the profits from its revenue-generating activities, and they plough back their profits from sales to the social mission. Their social and commercial goals are totally integrated, and this means that there are no contradictions between their aim to grow and also to maintain and expand their mission.

If they are working in a genuine hybrid of this kind, staff and management are not faced with the kinds of dilemmas between mission and profit which arise when an enterprise's revenue-generating activities are separate from the social ones, because both aims are fully integrated in the model (Battilana et al. 2012). Hot Bread Kitchen's website[3] shows this very clearly:

> While we are no longer business as usual, we remain steadfast in our commitment to supporting women, immigrants, and people of colour in the food industry. As of 2020 we have 280 women placed in jobs from

60 countries, 250 incubated, 500+ employment opportunities created by small businesses and reports $100 million+ in regional economic impact.

Hot Bread has been operating for ten years, and they are still quite a small operation, but they have successfully remained focused on their mission to enable people who are affected by gender, racial, social, and/or economic inequality in New York City to move forward, by using the potential of the food industry.

Genuinely hybrid models of this kind are of course not completely immune from the challenges of growth, and they are unlikely to be able to achieve their social objectives if it is not possible actually to employ the intended beneficiaries.

Nevertheless, there are an increasing number of innovations which might usefully be called the 'hybrid' type. Many social entrepreneurs are idealists; they start their social businesses with a strong commitment to achieve their social goals, but the day-to-day struggle for survival can soon overcome their passion for social change; they may give up, or leave, or the enterprise may move away from its social goals and become an ordinary profit-seeking business. Increasingly, however, some social entrepreneurs foresee this problem and try to ensure that the task of maintaining the balance between day-to-day survival and growth of the enterprise and the achievement of their social objectives is understood from the outset.

One example of this is a clean energy business called M-Kopa, which is based in Nairobi in Kenya. It was started by two friends who had studied for their MBA degrees together at Oxford University and had then worked for a short period in a microfinance and mobile-based payment services business called M-Pesa.[4] They then left M-Pesa and started their new business initiative in Nairobi. Their original intention was to assist poorer people to finance their purchases of solar energy–generation panels, but the business expanded to enable people to buy a large range of assets which they could not previously have afforded. These include refrigerators, mobile telephones, and television sets; M-Kopa also enables the same people to borrow money for whatever purpose they wish, such a school fees, once they have established their credit credentials by paying for a tangible asset such as solar panels.

M-Kopa was started in 2010, and by 2020 it was serving over a million customers in Kenya, Uganda and Tanzania and had also started operations in Nigeria. Their basic business model is to enable low-income people to acquire useful and productive assets through an initial deposit which is followed by daily or weekly instalments which can easily be made through customers' mobile phones using the company's innovative pay-as-you go on-line payment system. The M-KOPA website states:[5]

Our idea was to combine the power of digital micropayments with IoT (Internet-of-Things) connectivity to make financing more accessible, and solar was just the start. Since then, we have built one of the world's most advanced connected asset financing platforms. As of 2020, ten years after inception we have used it to provide nearly $400 million in financing that has enabled one million customers to access solar lighting, energy-efficient televisions and fridges, smartphones, cash loans, and more.

The asset-based pay-as-you go ownership system ensures that the credit is used to enable the company's customers to buy and in twelve months to own productive assets which save them money and are good for the environment. M-Kopa is very profitable, but the company is also making it possible for large numbers of people to own and benefit from productive assets which improve their lives and do not damage the environment, unlike the alternatives such as kerosene lamps or wood stoves. Investors include former vice president Al Gore's fund, as well as other mainstream international investors which look for substantial financial as well as social returns.

More and more social enterprises such as M-Kopa are achieving financial as well as social success and demonstrating by their example that is it possible to 'do well by doing good'; by learning both from traditional corporate businesses as well as charities, the traditional barrier between pure commercial and purely charitable organisations is beginning to be questioned. 'Ordinary' for-profit businesses should perhaps also be seen through a social enterprise lens when they claim to have taken on a social enterprise spirit in their operations.

It is of course positive that the boundaries between commercial and social enterprises are being blurred, but this also prompts some questions as to public attitudes, which can also affect many aspects of society's relationships with commercial entities. Should a social enterprise retain the label of 'social' merely because its founders had some social intentions at the beginning of its life cycle? Should not every enterprise, whether it is a traditional for-profit commercial business or a charity, have an equal potential to be a social enterprise or indeed to pay its way from its earnings, as it evolves and demonstrates that it can 'do good' or that it can also make a profit by selling its goods or services?

One example of this is the Walmart case, which was presented in the first chapter as an anonymous case. Walmart does indeed deliver on its mission "to save people money so they can live better" and also provides jobs for many people who might otherwise be unemployed or forced to work for even lower earnings. We may deplore the low earnings, harsh conditions and long hours which workers who manufacture many of the products which Walmart sells have to tolerate, but their alternative employment opportunities are usually much worse; companies such as Walmart make large profits, but in the process, they also promote economic development and generate enormous numbers of jobs. As of 2020, Walmart website[6] states:

> What started small, with a single discount store and the simple idea of selling more for less, has grown over the last 50 years into the largest

retailer in the world. Each week, over 265 million customers and members visit approximately 11,400 stores under 55 banners in 26 countries and eCommerce websites. With fiscal year 2020 revenue of $524 billion, Walmart employs over 2.2 million associates worldwide. It's all part of our unwavering commitment to creating opportunities and bringing value to customers and communities around the world.

Statements of this kind do not reflect the low wages and other aspects of the company's operations which we find less acceptable, but it is also undeniable that Walmart creates large numbers of relatively good jobs and satisfies the day-to-day needs of millions of its customers, probably including most readers of this book.

Similarly, the management of many non-profit charities demonstrate that they can be very business-like and enterprising in their operations, and some of them have successfully grown to the point where they are genuinely global organisations. They are known internationally for the quality and the positive impact of what they do, and although they have successfully scaled their impact to a global level, they are and are sustainably achieving a massive and positive global impact.

For example, Habitat for Humanity is a United States–based non-profit housing organisation which was started in 1976 using a housing partnership model which enables homeless poor people to build their own houses with their own labour, which acts as a down payment or 'sweat equity'. They can eventually acquire ownership of the homes through a number of different affordable financing options which carry no interest. The model was a huge success in the communities in the United States where it was initially employed, and large numbers of potential volunteers offered their time and labour because it was a sustainable solution to a large-scale and apparently intractable problem.

The founders of the organisation did not abandon their passion for the cause of community welfare, but they have successfully expanded its impact by encouraging and assisting other groups to adopt the same clustering and franchising approach. By 2020 Habitat for Humanity had franchise partners working in all the fifty states of the USA and in over seventy other countries; together, they have helped more than 35 million people to achieve strength, stability and independence through safe, decent and affordable shelter.[7] Their long-term vision is for everyone in the world to have a decent place to live in.

The Habitat homeowners help to build their own homes with the help of volunteers, and they pay for their homes with an affordable mortgage. Sustainability and social empowerment are both built into their model, and it has functioned effectively through the world.

There are many other very social entrepreneurs who have built not-for-profit organisations which show that traditional for-profit business entrepreneurs have no monopoly of innovative and globally replicable ideas. Sulabh

International[8] (Sharma 2017), for instance, is a global but community-based entity which has grown into is an internationally acclaimed pioneer in public sanitation. Its affiliates have built eight thousand public toilets in public places and in slums. The toilets are self-sustaining and remain clean and properly maintained because they are leased to local individuals who manage and maintain them and collect the very modest fees which are charged on a pay-per-use basis.

Like Sulabh International and Habitat for Humanity, many charities exercise their right to not completely embrace the neo-liberal principles of being a market-oriented social enterprise. Their founders know in their heart that their social cause is more pristine and protected with an enterprising charitable model. They explore sustainability principles but experiment and adopt only those market principles that align with their mission. Likewise, among social enterprises too, their founders should have no shame to experiment and evolve during the course of the enterprise's life cycle to decide what is best for the cause they stand for: stay hybrid or revert to fully commercial or charity-based models if they discover a path that best suits their vision for growth.

We conclude this chapter with the case of the Body Shop. The Body Shop is a successful business, as it offers good products, at good prices, in the right places. But it owes its financial success to its commitment to social and environmental causes. When the social business evolved during its life cycle and merged with a large commercial multi-national company, its management found that it was not easy to expand the business and at the same time to maintain the founders' original 'social' commitment. We leave our readers to decide whether the business should have remained small and committed to the founders' original social passion or whether it was right for the Body Shop to grow as it did. Was there really any choice; was growth and subsequent dilution of the social commitment inevitable? Was the subsequent evolution of the business consistent with the original vision of its founders, and does it matter if it was not?

10.2 Case study

Case 10.2.1 The Body Shop

In March 1976 Anita Roddick set up The Body Shop[9] in Littlehampton, a small town on the south coast of England; her husband, Gordon, was travelling in Latin America for some time, and she wanted to keep herself occupied while he was away, as well as to earn some money to keep herself and her two young daughters.

Anita had previously worked for the United Nations and had travelled extensively; she had noticed that village women in Africa and elsewhere used cocoa butter and other natural products as skin lotions; they usually had beautiful skin, with none of the problems which seemed to affect English women's complexions, so she decided to try to make a business out of this.

The business has grown to become one of the world's best-known providers of organic and fair-trade cosmetics, with a global reputation for its support of social and ethical causes. By 2020 The Body Shop had some 3,200 outlets, as well as over 20,000 home-based sales agents, in almost seventy different countries.

Anita Roddick received many prestigious awards, from institutions such as the United Nations, universities in the United States, the United Kingdom and elsewhere, and she was heavily involved in the development of the business, as well as in several charitable endeavours. She died in 2007, but she left behind many statements which summarise what she believed business and social enterprise should be about and what businesspeople should do with their success. These include:

> "A company should be active and endlessly excited."
>
> "The business of business should not just be about money; it should be about responsibilities, it should be about public good, not private greed."
>
> "Get informed; get inspired; get outraged; get active."
>
> "The art of giving is not simply doling out money nor dishing out things we assume people want. It is the ability to work with them. The art of development is helping people find the right tools, and the right approach, to develop themselves."
>
> "You educate people, especially young people by stirring their passions. So, you take every opportunity to grab the imagination of your employees. You get them to feel they are doing something important."
>
> "I think the value of money is the spontaneity it gives you. There are too many exciting things to do with it right now to bother about piling it up."
>
> "The original Body Shop was a series of brilliant accidents. It had a great smell, it had a funky name. It was positioned between two funeral parlours – that always caused controversy. . . . We recycled everything, not because we were environmentally friendly, but because we didn't have enough bottles. . . . What was unique about it, with no intent at all, no marketing nous, was that it translated across cultures, across geographical barriers and social structures. It wasn't a sophisticated plan, it just happened like that."

Anita Roddick and her husband, Gordon, had always been rather unconventional, and they wanted to run their own business. She was brought up in

Littlehampton; her mother was from Italy and had among other things set up and run a small café and a nightclub in the town.

Early on in their married life the Roddicks had managed a small hotel, and they also ran a hamburger restaurant, but Anita wanted to be able to spend more time with her children; she did not want to work round the clock. She decided that a retail shop would be less exhausting and time-consuming and would only involve working in normal business hours.

Anita decided to open a shop which would sell the natural products she had observed in Africa and elsewhere, and she decided to call it The Body Shop; the name was itself unconventional, because the term 'body shop' was usually used to refer to the workshops where damaged cars were repaired.

She went into a local bank to ask for a start-up loan of about six thousand dollars, but the manager turned down her request; Anita was not sure whether he refused her because her business idea was not properly presented with a neat business plan, or because she had gone into the bank dressed in jeans and along with her two little girls. She decided to take a different approach; her husband returned to the same bank a week later dressed in a proper business suit with a formally presented business plan in a neat folder, and the manager approved the loan.

The Body Shop's total sales on its initial day of business amounted to almost two hundred dollars' worth of lotions, but this was partly because of some fortuitous initial publicity; some local funeral homes had threatened to sue The Body Shop because they alleged that the name was insulting to their business, but Anita reported their threat to a local newspaper and the resulting report helped to make the shop known.

In spite of this initially fairly promising start, later results were disappointing, and in some weeks the shop brought only about $200 for all six days. Anita made all the lotions in her kitchen at home, and it hardly seemed to be worth all the effort involved in mixing the lotions and bringing the big twenty-five-litre containers of lotion down to the shop. After a while this proved to be too much hard work, so she then had them made by a small local chemical products manufacturer; they were allowed to use only the twenty-five natural ingredients which Anita had identified from her earlier work in Africa, and which were readily available from various local importers.

Littlehampton was only a small town, and there seemed to be little chance of doing much more business there, so Anita looked for a better location. She soon found a shop in a shopping area in the nearby town of Brighton, which is a major retail centre and has a number of fashionable shops. Sales soon started to pick up, but The Body Shop was still a very modest operation; Anita used to decant the lotions from the large commercial containers which the factory provided into small bottles which were actually sold for taking urine samples. These were not cheap and were not always available, so she then decided to offer customers the option of bringing their own bottles which were filled in the shop. This not only saved money, but it also began to build the reputation of The Body Shop as an environmentally sensitive place whose products and packaging presented a consistently responsible image.

Fortunately for the new business, the summer of 1976 was very warm by British standards, and the business started to improve. Anita decided to look for another shop, and she soon found suitable premises in Chichester, another relatively well-off town near Brighton on the south coast of England. She financed this with a six-thousand-dollar investment from a local businessperson, who is now a multi-millionaire thanks to the appreciation on the value of his shares. The next shop was opened in Hove, right next to Brighton, on a franchise basis, and this approach was generally followed in the subsequent years of expansion. This saved capital and also ensured that the shops were managed by people who were as committed as Anita herself to the success of the business and to the principles underlying the whole approach.

The Body Shop grew strongly after this initial somewhat faltering start, and after only eight years the business had reached the stage when it needed more capital than the Roddicks wished or were able to invest. In 1984 they therefore decided to 'go public' and to launch The Body Shop's shares on the London stock exchange.

The flotation was a great success. The Roddicks made several million dollars, and they both decided to intensify the social campaigning work which had always interested them even before they started The Body Shop and which had been closely associated with the business from the beginning. They had always stressed their commitment to fair trading principles, to pure organic raw materials, and they tried as much as possible to buy their materials direct from the producers, such as the African villagers whom Anita had observed during her development work before they ever started The Body Shop.

They also ensured that the business itself adhered to these principles. They played an important part in the international campaigns to ban testing of cosmetics of animals, and they established their UK soap manufacturing facility in Easterhouse, a needy suburb of Glasgow in Scotland, rather than in a more 'fashionable' and perhaps less problematic environment further south

The Body Shop was a large and successful international business, but the Roddicks felt that it would benefit from being allied to a larger multinational group, which might also enable them to spend more time on their campaigning for various causes which were consistent with their overall 'message', such as saving whales in collaboration with Greenpeace, promoting human rights with Amnesty International and working on environmental issues with Friends of the Earth.

They therefore responded favourably to an approach from L'Oréal, the world's largest multinational perfumery and related products business which owns a number of well-known brands such as Ralph Lauren, Giorgio Armani, Lancôme, Helena Rubinstein, Cacharel, Diesel and others, whose annual sales amount to around $30 billion, and whose annual profits at over $5 billion achieve one of the highest ratios of profits to sales of any large business of any kind, anywhere. After some tense negotiations, in 2006 The Body Shop was acquired by L'Oréal for almost $1 billion; Gordon and Anita themselves received almost $200 million for their share in the business.

This was not altogether a happy corporate marriage; Anita had perhaps over-optimistically anticipated that if The Body Shop was part of L'Oréal, it would be able to move the larger company towards the same social and environmental goals as its smaller acquisition, but this did not happen, and when Anita died in 2007, her husband felt even less able to maintain what he believed was her very special legacy.

His wife had started the business and had always been its main 'public face' and the driving force for its social mission. Gordon wanted in any case to devote more time to his work on social and environmental issues, but their colleagues who remained at The Body Shop, many of whom had joined the company because of its social commitment, found it difficult to work for the L'Oréal group. The Body Shop was by no means the biggest or most profitable member of the French group, and Gordon felt that if he moved away from direct involvement, the business and its unique culture would soon be submerged by the larger corporate environment. He felt sure that this would in time damage its business as well as discouraging the staff who had remained with the company after its acquisition.

He therefore made it known to the management at L'Oréal that he was unhappy with the situation; they had already realised that it was difficult for them to maintain and increase The Body Shop's profits without Anita's presence, and if they lost Gordon's support, the value of their acquisition would fall sharply. They therefore acceded to Gordon Roddick's request to look for a new home for the company, and finally, in 2017, L'Oréal sold The Body Shop to Natura, a large Brazilian cosmetics company, for a little over $1 billion. L'Oréal had not earned its expected return on the acquisition, but they had not lost money, and both L'Oréal's management and Gordon Roddick felt that this was the best solution.

Natura is a large and rapidly growing international cosmetics company, which had in 2012 taken a minority shareholding in Avon, the world's second largest direct sales business after Amway, but it was far smaller than L'Oréal, and it appeared more likely that The Body Shop would be able to affect its culture than that of the far larger L'Oréal. In 2019 Natura's sales volume was approximately $2 billion, well over that of The Body Shop, and its profits were about $150 million; by comparison, it was about twice the size of its acquisition, and its profitability as a proportion of its sales was less than half that of L'Oréal's; Gordon Roddick was thus rather more confident that The Body Shop's distinctive culture would survive than under the ownership of L'Oréal. He was also devoting even more of his time to social causes, such as The Big Issue, of which he was a co-founder in 1991.

The Big Issue[10] is a very successful social enterprise which enables needy people to regain their self-confidence and to earn a respectable living by selling a weekly newspaper; they pay the organisation about two dollars a copy and re-sell them for the cover price of about four dollars. In 2020 there were about fifteen hundred Big Issue vendors selling the paper in the United Kingdom, and the concept had been replicated in a number of other countries. The vendors work on the streets of London and other British towns, and their earnings average about six thousand dollars a year. This enables them to keep themselves and, more importantly, to re-enter society after periods of hardship.

The two dollars more or less covers the production costs, and The Big Issue has also set up Big Issue Invest, which is a major investor in social enterprises in the United Kingdom and elsewhere, and the organisation is also heavily involved in promoting and financing social housing.

In 2020 Natura, the new Brazilian multinational owner of The Body Shop, made a far larger acquisition when it finalised the purchase of the remaining share of Avon which it had not bought in 2012. It is not clear how this will affect the culture and operations of The Body Shop.

The history of The Body Shop raises a number of issues as to the effective meaning of 'social enterprise', and in particular about the durability of an organisation's culture and commitment as time passes and the nature of its ownership may change. The issues of discussion are:

1   The Body Shop has been registered as a conventional for-profit business since it was first established in 1976, and its two owners since that time have not changed its status. Does the company's history suggest that it might have been more 'social' if it had been incorporated in some other way?

2   In 2019 The Body Shop converted the registration of its United States operations into a so-called 'B Corporation', or 'Benefit Corporation'. This is a relatively new form of registration, which was initiated in Vermont and Maryland in 2010 and has since been adopted by over thirty other American states and in Italy and Colombia. This institutionalises some aspects of an organisation's social commitment but has little legal force. Are changes in legal status of this kind likely to make a significant difference to the operations of a company such as

The Body Shop, particularly when it is 100 percent owned by another company?

3 The co-founders of The Body Shop made enormous personal profits from the sale of the business, and they have used the money, and the personal independence it conferred, to pursue a variety of not-for-profit social causes. Is The Body Shop itself in any sense more of a social enterprise because its founders used some of its profits for social purposes?

4 How can the initiators of a social enterprise try to ensure that its 'social-ness' survives their departure when they retire or sell the business?

5 Is or was The Body Shop really a social enterprise in any useful sense of the term, or were its commitments not to use ingredients that were tested on animals and to other 'non-economic' behaviour anything more than effective marketing tools, which happened also to be 'good'?

10.3 Follow-up activity

Identify a local business which works for a social cause, or a social enterprise or charity which has been operating for more than a year or so. If you cannot find a local case, chose a national or international enterprise which has been operating for a few years but is not one of the well-known international institutions. Try to find out the extent to which it is a business, selling its services, or a 'charity', giving them away.

Ask its staff and try to judge for yourself how it will evolve over the next ten years. Will it move towards being more 'social' or more 'commercial' or will it retain its present balance? Will its management choose to change its legal form, to become a for-profit company or to move towards being a charity, or might they set up a separate but linked organisation, in either 'direction'? Or will the enterprise close down and disappear, because it has failed to achieve what it was set up to do, or because it has succeeded and is no longer needed?

Notes

1 One of the co-authors of this book taught social entrepreneurship to young people. The programme trained youth to start social enterprises while pursuing an academic course, and the observation is based on experience of start-up ideas in social entrepreneurship space.

2 Personal communication with Ms. Ishita Shah, senior associate of Catalytic Capital, Align Impact (impact advising organisation to social impact investors) on December 21, 2020. Align Impact. Accessed January 6, 2021. www.alignimpact.com.

3 Details sourced from: "Hot Bread Kitchen." Accessed January 8, 2021. https://hotbreadkitchen.org/.

4 M-Pesa (M for mobile, pesa is Swahili for money) is Africa's most successful mobile money service and the region's largest fintech platform serving 41.5 million people as on January 8, 2020. It is a mobile phone–based money transfer service, payments and microfinancing service, launched in 2007 by Vodafone Group plc and Safaricom, the largest mobile network operator in Kenya. Details sourced from: "M-Pesa." n.d. Vodafone.Com. Accessed January 8, 2021. www.vodafone.com/what-we-do/services/m-pesa.

5 Details sourced from: "M-KOPA SOLAR." Accessed January 8, 2021. https://m-kopa.com/.

6 Details sourced from: "Walmart." Corporate – US. Accessed January 8, 2021. https://corporate.walmart.com/our-story.

7 Details sourced from: "Habitat for Humanity." Accessed January 8, 2021. www.habitat.org/.

8 Details sourced from: "Sulabh International." Accessed January 8, 2021. www.sulabhinternational.org/.

9 Details of the case sourced from publicly available information: (a) The Body Shop website: "Beauty, Skincare, Bath & Body Products | The Body Shop." Accessed January 8, 2021. www.thebodyshop.com/en-us/ (b) "The Body Shop: What Went Wrong? – BBC News." n.d. Accessed January 8, 2021. www.bbc.com/news/business-38905530 and (c) "Body Shop Bought by Brazil's Natura, BBC News" June 27, 2017, Business. www.bbc.com/news/business-40417961.

10 Details sourced from: "The Big Issue." Accessed January 8, 2021. www.bigissue.com/.

10.4 References

Barney, Jay B., Judy Wicks, C. Otto Scharmer, and Kathryn Pavlovich. 2015. "Exploring Transcendental Leadership: A Conversation." *Journal of Management, Spirituality & Religion* 12(4): 290–304. https://doi.org/10.1080/14766086.2015.1022794.

Battilana, Julie, and Silvia Dorado. 2010. "Building Sustainable Hybrid Organisations: The Case of Commercial Microfinance Organisations." *Academy of Management Journal* 53(6): 1419–40. https://doi.org/10.5465/amj.2010.57318391.

Battilana, Julie, and Matthew Lee. 2014. "Advancing Research on Hybrid Organising – Insights from the Study of Social Enterprises." *Academy of Management Annals* 8(1): 397–441. https://doi.org/10.5465/19416520.2014.893615.

Battilana, Julie, Matthew Lee, John Walker, and Cheryl Dorsey. 2012. "In Search of the Hybrid Ideal (SSIR)." Accessed January 24, 2021. https://ssir.org/articles/entry/in_search_of_the_hybrid_ideal.

Brock, Debbi D., and Susan Steiner. 2009. "Social Entrepreneurship Education: Is It Achieving the Desired Aims?" *SSRN Scholarly Paper ID 1344419*. Rochester, NY: Social Science Research Network. https://doi.org/10.2139/ssrn.1344419.

Bull, Mike. 2007. "'Balance': The Development of a Social Enterprise Business Performance Analysis Tool." *Social Enterprise Journal* 3(1): 49–66. https://doi.org/10.1108/17508610780000721.

Clark, Cathy, Jed Emerson, and Ben Thornley. 2015. *The Impact Investor: Lessons in Leadership and Strategy for Collaborative Capitalism*. Hoboken, NJ: Jossey Bass.

Clark, Cathy, William Rosenzweig, David Long, and Sara Olsen. 2004. "Double Bottom Line Project Report: Assessing Social Impact in Double Bottom Line Ventures. Methods Catalog." *CASE*. Accessed February 2, 2021. https://centers.fuqua.duke.edu/case/knowledge_items/double-bottom-line-project-report-assessing-social-impact-in-double-bottom-line-ventures/

Guha, Samapti, Hemangi Patel, and Nadiya Parekh. 2017. "An Exploration of the Financial Practices of Tribal Communities in Jhabua, India." *Development in Practice* 27(6): 801–12. https://doi.org/10.1080/09614524.2017.1344187.

Lewis, Jonathan. 2017. "The Dirty Secret of Social Enterprise: Scale Is Overrated." *NextBillion*, July 5, 2017. https://nextbillion.net/the-dirty-secret-of-social-enterprise-scale-is-overrated/.

Marakkath, Nadiya, Francisco Olivares-Polanco, and T. Radha Ramanan. 2012. "Dangers in Mismanaging the Factors Affecting the Operational Self-Sustainability (OSS) of Indian Microfinance Institutions (MFIs) – An Exploration into Indian Microfinance Crisis." *Asian Economic and Financial Review* 2(3): 448–62.

MovingWorlds. n.d. "The Complete Guide to Growing and Scaling Your Social Enterprise." *MovingWorlds.Org.* Accessed January 6, 2021. https://movingworlds.orgsocial-entrepreneurship-guide.

Mueller, Susan, Taiga Brahm, and Heidi Neck. 2015. "Service Learning in Social Entrepreneurship Education: Why Students Want to Become Social Entrepreneurs and How to Address Their Motives." *Journal of Enterprising Culture* 23(3): 357–80. https://doi.org/10.1142/S0218495815500120.

Ormiston, Jarrod, and Richard Seymour. 2011. "Understanding Value Creation in Social Entrepreneurship: The Importance of Aligning Mission, Strategy and Impact Measurement." *Journal of Social Entrepreneurship* 2(2): 125–50. https://doi.org/10.1080/19420676.2011.606331.

Panwar, J. S. 2011. *Microfinance in India: Mission or Misery?* Responsible Research. Singapore.

Roy, Subir. 2019. "Microfinance Recovers from Andhra Nightmare." *Business Standard India*, July 13, 2019. www.business-standard.com/article/finance/microfinance-recovers-from-andhra-nightmare-113071300598_1.html.

Sharma, Jyothi. 2017. "Avoiding the Neoliberal Trap in Social Entrepreneurship (SSIR)." Accessed January 8, 2021. https://ssir.org/articles/entry/avoiding_the_neoliberal_trap_in_social_entrepreneurship.

Smith, Wendy K., Michael Gonin, and Marya L. Besharov. 2013. "Managing Social-Business Tensions: A Review and Research Agenda for Social Enterprise." *Business Ethics Quarterly* 23(3): 407–42. Cambridge University Press. https://doi.org/10.5840/beq201323327.

Tykkyläinen, Saila. 2019. "Why Social Enterprises Pursue Growth? Analysis of Threats and Opportunities." *Social Enterprise Journal* 15(3): 376–96. https://doi.org/10.1108/SEJ-04-2018-0033.

United Nations General Assembly. 2005. "2005 World Summit Outcome, Resolution A/60/1." Adopted by the General Assembly on 15 September 2005. Accessed January 8, 2021. www.un.org/en/ga/search/view_doc.asp?symbol=A/RES/60/1.

Zahra, Shaker A., Eric Gedajlovic, Donald O. Neubaum, and Joel M. Shulman. 2009. "A Typology of Social Entrepreneurs: Motives, Search Processes and Ethical Challenges." *Special Issue Ethics and Entrepreneurship* 24(5): 519–32. https://doi.org/10.1016/j.jbusvent.2008.04.007.

11 THE WAY AHEAD

11.1 Who invests in social businesses and why do they do it?

The total value of impact investment – that is, investment in social enterprises, businesses which aim to make a reasonable profit, but which, critically, also aim to achieve a measurable social return – has in 2020 been estimated to be anything between $300 billion and $715 billion (GIIN 2020). The wide range is understandable, given the lack of a firm definition of what does and does not qualify an investment as being 'social', or an 'impact' investment.

Whatever the definition, and the actual amount, this is of course a very large sum of money, but it must be remembered that it is still only a relatively modest amount when compared with the $3 trillion dollars, that is $3,000 billion, which is estimated to be the annual total of institutional investment.

This amount and the proportion of total investments which claim to be impact investments are both, however, growing very rapidly, and if present trends continue, it is likely that over half of all institutional investment will be able to claim some aspects of 'impact' by 2030, at least in their intentions if not their actual results. This does not, of course, mean that half of all businesses in which such investors invest their own and their clients' money will by that year be 'social', in their intent or their reality, since businesses and their policies and intentions are the result of many years of cumulative investment, not merely one year. Nevertheless, if this proportion is achieved, and maintained or even increased, we can expect business to become more and more social as time goes on.

This trend represents a major shift from the more passive or negative approach, in which investors avoid investment in activities which they perceive by some standard to have a bad impact, rather than insisting that all their investments have a positive social as well as a financial return, but the available evidence suggests that most investors in this relatively recent form of finance have thus far been satisfied that they are both 'doing well' and 'doing good'. It remains to be seen whether this will continue, or whether improved impact measurement techniques will lead to more critical appraisals, or whether would-be impact investors will be forced to compromise their standards as the 'low-hanging fruit' of obviously profitable and socially beneficial investment opportunities is taken by the earlier entrants.

DOI: 10.4324/9781003032229-11

As of 2020, most impact investment funds were still private, sponsored by wealthy families whose members want to 'give back', or by non-government organisations or other similarly motivated entities, but this was also changing, with more publicly available funds being launched, by more familiar and traditionally commercially oriented institutions.

India is an obvious location for businesses which aim to have a positive social impact and for those who wish to invest in them. It is home to what is by far the largest number of very poor people in the world, but it also has a vigorous and generally well-managed and sophisticated financial investment industry, and an already large and long-established tradition of socially responsible business, which goes back at least until the latter years of the nineteenth century, with well-known and very large and influential businesses such as the Tatas group.

McKinsey, the global consultancy company, studied the Indian impact investment scene over the period between the years 2000 and 2015, analysing the performance of fifteen different impact investment funds (Pandit and Tamhane 2018). The median internal rate of return was 10 percent, which was not dramatically different from the returns on regular for-profit investments, and the five best performing funds yielded an average annual return of 34 percent, which is very much at the higher end of the financial returns which are earned by investors whose aim is only to maximise their profits.

Investments in financial inclusion, including microfinance, yielded the highest returns. This was perhaps to be expected given the background of many of their senior management and the desperate need of hundreds of millions of low-income Indian households for reliable and secure financial services, and their willingness to pay a high price for them given that their only previous source for such services was extortionate local moneylenders or inadequate and often corrupt government 'schemes'.

Energy and agricultural businesses achieved average returns, while health and education performed relatively lower. Here again, given the nature of these services and the existing provision, this was perhaps to be expected, but the overall average return was satisfactory in relation to 'pure' 'for-profit' investments. The performance of this small and not necessarily representative sample of social enterprises and the impact investment funds which invested in them suggests that there may not be a need for compromise; it may be possible to do well and to do good at the same time (Pandit and Tamhane 2018).

In the earlier years of the twenty-first century, when social enterprises and the business of investing in them was in its infancy, the prevailing view was that there was an inherent trade-off between doing good and making a profit. Ten years later opinion seemed to be shifting. Assets under management devoted to impact investing – defined as investing in companies that intend to generate a financial return as well as a positive and measurable social or economic impact – grew to $715 billion as of December, up from $502 billion a year earlier, according to the Global Impact Investing Network (GIIN 2020). Nearly 90 percent of the 294 impact investors surveyed by the GIIN in this year said the socially oriented businesses and thus the funds which had invested in them had met or exceeded their financial expectations.

In its September 8, 2020, issue *Forbes* magazine, a well-known popular family-managed publication from the United States about business and finance, published a major feature about what they called 'impact investing', that is, investors and investment institutions that attempt to identify and invest in businesses which are financially profitable but which also claim to have a positive and measurable social impact.

In their 'Impact 50 list' of notable impact investors, the magazine included fifty individuals, mainly from the United States, who are involved in in ventures which aim to make a positive social or environmental impact, in the United States and internationally (Forbes September 8, 2020). Their list included wealthy Americans, some of whom had inherited their wealth and others who had earned it themselves in more conventional businesses, and they also covered several highly paid athletes and 'celebrities', and their survey covered a number of women as well as men. The final list excluded people who had been involved in impact investment for less than twelve months, and it included people who were responsible for investing their own personal capital and also capital from other sources.

The following brief summaries of the background, activities and social enterprise choices of a representative sample of fourteen of these people cover a wide range but in aggregate they give a useful picture of the type of people who are actively involved in impact investment and of the nature of the businesses in which they invest.

Ibrahim Al Husseini: Ibrahim Al Husseini's parents were Palestinian refugees who had fled from Palestine to Saudi Arabia. He was born and raised there and moved to the United States to go to college. He was always enterprising and entrepreneurial, as well as being inclined to natural and sustainable products, and he started his first venture when he was in college, distributing natural food supplements and health care materials.

He sold this business for a large sum in 1997 and went on to be an early investor in a number of businesses whose activities seemed to be consistent with his passion for environmental sustainability and also to be potentially profitable, such as the Tesla vehicle manufacturer. In 2013 Husseini started FullCycle, a fund which is focused on sustainable energy; he believes that there are already large numbers of social enterprises with the potential to remedy many environmental problems; what they need is recognition and finance, and Full Cycle can provide these.

Howard Buffett: Howard Buffett is the grandson of Warren Buffett, the so-called 'Oracle of Omaha' who was at one time said to be the richest or second richest person in the world, as a result of his long-term investments in often un-dramatic businesses which he believed would grow and yield high returns. The older Buffett then famously donated the majority of his fortune to the Bill and Melinda Gates Foundation, which is the world's largest charitable institution but is not generally a social investor; it donates money to good causes, globally.

His grandson Howard Buffett is a pioneer in social investment; he has published extensively on approaches to measuring non-financial and social rates of return and has created the 'impact rate of return', a widely used tool for the measurement of social and environmental impact. He has also invested in a number of for-profit businesses which aim to arrest climate change, to maintain and increase seed diversity and to reduce and re-cycle food waste.

Albert Gore: Al Gore was born in 1948. He was the vice president of the United States under President Clinton and beat George W Bush in the presidential election by half a million votes; nevertheless, he failed to secure a majority of the electoral college and thus lost the election. He is well known for his vital role in alerting the world to the threat of climate change, for which he has been awarded a Nobel Prize and many other honours.

Gore co-founded Generation Investment Management in 2004 to invest in sustainable, low-carbon companies. The fund was by 2020 managing almost $25 billion of investments, including, for instance, an investment of almost $100 million dollars in a new business which is developing and marketing newly 'designed' proteins to act as meat substitutes.

Irwin Jacobs: Irwin Jacobs was born in 1933, in New Bedford, Massachusetts. His early career was as an assistant and then associate professor at the Massachusetts Institute of Technology. He then went on to found the company which eventually became Qualcomm and was the originator of the technology which revolutionised satellite communication and is the foundation of much of modern communication technology. He has donated many billions of dollars to a variety of charitable causes, including education, public radio and classical music. In particular, he has donated large sums to Cornell University and MIT, where he was himself educated.

In addition to these donations, Jacobs has also invested in a number of new social enterprises whose objectives include action against climate change. These include Cyclopure, a company which is developing new and environmentally friendly technologies for water purification, and Tour Engine, which is working on a more efficient type of internal combustion engine.

Justin Kamine: Justine Kamine was born in 1989. His family had a solar energy business, and they later developed an investment company. He was from his childhood fascinated by the issue of waste, how to reduce it and to turn waste products into useful commodities which can be sold at a price which covers the cost of transformation.

He has initiated, financed and contributes to the management of a number of businesses which achieve this goal. They include KDCAg, which converts scrap meat and vegetable into a highly nutritious animal food, and Upgraid, which works with similar raw materials to manufacture human food. Additionally, Kamine has started Biodegr(edible), which aims to convert disposable packaging materials into foodstuffs.

He is also involved with the family investment business, the Kamine Development Corporation, which develops environmentally sustainable infrastructure and energy projects. They also work with other partners on a process which aims to produce cement with a process which itself generates energy, rather than the present highly polluting and energy-intensive process which is used worldwide.

Robyn O'Brien: Robyn O'Brien had a successful and very remunerative career in hedge fund management and then went on to co-found rePlant Capital with Don Shaffer and David Haynes. Together with her partners, she has pioneered creative financing methods, such as advancing credit to farmers on terms which are based on measurements of the health of the soil, in order to minimise emissions which contribute to climate change.

In early 2020 rePlant worked with Danone, the French-based multinational organic food company, to invest some $20 million of their impact funds with American farmers who are committed to supplying Danone North America with certified food raw materials as they move from traditional farming methods to more organic and regenerative farming.

Amy Novogratz: In 2013 Amy Novogratz together with her husband and business partner, Mike Velings, started Aquaspark, a Netherlands-based global fund which focuses on sustainable aquaculture. Amy had many years of experience in enterprise selection, in part through her work managing the TED Talk institution, and Mike Velings was a serial entrepreneur who had worked and invested in a wide range of innovative and successful enterprises.

They aim to combine commercially competitive returns with a positive environmental and social impact. Global demand for fish is growing steadily and has doubled since 1970. This means that existing wild natural fisheries cannot sustain the present rate of depletion, but there is an enormous potential for fish farming which, unlike traditional fishing, can be self-sustainable or even positive in its environmental impact.

The world's appetite for fish is growing, and we are now eating twice as much fish as fifty years ago. There is a need and indeed a profitable market for more than twice the present demand. There are many new types of fisheries that can earn substantial profits as well as being fully sustainable and more, and Aquaspark is involved with about twenty such enterprises, such as sustainable fish farms. Many of the fund's investees are also able to work together to achieve even better results.

By 2020 their fund had invested approaching $200 million in minority stakes in more than twenty such enterprises. The funds had been contributed by 190 investors who were themselves based in about thirty different countries. In 2019, the fund achieved a net internal rate of return of about 22 percent.

Valerie Rockefeller: The Rockefeller Brothers Fund, whose business policy and choices of enterprise are still manly directed by members of the well-known Rockefeller family, has committed over $200 million dollars to social enterprises which aim to earn a reasonable profit but also to achieve a positive social impact.

One central focus of the fund is to invest in areas such as climate change and sustainable agriculture, and in 2015 the family fund's decision makers made the historically dramatic decision to divest from fossil fuels such as coal and notably from petroleum, which was of course the industry which had been the means whereby the family achieved their fortune a hundred years earlier.

The Rockefeller family's fund has also invested in an institution which promotes female-led technology, in an effort to redress the heavy male domination of venture funds, both in their management and in their choice of businesses to support, but also in order to improve their own fund's returns by investing in women-owned businesses. The Rockefeller family's fund has achieved an annual return of nearly 8 percent.

Eric Schmidt: Eric Schmidt was the chief executive of the Google search and information company, and his personal wealth is said to be over $15 billion. He and his wife have set up the Schmidt Family Foundation, which has invested nearly $40 million in a variety of businesses which aim to enable poorer communities to access 'clean' energy and clean fresh water.

Their businesses also develop new technologies which aim to recue marine pollution and to improve the health of the world's oceans. The fund also invests in solar power, in particular to serve Native American communities.

Jeff Skoll: Jeff Skoll was appointed president of e-Bay, the on-line trading business, in collaboration with the company's founder, Pierre Omidyar. Under his leadership, e-Bay invested in other innovative companies such as PayPal, Craigslist and Skype. Skoll's personal wealth was estimated to be over $5 billion.

Skoll set up Capricorn Investments to manage his personal investments, and it has become one of the world's largest mission-aligned investment businesses. Capricorn aims to be involved in businesses which provide solutions to global problems, and at the same time to out-perform the investment market by earning a high long-term rate of return. The firm also manages the personal wealth of a number of other high-net worth individuals.

It has supported businesses which work in a number of socially positive fields, such as clean energy, including a joint venture with Volkswagen to produce batteries for its new range of electric vehicles, and a satellite imaging business which provides images to monitor activities in farming, forestry, power generation and many other fields.

Will Smith and Jada Pinkett Smith: This apparently well-known 'celebrity' couple are both very successful actors onstage and in cinema, and they have successfully built a substantial fortune largely by being 'celebrities' who are well-known for their personal lives and have as a result been very substantially rewarded merely for 'being famous' and for appearing on a wide variety of entertainment platforms.

They have set up a family foundation, which has supported a number of sustainable ventures. These include a company called Quidnet Energy, which is developing an innovative storage system for excess electricity produced by renewable-energy systems, and a substantial investment in the multi-million-dollar Prime Impact Fund, which itself invests in a number of businesses whose focus is environmental sustainability. These include Lilac, which has developed a more environmentally friendly method of extracting lithium, a key component in electric car batteries. Prime's backers include this couple and other perhaps more conventional people and institutions, such as the well-known Indian investor Hindawi, the Packard and the Hewlett Foundations and the United States–based Sierra Club Foundation.

Tom and Taylor Steyer: Thomas Steyer was born in 1957 and is a very successful hedge fund manager in the United States. His family's wealth is estimated to be well over a billion dollars. He founded and directed Farallon Capital, which is well known for its successful management of university and wealthy individuals' funds and was at one time considered to be the world's largest hedge fund.

Steyer has used his wealth and position to become heavily engaged in philanthropy, environmental issues and a number of related causes. He also founded and managed Onecalifornia Bank, which was later renamed as Beneficial State Bank, and is a leading low-cost social housing and community development institution in California.

His wife, Taylor Steyer, is now chief executive of the Beneficial State Bank and has also served on the management board of the Harvard University investment fund. She later resigned from this position because her colleagues on the board were unwilling to support her demand to divest the fund from investment in fossil fuels.

The couple also co-founded Radicle Impact which invests and works with large companies such as Proctor and Gamble and Unilever to help them to grow and enter new fields. They also own and run a large farm near San Francisco which aims to demonstrate how it is possible to regenerate degraded land and to use new sustainable farming methods to bring it back into productive use.

Ben and Lucy Ana Walton: Ben Walton is the grandson of Sam Walton, who founded Walmart, the world's largest retail business. His wife, Lucy Ana Walton, is from Chile and is a qualified psychologist.

They have together founded Zomalab, a socially conscious institution that invests in community-oriented businesses such as low-cost housing and childcare institutions. Their enterprises are concentrated in the founders' origins, the state of Colorado in the United States and in Chile in Latin America.

In both areas they focus on investment in power generation, where they aim to encourage facilities which do not depend on coal or oil consumption, and in more efficient and equitable grid distribution, and water, where they aim to improve low-income communities' access to low-cost, high-quality household water supplies. They assist socially oriented businesses and other entities which work with children from disadvantaged communities and in improving long-term employability.

The couple have also invested in Credly, a for-profit business which enables people to develop convincing digital credentials even if they have not obtained a traditional university degree.

Evan Williams: Evan Williams was one of the founders of Twitter, and his personal net worth is said to be over $2 billion. His personal investment vehicle is Obvious Ventures, which aims 'to combine profit and purpose for a better world'. This company has invested in a number of businesses whose activities relate to environmental issues, and Williams is himself personally active in a number of the companies in which he has invested.

These include the 'artificial' meat business Beyond Meat, which produces plant-based protein products and is the global pioneer and leader in this fast-growing but little-known field, in which another of our case study subjects is also involved. Other enterprises in which he is involved include a business which offers a variety of financing options for homeowners who want to install solar panels to generate their own electricity, and in a producer of electric mass-transit vehicles.

These brief case studies suggest that most of these impact investors, but not all, invested family money or money they had themselves made earlier before they became more explicitly 'social'; most of them incurred no substantial risk, because they had large amounts of other money. We may tend, perhaps almost unconsciously to downgrade the genuine 'social-ness' of these investors, and perhaps even of the enterprises themselves, because they did not take a major personal risk, unlike many of the other social entrepreneurs whom we have discussed.

We should question our scepticism, because the social achievements of the companies are usually not directly related to the motives or personal position of their investors, and their personal wealth may indeed allow them to be more patient than a 'bootstrap' investor. The Holy Bible tells us that it easier to put a camel through the eye of a needle than for a rich man, or presumably a rich woman, to enter the Kingdom of Heaven, but are rich peoples' investments any less social because of their wealth?

We should of course question the motives behind these people's activities; they may wish merely to polish their credentials, or possibly in some way to 'atone' for the for-profit businesses which enabled them to acquire such wealth. We should nevertheless honestly confront the issue as to whether it makes any difference to the 'socialness' of an enterprise or a 'social' investment institution whether the entrepreneurs were taking a personal risk in terms of their wealth, their career and their income or were not.

A more fundamental and perhaps more important issue relates to the long-term impact of the social enterprises which have been supported by these people. Many of the enterprises are engaged in activities which some people consider should be the role of government, such as waste disposal, low-cost housing or basic education for children from disadvantaged backgrounds. Are these not activities which should be undertaken by governments? Might such enterprises run the risk of letting governments 'off the hook' by undertaking tasks which are properly the job of government?

This is a very broad and politically loaded question, but these impact investors are mainly from the United States, although some of the businesses in which their funds invest may have global impact. The USA is dropping down the hierarchy of social progress (Kristof 2020), particularly in fields such as basic education and health care, and ranks well below countries such as Estonia and Greece and is at a similar level as Chile, Uzbekistan and Mongolia. Can or should privately financed social enterprises ever replace the public sector? Are these privately financed social investors in some way 'crowding out' government interventions, in spite of the fact that their total impact is far below the scale that could at least in theory be achieved by public sector interventions? These are not easy questions, but they are important.

We have included a number of case studies in this book; a subject which is so broad, and as vaguely defined. as social enterprise is most effectively dealt with, and understood, by reference to individual real-life examples, or case studies. This final chapter concludes, therefore, with two case studies; the first is about a quite modest social enterprise which offers a service to the secondary schools of one city in the United Kingdom. This has been devised and is led by a schoolteacher who is also a social entrepreneur, and he is attempting to remedy an important but little understood weakness in secondary education.

The second and final case study is about an initiative, which might better be described as a bundle of initiatives, which are being planned and, in some cases, actually introduced by one of the world's most visible and controversial entrepreneurs.

These cases are fundamentally different in their scope, but both examples raise a number of important issues. These relate not so much to the definitional issue of what is and what is not a social enterprise, but more to the broader topic of what is the best way for social innovations to be introduced and to be managed. Should society rely on governments to undertake what may to some people seem risky or unimportant or even undesirable social ventures? Should we on the other hand expect businesses to do what they have done so successfully for so many new activities: to take a risk, to be prepared to fail if the idea proves not to be viable but also to reap a commensurate reward if it succeeds?

New initiatives whether they are 'social' or not, are risky and may fail, because they are untried, and they are inevitably expensive, if only in terms of the innovators' time. It is therefore not unreasonable for the entrepreneurs who have taken the risk to expect a commensurate reward if their idea proves to be successful. This is acceptable for innovations where there are potential customers who will be willing and able to pay a price for whatever new product or service is being introduced, but the 'market' for the products or services provided by social innovations does not operate in the same way.

State institutions tend not to be great risk-takers, nor should they be; hence there is a need for so-called 'social entrepreneurs' to fill the gap, at a local, national or even international level. The following two examples describe how two social entrepreneurs are trying to fill it.

11.2 Case studies

Case 11.2.1 Worktree – a social enterprise at many crossroads

Tom Bulman[1] was at one time a schoolteacher, and in many ways, he still is one. He is also a talented saxophonist, a footballer, a father and a trick cyclist, and, perhaps inevitably given the range of his interests and ambitions, he is a social entrepreneur.

Tom's first teaching job was in London; he felt that he was doing a reasonably good job in teaching the required syllabus, and getting children through the exams, but he was deeply dissatisfied with what seemed to him to be the school's failure to deliver the 'non-academic' components of education in its widest sense. There were many things that were wrong or were missing from the curriculum, but in particular, he believed that school was totally failing to prepare young people for the real world beyond school.

Many of them seemed not to have any idea of what their own parents did; 'my dad goes to an office' or 'my mum works at the supermarket' was about as much as they knew, and there seemed almost to be a taboo about the subject; passing or, better, getting good marks in school and then public examinations were the dominating, official focuses of what school was all about.

Every school had some kind of careers teacher or advisor; this was usually a part-time responsibility for a teacher whose main focus was naturally on whatever subject she or he was teaching, and most teachers, like Tom himself, had no experience of any full-time employment other than schoolteaching.

Or there was sometimes a full-time careers advisor who dealt with many different schools, who also usually had no personal experience of the world of work apart from teaching. These advisors did what they could, including inviting local employers to give talks about what they did, but these sessions were generally given low priority by the schools and by the pupils themselves. Fundamentally, formal secondary education was a closed circuit, whose success was measured by its pupils' examination results, and where nobody seemed either to know or to be very much concerned about the world of work.

After teaching at a number of different schools, Tom concluded that this problem was more or less universal; he decided to do something about it. He had by this time moved out of London to a new city called Milton Keynes; he resigned from his teaching position in a secondary school in the city and set up a new registered charity which he called Worktree. Its goal would be to try to overcome the barriers between school and work which Tom had observed. He persuaded the local Chamber of Commerce to allow him to base himself at their office and to offer local secondary schools a new and unique form of brief but intensive exposure to the world of work, to which Tom gave the brand name of Career Workout.

Tom's first attempt to break down the barriers between school and work was quite simple. He persuaded secondary schools to accept class sessions with a speaker from a local employer but with an unusual pupil-led approach; the speakers were not expected or even allowed to give traditional 'talks', the pupils had to lead by asking their own questions, and the visitor was merely expected to answer them and then to move on to the next question. This did not generally work very well; the visitors tended to give long answers, which were little different from the usual visitors' talks, and very few pupils had an opportunity to ask questions.

It was clear that a more structured approach was needed, and Tom eventually evolved what has come to be called the Career Workout. People who work in a wide variety of jobs in the city are invited to spend an hour at a local school. They are told that the children will be asking them questions about their jobs; the visitors are specifically asked not to prepare anything, not in any way to make a presentation; all they have to do is to answer the children's questions, and if necessary to try to ensure that every child in the small groups they meet had a chance and is if necessary encouraged to ask a question.

Around a dozen visitors come at one time; they sit in a large circle in a suitable room in the school, facing outwards, and each is faced by four or five chairs. Some sixty children then come into the room, between the ages of eleven to eighteen; they are usually from one year's classes at the school, and four or five sit facing each visitor. After a brief introduction, they are given five minutes to ask the visitor whatever questions they want about their jobs; how they got them, what qualifications and skills they had needed, what they like and dislike about them, how much they are paid (guests were told in advance that they could if they wished decline to answer any questions which they preferred not to answer) and so on. After five minutes the children stand up, thank their visitor and move around the circle to the next visitor.

In that way each child has the experience of meeting ten or twelve adults whom they have never met before, not to listen to them but to ask them questions about their work. This is in itself a valuable exercise in overcoming their natural shyness, in speaking to adults whom they have never met before. Most importantly, the children learn something about the kinds of jobs which people do and to which they themselves might (or might not) aspire.

The children and the visitors are asked to complete short feed-back papers to share their opinions about the experience. These are almost universally favourable, and the visitors as well as their employers nearly all agree that it has been a valuable experience for them as well as being a useful opportunity to publicise their organisations to potential employees and to the school. Worktree has run Career Workouts in most of the secondary schools in Milton Keynes, and it is hoped that all the children in the city can have this experience once a year for five or six years. Tom and his four part-time colleagues have not been able to measure the long-term impact of Career Workout on the children, nor do they pretend that such a short albeit intensive experience is likely to make a fundamental difference to a child, except in occasional cases. The schools, the visitors' employers and the children themselves, however, all welcome the experience.

This approach was initiated in 2014, and by 2019 more than ten thousand children had experienced a Workout session, and every one of the fourteen secondary schools in Milton Keynes was involved. The aim was for every pupil aged eleven to eighteen to participate in a session once a year, and this is nearly halfway to being achieved. More than eighteen hundred visitors have taken part in these sessions, many of whom participate quite regularly, and they are generally encouraged to participate by their employers. They are all volunteers, and Worktree's staff are modestly paid.

The schools pay a small fee of about five dollars for each session, but this does not cover all the costs, and Worktree also depends on grants from the Local Council and from some employers, on occasional fund-raising events such as a sponsored long-distance cycle ride, on consultancy fees paid to Tom for advice on particular issues such as employability for children with special needs, and from sales of books and games and other learning resources which they have produced.

Worktree's total income was about $110,000 during 2019, and their expenditure was around $115,000. Worktree has been losing money for some five years, and it is becoming urgent to find new sources of income and/or to reduce costs, which are mainly for staff and for travel and general administration.

Some issues for discussion from this case are:

1   Should Worktree continue to rely mainly on earnings from sales of its services, or should it also attempt to raise more money from grants and donations? Are there other ways whereby Worktree could raise money?

2   If they decide to focus on revenue from sales, how should they do this? By 'deepening', working more deeply with local schools, or by 'spreading', extending its activities beyond Milton Keynes (and if so how), or in some other ways?

3   It might be argued that Worktree has done its job; it has developed a novel and apparently effective method of introducing schoolchildren to the world of work, which should perhaps be implemented by schools' own staff; should Worktree produce a manual to guide them to do this, and then wind up?

We conclude the chapter, and the book, with a case study about a much more famous person who is perhaps one of the world's best-known entrepreneurs and innovators.

Case 11.2.2   Elon Musk – visionary, multi-billionaire: is he also a social entrepreneur?

Elon Musk[2] is said to be worth about $100 billion dollars, and to be the fifth richest person in the world. His businesses have ranged from Tesla electric vehicles, Space-Ex space transport, solar power generation and PayPal payment systems, and he says that his passion is to secure the future for mankind. Who is he, really?

He was born in 1971 in Pretoria in South Africa; his parents were divorced, and he appears to have had an unsettled childhood; he chose to live with his father although he loved his mother, because he felt sorry for his father. He played with the early computers as a child, and he even built his own computer at the age of ten. He stayed with his father for his childhood years and went to primary and secondary schools in Johannesburg, where he is said to have been severely bullied, but he soon fell out with his family and moved to Canada when he was eighteen years old. This was in part to get away from his family, but also to avoid having to serve in the South African army, which supported apartheid, and to access a better college education.

He undertook an undergraduate degree in Canada, and then moved to do post-graduate work at Stanford University in California, but he dropped out of the course after only a few days to become part of the already booming San Francisco technology area and to pursue his own career in electronics and software development.

He married a Canadian author in the year 2000; they tragically lost their first child but they were married for eight years and had five children, including a set of triplets, all by IVF. They were divorced in 2008, although they remain in touch; both he and his ex-wife agree that he was so totally focused on his business ventures that the relationship was never easy. Since his divorce, Musk has become part of the 'celebrity' world, and he married a British actress after various difficulties, but this ended in divorce and he has since been linked to various 'show business' personalities.

Musk developed a software device to help city businesses to relate to media and other businesses; this was called 'Zip2' and was soon sold for a total of $307 million, from which he himself earned $22 million. He then became involved in the business which later became PayPal, and when this was sold Musk made a further $165 million. He has also started or participated in a number of new technology-based enterprises, including X-Comm, Stripe, an internet payment business, a tunnelling company called The Boring Company, and several others.

He says he has a passion to ensure the preservation of humanity, both by reducing carbon emissions and by designing and constructing rockets and systems for space travel which he hopes will help to make humans into an 'inter-planetary species', but which can in the meantime generate a profitable business out of placing satellites with reusable rockets, thus vastly reducing the cost of space transport. He initially planned to buy rockets and other technology for this from Russia, but this proved impossible; Musk then successfully built his own rockets, and he is confident that there will be a human colony on Mars by the year 2040.

Musk's career has not been without setbacks. He developed a proposal to build a supersonic train which would cover the 380 miles between Los Angeles and San Francisco in thirty minutes but failed to secure the necessary backing from government or financial institutions. In 2019 he claimed that he had secured the necessary funding to take the Tesla vehicle company private; this was not true, and the authorities levied a fine of some $40 million and ruled that he had to stand down as chair of the company.

Musk also started Solar City, which has become the United States' largest suppliers of domestic solar panels for power generation; like many of his ventures, this came close to disaster but is now a successful and profitable business.

His greatest success to date (that is late 2020) has been the Tesla vehicles. Musk invested in the company in its early years, and when it appeared to be foundering, he ousted the chief executive and took over himself. The company started with a highly priced car, and then moved down to a more affordable model, of which about half a million have been sold. Unlike other vehicles, Tesla cars do not sell through agents or distributors but sell direct to the consumers; this has proved to be effective in part because the demand is so great and customers have been willing to pay substantial deposits and to wait several months or even years for their cars.

This venture has also involved the construction of the world's largest factory, to make the batteries. If it is assumed that the purchasers of these cars would otherwise have driven traditional cars with petrol or diesel engines, it is reasonable to assume that Musk has made a greater contribution to the reduction of carbon emissions than any other human being.

Musk claims that his main focus is on environmental issues and on the survival of humanity, rather than on building great wealth for himself. He has offered to allow General Motors and the Ford company to have full and free access to the technology which has enabled Tesla to become the world's leading electric vehicle manufacturer.

He is said to have an extraordinary memory for technical detail, but at the same time he remembers the larger picture so that he does not become bogged down in detail. He is clearly determined, in his personal life, where his first wife recounts his persistence in wooing her, and in business also, as when his Space-Ex rocket failed three times, he insisted on trying again and was successful at the fourth attempt. He hires the best people and expects them to work with the same determination and commitment as he does, and he is not impressed by paper qualifications or prestigious degrees.

This case presents a number of issues for discussion, including the following:

Musk's career has certainly involved many rather dramatic 'ups and down'; his businesses and his personal life may in a few years or even a few months be very different from what is described in this short case study. Readers may have kept themselves up to date as a matter of personal interest, but we suggest that they should at least take a brief look at Musk's current situation before attempting to draw any conclusions from the case study.

Musk's career is very different from that of most of the social entrepreneurs whom we have examined in this chapter and in earlier parts of the book; it should prompt us to question some of the assumptions which may underlie our view of what is 'social' and what is not.

1   Is Musk a social entrepreneur? Does his acquisition of astronomical personal wealth, at least on paper, in any way erode the 'socialness' of what his business ventures have already achieved or may achieve in the future?
2   Does Musk's personal entry into what might be called the 'celebrity' circle of the super-rich in any way reduce our respect for the man and for his businesses?
3   Musk made a serious mistake when he claimed that he could take Tesla private, and he and the business were fined very substantial amounts for securities fraud by the United States Securities and Exchange Commission. Musk was compelled to invest a further $20

million in the business, by buying shares so that the company could afford the fine. Paradoxically, Tesla's shares appreciated substantially soon after Musk made this investment, so that his personal wealth was massively increased. Does this offence and its outcome in any way reduce our respect for Musk and for his company?

4 Musk's career is very different from that of most of the social entrepreneurs whom we have examined in this chapter and in earlier parts of the book. Space travel, electric vehicles and solar energy are very different fields from most of the areas in which social enterprises are engaged. Does Musk's financial success (at the time of writing) and the 'blue skies' nature of the businesses in which he is engaged imply that his ventures are in some way more (or perhaps less) genuinely 'social' than the more conventional businesses in which most social enterprises are engaged?

11.3 Follow-up activity

Think about your own community and identify one or more services which are not presently available and would benefit some local people, but for which these people would not be able to pay the full cost. Approximately what 'mix' of methods would you propose for raising the necessary funds, including selling the services to the proposed beneficiaries or to others, charitable donations, grants from local government authorities, from local businesses or from private donors?

11.4 Conclusion

In conclusion, we hope that this book with its case discussions and activities, will in some sense change the narrative in the emerging discipline of social entrepreneurship by reminding us that the merit of the rather novel concept of 'social enterprises' is not merely to try to fit as many enterprises as possible into a narrow new theoretical distinction which emphasises the differences between commercial businesses and traditional charities. The concept should rather assist us to think critically through the practical issues of trying to do good and to do well that every social entrepreneur has to face. For this, we have attempted to explore the question of 'What enterprises are really social?' by using case study examples. The experiences of the social entrepreneurs in our case studies, and of the impact investors who have invested in their social enterprises, have provided us with a basis for the discussion and analysis issues which go back for centuries but which are totally contemporary. We hope that the book will remind all our readers that every investor or would-be entrepreneur, regardless of whatever label society or the founder or others put on the enterprise, has to appreciate the social implications of its value proposition.

Notes

1 Details of the case sourced from (a) Personal interview with the Founder of Worktree, Mr. Tom Bulman on January 20, 2021, and (b) publicly available information on the Worktree website and (c) "Worktree." Accessed February 16, 2021. https://worktree.org/about/.
2 Details of the case sourced from publicly available information on the Tesla website (a) "Elon Musk | Tesla." Accessed January 15, 2021. www.tesla.com/elon-musk; information about Tesla in the book (b) Vance, Ashlee. 2017. *Elon Musk: Tesla, SpaceX, and the Quest for a Fantastic Future*. Illustrated edition. New York. Harper Collins Publishers and from publicly available article and (c) Benjamin, N. Alexander, Coget, Jean-François, and C. Dahm Patricia. 2018. "Does Elon Musk Rank?" *Journal of Case Research and Inquiry* 4. Accessed January 15, 2021. www.jcri.org/cases/2018/Elon%20Musk%20JCRI%20CASE.pdf.

11.5 References

Forbes. 2020. "Impact 50: Investors Seeking Profit – And Pushing for Change." *Forbes*, September 8. Accessed February 15, 2021. www.forbes.com/sites/forbeswealthteam/2020/09/08/impact-50-investors-seeking-profit-and-pushing-for-change-diversified/.

GIIN. 2020. "2020 Annual Impact Investor Survey." *The GIIN*. Accessed December 4, 2020. https://thegiin.org/research/publication/impinv-survey-2020.

Kristof, Nicholas. 2020. "Opinion | 'We're No. 28! And Dropping!'" *The New York Times*, September 9, 2020, sec. Opinion. www.nytimes.com/2020/09/09/opinion/united-states-social-progress.html.

Pandit, Vivek, and Toshan Tamhane. 2018. "Understanding Impact Investing" | *McKinsey Quarterly*. Accessed February 15, 2021. www.mckinsey.com/industries/private-equity-and-principal-investors/our-insights/a-closer-look-at-impact-investing#.

INDEX

Note: Page numbers in *italics* indicate a figure and page numbers in **bold** indicate a table on the corresponding page.

Aavishkaar (case study) 70–4
Acumen investment fund 106–7
Al Husseini, Ibrahim 169
Annual Impact Investor Survey 88, 90
asset-locked social companies 6

BACO *see* Best Available Charitable Option (BACO)
BASIX (case study) 126–31, 150, 153–4
Battilana, Julie 154
Ben, Lucy Ana 173–4
Ben and Jerry's (case study) 20–2
benefit corporation 41, 123, 163
Best Available Charitable Option (BACO) 106–7
Better Meat Company (case study) 79, 84–6
Blue Hub 68
Body Shop (case study) 158–64
British Social Enterprises 6
Brock, Debbi D. 145
Buffett, Howard 169–70
Buffett, Warren 170
Bulman, Tom 176

Caninianville 116–17
carceral state 92
Career Workout (brand) 177–8
charitable incorporated organisation (CIO) 124
charity 1, 10, 29, 40–2, 44, 69, 118, 148, 177; traditional 2; traditional donation to 107
children 18–19, 178
CIC *see* community interest company (CIC)
CIO *see* charitable incorporated organisation (CIO)

Columbus, Christopher 66
community interest company (CIC) 7, 124
Community Reinvestment Act (CRA) 64
companies limited by shares 7
Cornerstone Capital Group 104
corporate social responsibility (CSR) 92–3
COVID epidemic 89
CRA *see* Community Reinvestment Act (CRA)
CSR *see* corporate social responsibility (CSR)

Development Impact Bonds (DIBs), finance development programs 93
Dharmasthala Trust 47
Double Bottom Line Report 103

Edelman Trust Barometer survey 28
Educate Girls 93
employment 13, 19, 22, 58, 155–6
environmental/environment: damage 4; dimension 18; intervention 88–9; stewardship of 69–70
Equitas Microfinance 71–2
ESG lens 78
Eton College (case study) 34–6
Excellence Bond 94

Facebook 41–2
faith-based institutions 63
family offices 69
FASB *see* Financial Accounting Standards Board (FASB)
Financial Accounting Standards Board (FASB) 106
flexible purpose corporation 123

FMO 72
Foreign Contribution (Regulation) Act (FCRA) 125
Franklin, Benjamin 66
Friedman, Milton 5, 13

Generally Accepted Accounting Principles (GAAP) 106
Generation Investment Management in 2004 170
GIAN see Gujarat Grassroots Augmentation Innovation Network (GIAN)
GIIN 105 see Global Impact Investors Network (GIIN)
GIIRS see Global Impact Investment Rating System (GIIRS)
Global Impact Investment Rating System (GIIRS) 105
Global Impact Investors Network (GIIN) 60, 88, 90, 103–4, 168–9
Goldman Sachs 92
Gore, Albert 170
Gujarat Grassroots Augmentation Innovation Network (GIAN) 70–1

Habitat for Humanity 157–8
health care 68, 72, 94, 113, 175
homelessness 18, 91, 93, 108, 110
Hot Bread Kitchen 154–5

impact assessment: Not for Profit Finance Fund (NFF) (case study) 107–13
Impact Reporting and Investment Standards (IRIS) 104
Impact Value Chain Model 103, 103
Income Tax Act of 1961 125
incorporation, forms of 122; Indian social enterprise incorporation guidelines 124–6; UK social enterprise incorporation guidelines 123–4; USA social enterprise incorporation guidelines 122–3
Indian Institute of Forest Management 70
Indian Institute of Management in Ahmedabad 70
Indian social enterprise incorporation guidelines 124–6
Industrial and Provident Society 124
industrial provident societies 7
inflation 62, 69
insurance 72
International Finance Corporation 72
IRIS see Impact Reporting and Investment Standards (IRIS)

Jacobs, Irwin 170
J Paul Getty Trust 98
JP Morgan Chase Bank 77

Kamine, Justine 170
Karnataka Land Reform Act 43
Kings Active Foundation (case study) 22–5, 25

L3C see Low Profit Limited Liability Company (L3C)
Lewis, Jonathan 148
Loving Dogs' Home 116–18
Low Profit Limited Liability Company (L3C) 123

Mahajan, Vijay 126–31
McKinsey global consultancy company 168
Merchant of Venice, The (Shakespeare) 61
microfinance 39, 47–8, 51, 168; 'bubble' in Indian state of Andhra Pradesh in 2008 147; businesses in India 153–4; enterprise initiative 144; impact measurement in 146–7; institution 17, 146; SKDRDP 149
Micro-finance Credit Rating International (M-CRIL) (case study) 31–4
Milk Mantra (case study) 79–84
Milton Keynes 177
M-Kopa 155–6
M-Pesa 155
Musk, Elon (case study) 179–82

New York Metropolitan Transport Authority 4
non-religious investment funds 63
Not for Profit Finance Fund (NFF) (case study) 107–13
Novogratz, Amy 171

O'Brien, Robyn 171
One Service organisation 98
Ormiston, Jarrod 146

partnerships 123
performance payments 94
Peterborough Social Impact Bond (case study) 94–100
Pioneer Fund 63
Porter, Michael 13–14
portfolio decision-making 107
prison: components of 119; sentence 118–19; services 95

private equity 78, 105
Public Charitable Organisation 125
public health 89–90
public-private partnerships 91

Qur'an 62

Rang De (case study) 131–40
Rangsutra 71, 74
recidivism 91–2, 119
Rikers Island Prison in New York 91–2
Rockefeller Brothers Fund 171–2
Rockefeller Foundation 98
Rockefeller, Valerie 171–2
Roddick, Anita 159–60
Rural Development and Self
    Employment Training Institute
    (RUDSETI) 45, 149

Schmidt, Eric 172
SDGs see Sustainability Development
    Goals (SDGs)
Seymour, Richard 146
Shri Kshetra Dharmasthala Rural
    Development Programme (SKDRDP)
    42, 150
SKDRDP 43–59
SKDRDP see Shri Kshetra Dharmasthala
    Rural Development Programme
    (SKDRDP)
Skoll, Jeff 172
Slow Money 30–1
Smith, Jada Pinkett 172–3
Smith, Will 172
SOCH (Society for Children) 29–30
social equity 19; Ben and Jerry's (case
    study) 20–2; follow-up activity 25;
    Kings Active Foundation (case study)
    22–5; through entrepreneurship
    16–19
Social Finance 2010 98
social housing 90
social impact bonds (SIBs) 90–3; critical
    aspect of 90; experiment 100
social outcome 90–1
social responsibility 63
social value 5, 145
social welfare system, components of
    119
Sodexo Justice Services 95
solar energy–generation panels 155
sole proprietorships 7
sole traders 123
stakeholders in impact creation process
    103
Steiner, Susan 145

Steyer, Taylor 173
Steyer, Thomas 173
St. Giles' Trust 96
sub-prime loans 68
sub-prime mortgage crisis 64
Sulabh International 157–8
Sustainability Accounting Standards
    Board (SASB) 106
Sustainability Development Goals
    (SDGs) 73, 103–5; Access Impact
    Framework 104; principles of 104
sustainable investment 2
Swain, Manoj Kumar 29–30

Transport for London 4

UBS Optimus Foundation 93–4
UK: Government's Financial Services
    Authority (FSA) 124; social
    enterprise in 5–14; social enterprise
    incorporation guidelines 123–4; Social
    Finance Ltd. 91
Unilever group 20–1
unincorporated registered charity 124
United Nations Development
    Programme 28
United Nations Environment
    Program 79
United Nations Global Goals 103
United Nations Principles for
    Responsible Investment (UNPRI) 65
United States Sustainable Investment
    Forum (USSIF) 65
UNPRI see United Nations Principles for
    Responsible Investment (UNPRI)
USA: carceral state of 92; Declaration
    of Independence 66; hierarchy of
    social progress 175; social enterprise
    incorporation guidelines 122–3
USSIF see United States Sustainable
    Investment Forum (USSIF)
Utkrisht 94

value chain model 103
venture capital 62, 78, 105

Walmart 13, 39, 41–2, 156
Walton, Lucy Ana 173–4
Williams, Evan 174
Worktree 175
World Bank 72
World Summit on Social Development
    2005 142
World Vision 28

XYZ (case study) 10–14